Praise f

MW01502883

"*Jean-Luc is a Bitcoin/blockchain pioneer and one of our most knowledgeable experts in the firm. He is able to translate complex topics, such as blockchain, into tangible ideas and examples.*"

Eric Piscini, Global Blockchain Lead, Deloitte

~

"*This book strikes the perfect balance between the inner workings of the technology and its potential. Well-written, concise, yet exhaustive. Perfect for all audiences.*"

Shermin Voshmgir, Founder, BlockchainHub

~

"*PS – I thought you might like to know that I gave my husband a bitcoin for Christmas, I have been telling him about what I learned from your book, and he is all revved up about the system.*"

Mallory Miles, Copyeditor of this book and first reader

Bitcoin, the Blockchain and Beyond

The 360-degree onboarding guide to
the future of money and blockchain

By Jean-Luc Verhelst

Copyeditor: Mallory Miles, Anita Vermaak
Proofreader: Vidya Vijayan
Cover: Ilian Georgiev
Interior Designer: Jean-Luc Verhelst
Illustrations: Jean-Luc Verhelst, Julien Bayot, Jill Roex
Self-Published

Credits for illustrations: Aleksandr Vector, AlePio, Alice Noir, Alrigel, Creative Stall, Erin Battersby, Guru, Murthy2819, Roman Shvets, Symbolon, To Uyen, and Useiconic.com from Noun Project. Freepik from flaticon.com. Picture of boxes: Jérémie Denis.

First edition published in September 2017 - v1.083

ISBN paperback version: 978-2-930971-00-1
ISBN e-book version: 978-2-930971-01-8

To those who dare to dream.

But even more, to those who pursue their dreams.

Contents

Preface

They say that a Google search can change your life. That was the case for me back in 2011, when I discovered Bitcoin. At the time, I was a student about to start university.

In 2013, when I had to choose a subject for my master thesis at the Louvain School of Management, I decided to dedicate my research to Bitcoin. I discovered a new world, a world in which a community of enthusiasts was changing the concept of money. I was fascinated by the philosophy behind Bitcoin and was eager to investigate the working of the Blockchain, the technology behind Bitcoin. Writing my master thesis changed me. It opened my mind and made me realize that my understanding of what money truly is was incomplete. I started to understand how valuable—or should I say, invaluable—money is, and this shift changed my perspective on quite a few things in life.

By 2014, I completed the thesis and was amazed by Bitcoin's potential to change the world. I remember taking some positions, which were unconventional at the time, at least outside the community. I can still hear myself saying, "The payment industry will be disrupted by this technology and banks better start looking into it. The smartphone has become our agenda, our mailbox, our alarm clock, our MP3 player, our camera, and so much more. It is only a matter of time before it becomes our wallet."

Given my excitement about Bitcoin, I was confused by the conservative positions from governmental administrations toward Bitcoin. I understood that they were concerned about a currency out of their control, but I could see how the technology could reduce fraud and benefit central banks, governments, and the financial system. How long would it take before they caught on? I made a conservative guess of five years but the speed of innovation proved my naïve mind wrong. Against my expectations, only two years later, central banks started looking into blockchain technology. Today, the idea of a central bank adopting some kind of cryptocurrency will definitely not surprise me.

Many aspects of Bitcoin absorbed me. Studying this new currency has been a rewarding intellectual journey filled with questions. Moreover, from every such question that has been answered, more questions have emerged. Bitcoin touches upon so many fields: monetary policy, banking, cryptography, network security, the adoption of disruptive innovations, business, and society. In many of these fields, I already had an interest, while in fields like cryptography, where at first I did not have a particular interest, I developed one. I was so amazed by the power of cryptography that it kept me awake at night. Unexpected is the least I can say.

Gradually, my interest started to shift toward the technology behind Bitcoin: the distributed ledger technology (more commonly referred to as the blockchain technology). My passion for the subject reached new heights when I realized, at the end of my thesis, that distributed ledgers could affect many industries and reshape society.

I had long harbored the idea of writing a book, but the feeling became more acute when I realized the potential of cryptocurrencies. I could no longer keep this knowledge for myself. I felt it was my duty to share everything I had learned, and I have done so through this book.

As is often the case, things really took off when I was given a deadline. At the end 2015, I was contacted by Frederic Helsen, a Ph.D. in Law at the Catholic University of Leuven. He asked me to make a Dutch contribution to a book titled *Innovation and Disruption in Economic Law*.[1] The book addresses multiple innovations—such as online dispute resolution and the sharing economy—and their implication from a legal perspective. It is published by Intersentia, a scientific publisher specializing in law, business, and economics. My contribution consisted of providing an understanding of what Bitcoin is, how it operates, and whether it can be considered money.

I started to combine my day job with writing in the evenings and during weekends. By the summer of 2016, I submitted my contribution. However, I was not finished yet. There was much more I wanted to share, and I decided to pursue my writings to publish a more exhaustive version—the same version you are now holding in your hands.

Now, writing is not something I am used to. The most comprehensive writing experience I had is when I completed my master thesis. For someone who never was a natural with the pen, writing a book was definitely a challenge! After having spent many weekends over the course of 2016 and 2017 writing, reviewing, rearranging, and reworking, the book is finally ready for its first edition in the summer of 2017. This exercise required quite a lot of effort, and it was challenging to break down the more technical concepts step-by-step. As you will discover in a couple of chapters, many of them are linked to each other.

I used my master thesis as a starting point. For the purpose of this book, I started to update my writings to include a deeper understanding of the subject and recent developments. My main ambition was to provide you with the smoothest possible reading experience while presenting all relevant concepts to you in an understandable way, one by one. This book aims to define what Bitcoin is and what it is not and to introduce not only the opportunities but also the challenges facing Bitcoin. With this book, I hope to bring something of value to the amazing community of Bitcoin developers, Bitcoin users, Bitcoin entrepreneurs, and all enthusiasts of blockchain technology. I hope this book makes things more accessible by providing a 360-degree view of Bitcoin, the blockchain, and everything beyond it.

I hope that my mission will be successful and that you will enjoy the read while discovering the future of money.

It all started with a Google search.

READING TIPS

The structure of the book is designed in such a way that you discover all concepts in a sequential flow. Some chapters might be of more or less interest to you, and you are free to skip some chapters and move on to the ones that interest you.

The chapters explaining the working of Bitcoin and the Blockchain are, however, essential to help you make up your opinion about Bitcoin. Many of the concepts discussed in these chapters will be discussed again in following chapters; they are therefore important to read if you want to capture all the nuances of the following chapters. The chapters in the ecosystem part are more descriptive and provide an overview of Bitcoin's possibilities. In particular, the chapter on wallets can be skipped if you have no interest in understanding all types of wallets. It remains, however, a must-read if you decide to buy bitcoins and want to know how to store them safely. The remainder of the book builds upon the previous chapters and gives a better perspective on Bitcoin and the potential of the underlying technology. Enjoy the read!

Acknowledgments

"No man is an island,

Entire of itself,

Every man is a piece of the continent,

A part of the main."

~ John Donne

These verses from John Donne perfectly articulate how nothing can be achieved by one person alone. Everything we are and everything we do is shaped by our environment, the people inspiring us, the people surrounding us, the people helping us, and the people supporting us.

This book is no different.

You are holding in your hands the achievement of a four-year journey. It would, however, not exist had it not been for the many people involved in the process.

First, there are those who contributed to my environment. I am grateful to **my parents** who made it possible for me to study what I wanted and who respected the choices I made. I am thankful to **my professors** for their lessons in an academic environment fostering intellectual challenge. To **the Jury of the ING Thesis Award** and **Frederic Helsen**, who confirmed the quality and uniqueness of my message.

Then there are the people who inspired me. This list would be endless, and most of the people on it are people I have never met. These are world leaders in their domains, entrepreneurs, and people who changed things; those who hold a passion or a message and do not give up.

Finally, thank you to the people surrounding me, the many **colleagues** across all levels at Deloitte who were positive and interested in this adventurous project, and who welcomed my different initiatives with enthusiasm and trust. To **my friends** in Belgium and the people I met in Dublin, for being there when I needed small "escapes" from the "overloaded life."

Thanks to:

Moe **Adham** (Co-founder, BitAccess)

Dr. Adam **Back** (Co-founder and CEO, Blockstream)

Damian **Barabonkov** (Slimcoin)

Thomas **Bertani** (CEO, Oraclize – Founder, InsurETH)

Iddo **Bentov** (Cornell University)

David **Birch** (Director of Innovation, Consult Hyperion)

Michelle **Brinich** (Head of Marketing, Blockstream)

Francisco **Cabañas** (Monero)

Luke **Dashjr** (Bitcoin Core developer)

John **Frazer** (External Relations Lead, Ethereum Foundation)

Nick **Gogerty** (Solarcoin and MIT Media Lab)

Cedric **Hauben** (Lawyer, DLA Piper)

Haitch (member of forums.burst-team.us)

Eitan **Katchka** (Founder of La'Zooz and Commuterz)

Arnaud **Kodeck** (Founder, EBTM)

Claire **LaRocca** (Everledger)

Louis **Larue** (Basic income, Catholic University of Louvain)

Christophe **Lejeune** (Catholic University of Louvain)

Christoph **Jentzsch** (CEO, Slock.it)

Daniel **Kraft** (Namecoin)

Sunny **King** (Founder, Peercoin)

Gilles **Mitteau** (Founder, YouTube Channel Heu?reka)

Bach **Nguyen** (SatoshiLabs)

Jean-Grégoire **Orban de Xivry** (Co-founder, Solarly)

David **Osojnik** (CTO, Bitstamp)

John **Quinn** (Co-founder, StorJ)

Luca **Pensieroso** (Macroeconomics, Catholic University of Louvain)

Paige **Peterson** (Zcash)

Andrew **Poelstra** (Mathematician, Blockstream)

Joseph **Poon** (Lightning network)
Veena **Pureswaran** (IBM)
Jeremy **Rand** (Namecoin)
Ripple
Ted **Rogers** (President, Xapo)
Pavol **Rusnak** (SatoshiLabs)
Fabian **Schuh** (BitShares)
Matthew **Spoke** (Co-founder and CEO, Nuco)
David **Schwartz** (Member of bitcoin.stackexchange.com)
Martin **Swende** (Ethereum Developer)
Alan **Szepieniec** (Cryptographer, KU Leuven)
Ryan **Taylor** (CEO, Dash)
Susanne **Tarkowski Tempelhof** (Founder, Bitnation)
Stephan **Tual** (COO, Slock.it)
Roger **van de Berg** (Lawyer, Baker & McKenzie)
Patrick **van der Meijde** (Founder, BitKassa)
James **Walpole** (BitPay)
Tyler **Welmans** (Deloitte Digital)
Bas **Wisselink** (Nxt Foundation)
Lon **Wong** (President, NEM.io Foundation Ltd)
Vasja **Zupan** (COO, Bitstamp)

For their help, insights, content review, and feedback to this book.

Special thanks to **Mallory Miles** and **Vidya Vijayan**, for helping in the editing process and answering my endless requests. Your feedback and work have truly made a difference and contributed immensely to the quality of this book. Thanks to the **teachers** of universities who trusted me to be a guest lecturer and to **Deloitte** for bringing me to the executive boards.

To my dear friends: **Gerard Salvador** for his continuous and extreme enthusiasm: every author needs someone like you around. To **Jérémie Denis**, for his feedback, ideas, positivity, and the time he invested voluntarily. To **Quentin Nederlandt** for his feedback.

Thanks to **Kim Bracke** and **Lieven Verbrugge** for their personal time investments in creating the first YouTube video.

On an almost final note, I would like to thank many people in the Bitcoin and blockchain **community** who helped me in the writing of my thesis during 2013-2014. The **developers** of the community who make things real as well as the **connectors** for connecting, opening doors, and giving me opportunities. To all the people who believed I was not crazy after receiving my speeches and who welcomed my opinions with great enthusiasm and challenge.

A huge thank you to **all those who like, follow, share, and subscribe** to my social media pages for spreading the message! Your impact is much larger and more valuable than you would expect. I will be extremely grateful if you post a picture of this book and let me know what you think!

Finally, I would like to thank **you as a reader** for believing this work is worth your time. I am grateful and humbled by your attention, and I hope this book will meet your expectations.

Introduction

Money rules our lives. Created at the dawn of civilization, it is probably one of humankind's most ancient and impactful innovations. It has funded many battles. It has the power to enable or disable experiences, opportunities, and even survival. It gives us social status and material satisfaction. It can enable us to take shortcuts, impress people, avail services, spread messages, care for the people we love, and, in some cases, have power.

Although the current monetary system has its dysfunctionalities and incoherencies, money is a peaceful tool to avoid anarchy. It organizes and shapes our society. It moves things around. It is everywhere, in every town all over the country, in every business on the street, in every household. Today, 99.9% of all people on earth deal with money. After water and food, it is probably humanity's most common daily-used item. Yet, few of us understand what money really is. It is embedded in our life from the moment we are born, and we plan our lives expecting it will be there when we die. A society without money would be unthinkable.

Who knows what money really is? Is it more than a bunch of numbers on your bank account? What is the story behind the coins and notes that bring food to the table? Money has taken on various forms throughout history, and many different currencies—the most common form of money—have emerged and vanished over the centuries.

Who controls it? Is money serving its purpose? Is money, in its current most popular form, sustainable? Should we be looking for alternatives; currencies that would suit the digital age?

Could Bitcoin, "the currency of the Internet," be the solution we have been waiting for?

In the autumn of 2013, it was impossible to open a financial newspaper without seeing the word Bitcoin:

> *"The future of money: The Bitcoin"*
> *(BBC)*

> *"It is not different from the tulip mania of the sixteen hundreds"*
> *(Bloomberg TV)*

> *"It is going to change the world but probably not in the way we expect"*
> *(IBM Executive)*

What was once seen as "play-money for geeks" became front-page news in the *Financial Times* and was presented to the world as the next global currency. In a time when banks were going bankrupt or needed to be backed by governments, Bitcoin's most impressive innovation, decentralization, was (and still is today) appealing. The fiat currencies we use today are losing their credibility and some have announced that Bitcoin will be the next generation of money. Mass media outlets are claiming that Bitcoin can revolutionize the way we think about money and financial systems.

At the same time, many people are dubious about Bitcoin because of its alleged connection to illegal trade, its apparent lack of intrinsic value, and its price that can skyrocket one day and flash-crash the next. Additionally, soon after Bitcoin was announced as "the next big thing," bitcoin exchange platforms were subject to attacks and filed for bankruptcy, leaving thousands of Bitcoin-believers stranded.

So what is Bitcoin really? Is it money? Is it a currency? Is it Gold 2.0.? Will it survive? Or is it all hype? What will Bitcoin's future look like?

Can it change the world? These are the questions this book will try to answer.

In order to do so, this book will be divided into four distinct parts.

The first part will focus on understanding how Bitcoin and its Blockchain work under the hood. The aim here is to get a conceptual understanding of what Bitcoin is and what it stands for today. What makes Bitcoin unique? How does it operate? How secure is it? Does it face any challenges? This part will touch upon some concepts of cryptography to provide a deeper understanding, but we will try to keep things simple. At the end of this part, the reader should have an understanding of what Bitcoin is and how it functions.

In the second part, we will introduce some key elements of Bitcoin's ecosystem such as wallets, solution providers, etc. This will enable you to have a better understanding of the maturity of the bitcoin landscape, which is essential for its adoption.

The third part will build upon the first part and assess whether Bitcoin qualifies as money and/or as a currency. Before reaching a conclusion, we will use a historical lens to understand what makes good money and a good currency and whether Bitcoin is or has the potential to be good money/currency.

Finally, we will look beyond Bitcoin and discuss the environment in which Bitcoin evolves as well as the innovation Bitcoin brings about. What are the drivers of success for Bitcoin? What are the odds of seeing Bitcoin succeed? Can bitcoins be regulated? Will Bitcoin be replaced by another cryptocurrency? What are the alternatives? We will also look into what the blockchain technology has to offer beyond Bitcoin, as well as how it can redefine not only money but also multiple other aspects of our lives, such as contracts, identity, business operations and, eventually, democracies.

PART I

The core of Bitcoin and the Blockchain

Chapter 1

Introduction to Bitcoin

In 2008, at the dawn of Bitcoin, a mysterious inventor, nicknamed Satoshi Nakamoto, shared a paper,[2] in which he detailed his design for a peer-to-peer electric cash system: Bitcoin. According to one of his posts, his reflection started in 2007.[3] In 2009, he released the software and became active on forums,[4] presenting his idea and helping to understand and improve the open-source code. Then, slowly, Nakamoto started to disappear from the forums. By the spring of 2011, he declared that he had "moved on to other things."[5] To this day, Nakamoto's identity remains a mystery.

By 2013, Bitcoin was splashed across the front pages of newspapers all over the world—and it had acquired a bit of a nasty reputation. The currency was associated with illegal activities on the dark web, and the belief that it could maintain the anonymity of its users raised many eyebrows. Moreover, people were mystified by the fact that bitcoins were created out of thin air and that the creator of this growing empire still refused to step out of the shadows. How could Bitcoin be trustworthy? How could it be put to good use?

Against this backdrop of public suspicion, the Bitcoin community began making efforts to clean up Bitcoin's reputation by educating the public about how Bitcoin really works. These efforts paid off. In a landmark review, the BBC declared that Bitcoin was the future of money. Bitcoin users began to speak out in defense of the currency, pointing out that, while it was true that Bitcoin had been used to fund drug-trades, hire murderers, and pay for child pornography, fiat currency had been used for the same dark purposes for centuries before Bitcoin. These early champions of Bitcoin claimed that the currency had a place in normal trade and that it was a revolutionary invention that would change the world.

Although Bitcoin has certainly gained a better foothold in public opinion, many misconceptions still exist, and there is still a general lack of understanding about how Bitcoin operates. This part of the book will give you a conceptual understanding of how Bitcoin and the underlying Blockchain operate. The aim is to give you a basic understanding of the mechanics, the security, and the challenges of Bitcoin. We will not go into the technical details that are required for developers. If you want to go beyond a conceptual understanding and are interested in the programming language behind Bitcoin, I recommend reading *Mastering Bitcoin* by Andreas M. Antonopoulos.

This being said, to properly understand Bitcoin, this section will inevitably touch upon some subjects such as cryptography. It will be explained in a comprehensive way for non-technical readers.

THE END OF THE FINANCIAL INTERMEDIARY

Throughout history, money has taken on many forms. In the early days, shells and spices were used as currencies. Later, standardized gold coins were minted before being replaced by paper money backed by the gold standard. Today, money is represented by bits on computer servers.

Banks were created centuries ago by renowned families, like the Medicis, who were trusted by people to keep their money safe and to oversee their transactions. Remarkably, that premise has changed very little over the years. Today, banks still act as intermediaries, with the same responsibilities as the renowned families of old. They protect our "accounts," and when we want to make a transaction, they bounce our money from place to place until it finally lands in the correct account, somewhere else. In some cases, multiple intermediaries can be involved in one transaction!

Let us look at an example. Say you buy something online and decide to pay with PayPal. Unless you have credit in your account, PayPal will either charge your credit card for your purchase, which will then charge your bank account, or charge your bank account directly. Next, the money will be transferred to the financial institution used by the online store. If this financial institution is different from yours or is located in another country, the transfer might involve a couple of other trusted intermediaries.

This web of trusted intermediaries works most of the time, but it is slow, work-intensive, and costly. Still, these intermediaries are often required to make transactions both online and offline. The only transactions where no intermediary is involved are the ones paid in cash.

Many attempts have been made to create a digital, Internet-friendly form of cash, but all of them, until Bitcoin, have failed. Why did they fail? When you transfer something in digital space, you do not *really* transfer it. You simply create a copy of it. You can see this principle in operation when you send an email attachment. In order to transfer that file to someone else, you actually create a copy of the file, which you attach to your email, but notice: *you still have a copy of the file on your computer.*

So, in essence, you do not transfer, you copy. This conundrum of transferring vs. copying is why we have always needed trusted intermediaries when dealing with money on the Internet. If we transferred money the way we transfer files, we would end up copying our money, and we would be able to reuse it as many times as we wanted. This is known as the double-spending problem. In a system where money could be endlessly copied and reused, it would lose its scarcity and, as a result, it would become worthless.

Bitcoin was the first to solve the transfer vs. copy conundrum, and so it became the first Internet currency to make direct payment from one person to another possible without the need of an intermediary. In the next seven chapters, we will see how this is achieved, but before we get mired in the ins and outs of Bitcoin, let us have a peek at what a world that has embraced Bitcoin would look like.

A WORLD WITH BITCOIN

In a world ruled by Bitcoin, there is no debate about whether the central banks should increase or decrease the monetary supply. In fact, there are no central banks anymore. You can barely remember a time when you had to wait multiple days before receiving the payment someone sent you via a wire transfer. A local bank that closes early for every minor holiday? Gone. An overly expensive Western Union? Gone. Everything has been replaced by the first digital currency operating globally 24/7: Bitcoin.

In the Bitcoin world, most people use their smartphones to make payments, but paper is also an option for traditionalists. When you want to buy something, you scan a QR code generated by the seller. Almost instantaneously, the payment is validated, executed, and recorded on the Bitcoin network. Your money no longer needs to pass through PayPal, banks, or other intermediaries before it arrives at its destination. Instead, your money moves straight from your Bitcoin wallet to the seller's wallet, and no one else is involved. Remember, Bitcoin is not a person or a corporation out to make a profit. Bitcoin is simply a network, just like the Internet. It is not controlled by a central authority, and the only way to stop it from operating would be to shut down the Internet.

Chapter 2

The concept of blockchains

Blockchain, the platform on which Bitcoin is built, is one of the greatest advents of the Internet, right up there with mobile Internet, social media, the Internet of things, and artificial intelligence. Blockchain gives a new dimension to the web; it rethinks the way we operate and enables new types of interaction between complete strangers.

Blockchains make it possible to share a collection of records with a large network of participants. In the case of Bitcoin, this collection of records is a shared account ledger keeping track of bitcoin ownership. It shows who owns how many bitcoins at a certain point of time. The ledger is distributed across the network, meaning that every participant in the network has a copy. Think of it as a database that is replicated on many computers.

Sometimes the term "distributed ledger technology" (DLT) is interchanged with "blockchain" or "blockchain technology." Let us clear up that relationship. A distributed ledger is a database where records are stored one after the other. It is spread amongst different participants where the people entering records are trusted by everyone. Blockchains are distributed ledgers where trust is *enforced by the rules* governing the blockchain. Blockchain, with a capital B, is the name of one specific distributed ledger: Bitcoin's distributed ledger. Because of Bitcoin's ingenuity and success, the term blockchain has become so popular that other distributed ledgers, which are often inspired by the Blockchain, are referred to as "blockchains." When distributed ledgers follow the same principles as blockchains (described in this chapter), we can say that they apply the "blockchain technology." In this book, we might use the term "blockchain" (without a capital B) or "blockchains" when referring to them. When distributed ledgers do not use the same principles as blockchains, we will not qualify them as blockchains.

Since Bitcoin's creation, multiple distributed ledgers inspired by the Blockchain have emerged, and most of them use the blockchain technology. As of today, the Bitcoin Blockchain is still the largest and most reliable of all blockchains worldwide. As the title of this book implies, we are going to talk about *the* Blockchain: Bitcoin's Blockchain. After explaining Bitcoin and its Blockchain, we will briefly discuss the distributed ledgers of other cryptocurrencies, as well as other potential applications of the distributed ledger technology, in the fourth part of this book.

As the aim of this book is to understand Bitcoin, we will focus on understanding the working of Bitcoin's distributed ledger (aka *the* Blockchain) in the next chapters.

STORED IN A DISTRIBUTED FASHION

Before moving on, let us pause to think about the term "distributed."

We mentioned that you can think of blockchains as distributed databases. Distributed means that the data contained within a blockchain is neither stored nor managed by one central entity. Instead, a copy of the blockchain, with all its data, is stored on each full node of the network. A node of the network consists of a computer or device connected to the blockchain. A full node stores and maintains a full copy of the blockchain. Anyone can become a full node; you just have to decide to store a complete copy of the blockchain (the complete history of bitcoin transactions in the case of the Blockchain) on your computer.

Because there is no central entity keeping track of the blockchain's data, there is also no single point of failure and no third party or intermediary in whom you have to trust. The entire network of Bitcoin participants collectively maintains the Blockchain.

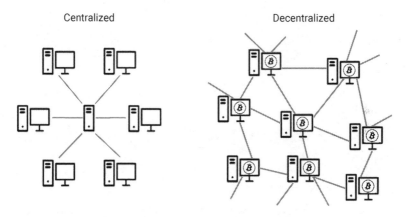

Figure 1. Centralized vs. Decentralized model

A CHAIN OF BLOCKS

Now that you know that blockchains are stored on multiple computers, not only one computer, let us take a look at the structure of the data stored on each of these computers. In other words, let us take a look at the blockchain itself.

Blockchains are sequential chains of blocks where:

- Each block is indissolubly linked to the previous block.
- Each block contains data. In the case of Bitcoin, this is a list of transactions, tracking the movement of bitcoins from one user to another.
- Every couple of minutes (10 minutes in the case of Bitcoin), one new block is created and added to the chain.

- Each new block spreads across the network and is stored on each full node.

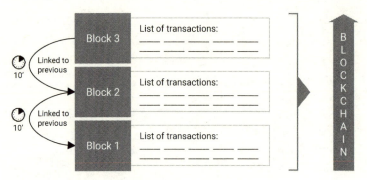

Figure 2. Graphical representation of the Bitcoin Blockchain

BLOCKCHAIN EXPLORERS

Websites allow everyone to consult the information within a blockchain. For the Bitcoin Blockchain, blockchain.info or blockexplorer.com allows everyone to follow the creation of blocks and the flow of bitcoin transactions.

Chapter 3

Building consensus

In the previous chapter, we discovered that a blockchain is a sequential chain of blocks, where new blocks are built on top of previous blocks. In this chapter, we will take a closer look at the mechanism that creates these blocks in the Bitcoin Blockchain and ensures consensus on the network. Such a mechanism is referred to as a "consensus mechanism." Bitcoin's consensus mechanism is called proof-of-work (PoW).

THE CREATION OF A BLOCK

On average, a block is created every 10 minutes through solving a mathematical puzzle. Everyone is free to join in and try to solve this puzzle. People who try to solve these puzzles are called miners.

Before we can explain what the mathematical puzzle is all about, you need to understand the magic of a cryptographic hash. Hashing might sound a bit technical, but it is one of the most crucial pieces of Bitcoin's working, so understanding it is key.

Cryptographic Hash

A hash is the output value returned by a hash function.[6] A hash function is a function that transforms any string of data of arbitrary size to a string of data with a fixed size. A good hash function meets three requirements, namely:

- It has *preimage resistance*, meaning that it only operates in one direction; the hash value can easily be computed from the input data, but the input data cannot be computed from the hash value.
- It is *collision resistant*, meaning that it is unlikely to generate the same hash twice. Let us say the odds of a meteor hitting our planet in the next two seconds are higher!
- There is *avalanche effect*, meaning that a slight change in the input data will significantly change the hash value.

When given an initial set of data, the hash function generates the corresponding hash value. This type of data manipulation is often referred to as "hashing data."

Since a good hashing function has avalanche effect, changing even one bit of the initial content will generate a completely new hash. Let us take a concrete example of a hash function used by the Bitcoin protocol (SHA256).

Given input data	Generated hash (SHA256 algorithm)
Sun is shining	AC46B9B7E7991E0BC876C0DB64A1F4DE 142D4A20AA74727DD4408E64F75E1DC3
sun is shining	475C228C53BA62DE0B19B5416690F4D 65DAB1A91A3A596CF9B61C06122147 13D
Sun is shining!	704B5DA828C94FE864C51A5FD77A464 D2BD494610893A7517EBA065E40C3D711

Table 1. Avalanche effect

As you can see, similar input data can generate completely different hashes. In this case, capitalizing the letter "s" or adding an exclamation mark at the end of the input data changes the hash completely.

The most efficient way to regenerate initial data from its hash value is to try inputting random data until you find data that returns your desired hash. However, given the number of potential input possibilities, it is almost impossible that you will ever stumble upon the hash you are looking for. Even if you did manage to find input data that generated your desired hash, you could not be certain that it matched the original input data. In some cases, multiple inputs can lead to the same hash.[7]

Competition to generate a valid hash

To create a new block in the Bitcoin Blockchain, you must be able to generate a hash that satisfies certain constraints. The process of searching for valid hashes is known as "mining," and it is performed by nodes (computers connected to the Bitcoin network) called "miners." Note that nodes are not required to participate in mining to use Bitcoin. Nowadays, most nodes only verify blocks created by other miners, without mining themselves at all.

Mining can be considered a competition to solve a mathematical puzzle before anyone else. In this competition, the puzzle is to find an input that will generate a valid hash. The miner who solves the puzzle first is rewarded with bitcoins (more on this later). This reward creates competition between miners.

So what constitutes a valid, reward-winning hash? It has to start with a certain number of zeros. To find a hash with the appropriate number of zeros, a miner must make multiple, random guesses using different input data until he finds a valid hash. This concept is known as *proof-of-work*; a valid hash proves that work was performed by a miner. Otherwise, they could not have guessed the hash!

Once a valid hash is found, the mathematical puzzle is solved. The winning miner is declared, and he will spread the block he created to announce his victory. The hash he found, which in turn created the new block, will serve as the unique fingerprint for the block.

In a competition where the purpose is to find the solution to a mathematical puzzle before anyone else, everyone should start solving the puzzle at the same time with the exact same information.

However, if a hash only requires a certain number of zeros to be valid, a miner could easily reuse the same input, generate the same hash, and create another valid block. He could win the competition over and over again! Miners could also store a series of valid hashes they found in the past, but kept secret, and then suddenly decide to use them all to create multiple blocks, one after another. In a race to find the first valid hash, this would be cheating because some people would start off with the advantage of having more data than other people.

To set everyone at the same level when the competition for a new block begins, the inventor of Bitcoin added a second requirement for the hash to be valid: it must also incorporate the fingerprint of the previous block. Let us look at how that works.

Remember that a hash is generated from input data. This input data can be a combination of different pieces of data. For example, one application could require that the input data always include the following: first name, last name, and year of birth. In this case, the first name, last name, and year of birth would represent the constant part. However, hashing this data might not lead to a hash starting with the desired number of zeros. Therefore, a variable part should be added to the constant part. The variable part can be a number that changes until it generates a hash with the desired number of zeros when combined with the constant part. This number is called a nonce.

To reset the game every time a new block is created, Satoshi Nakamoto designed the rules of the Bitcoin Blockchain so that, in order to produce a valid hash, the input data must include the fingerprint, or hash, of the previous block. Since no two blocks have the same hash, Bitcoin miners are forced to change their input data (so that it includes the appropriate hash), every time a new competition begins. No one can reuse old input data. No one has a head start.

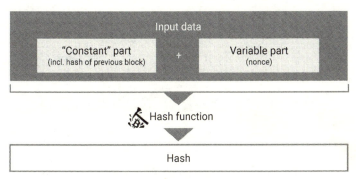

Figure 3. Generation of the block hash

This means that the miner will make his guesses for finding a valid hash by combining the constant part of the input data (the previous block's hash but also a couple of other constant inputs—see Appendix 1 for a full list) with a variable part (the nonce). By changing this variable part, the miner will be able to generate a completely new hash. He will change the nonce of the input data as many times as necessary, until he finds a hash starting with the correct number of zeros. Once he has found a nonce, which, when combined with the constant part, gives a valid hash, he will spread both pieces of information to the other nodes of the network. The receiving nodes will verify that (1) the hash of the previous block is correct and (2) when combined with other constants and the nonce, the hash function generates a valid hash.

Using the hash (fingerprint) of the previous block as an input for the hash (fingerprint) of the new block creates an unbreakable link between the two blocks. The new block is chained to the previous block, which is chained to the previous block, which is chained to the previous block... hence the name blockchain.

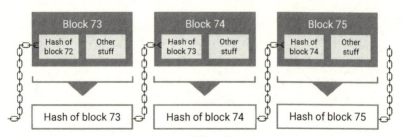

Figure 4. How blocks are chained

The 10-minute rule

As the amount of computing power available in the Bitcoin network increases (because more and more people are connecting their computers to the network), miners as a group can generate more guesses per second. The increase in guess-rate means that valid hashes can be discovered faster and faster. It is like 5 million people deciding to buy lottery tickets instead of only five; the odds of *someone* winning the lottery soon go way up!

To counter this phenomenon and keep the average time between blocks at 10 minutes, the difficulty of finding a valid block is linked to the amount of computing power available in the network. The more computing power available, the more zeros are required at the beginning of the valid hash, thus making it more difficult to find a valid solution because more guesses are required. Bitcoin wants the difficulty to be set at a level that will take two weeks to compute the next 2,016 blocks (that is, approximately one block every 10 minutes). Therefore, the number of required zeros is redefined every 2,016 blocks, based on the time it took to compute the last 2,016 blocks.

MINING EVOLUTION AND MINING POOLS

Computing power increased

As more and more mining nodes started competing against each other to find the hash before anyone else, mining material became more and more professional. Central processing units (CPU) were replaced by graphics processing units (GPU), which are able to generate hashes 50 to 100 times faster, going up to 800 Mhash/s. At the end of 2011, GPUs started to be replaced by specialized mining processors called field-programmable gate arrays (FPGA), which were then replaced by application-specific integrated circuit (ASIC) cards. Each generation enabled miners to guess more hashes, in the hope of beating the competition to a valid hash and collecting the reward. Over time, mining shifted from the amateur using his personal computer to the professional investing in large-scale mining equipment.

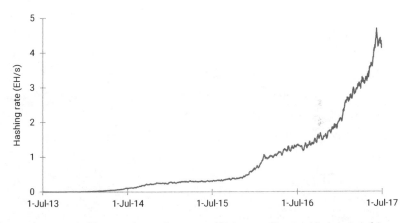

Figure 5. Hashing rate from July 2013 until July 2017 (Source: blockchain.info)

Due to the increasing amount of computing power devoted to finding each new hash, the difficulty of finding a valid hash (defined by the numbers of zeros) increased in a similar fashion to uphold a mining time of 10 minutes per block.

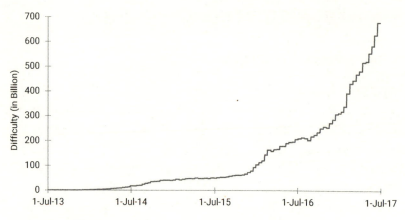

Figure 6. Difficulty rate from July 2013 until July 2017 (Source: blockchain.info)

Mining pools appeared

Eventually, miners started to group into communities, better known as "mining pools." The idea is that, together, they have a better chance of finding a valid hash. Each member of the community contributes a number of guesses, depending on the computing power he has. When a block is solved, the pool broadcasts the solution and gets rewarded. The reward is then split between the members of the community in proportion to the computing power they brought to the mining pool. Miners are therefore less subject to random luck in finding the solution and have the guarantee of a more stable income.

CONSENSUS

In this section, we will study how blockchains are formed. Let us start with a chain of three blocks, waiting for the creation of a fourth block.

The newly solved block (block 4) spreads across the network and is added to the blockchains of the different nodes that receive and validate it. If the block is considered valid under the constraints set by the protocol, it is added to the chain.

In the event of a second valid block (block 4') being created at the same time by someone else in the network, each node will accept the first block it receives and refuse the second block, since it already has a block referring to the hash of the previous block. At this point in time, two blockchains with different last blocks might exist in the network.

For example, node A, which receives and validates block 4 first, will include block 4 in its blockchain and therefore refuse block 4' because it already accepted a block referring to block number 3.

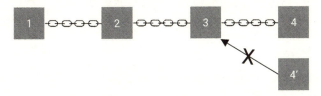

Another node, node B, which receives and validates block 4' first, will include block 4' in its blockchain and will refuse block 4 because it already accepted a block referring to block number 3.

How is this difference reconciled?

The consensus rule is that the longest valid chain, with the most proof-of-work, sets the standard for all other chains. If a node receives a block from a chain that is longer than its own, thus having more proof-of-work, it will accept the block and, if necessary, replace the previously accepted block with the block present in the longest blockchain (as long as all the blocks are considered valid by the receiving node, of course).

In our example, we will imagine that the mining node that finds block 5 has the same blockchain as node B presented above. In other words, the node that finds block 5 previously accepted block 4' and refused block 4. As a result, block 5 will be chained to block 4'.

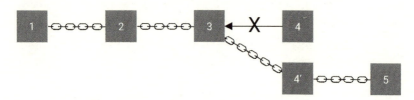

All nodes on the network will now receive block 5 for validation. As a chain with five blocks is longer than a chain of four blocks and has more proof-of-work, all nodes will consider this longest chain as the valid one. Nodes such as node A, which previously accepted block 4 and not block 4', will replace block 4 by block 4'. Remember, block 5 was made with the unique hash from block 4', so it would be impossible to link block 5 to block 4. That is why block 4 has to be replaced!

Ultimately, the blockchain will always stabilize when miners reach a consensus by following the longest chain available. The general consensus states that a user should wait for six blocks (one hour) to be sure that the blocks will no longer be subject to change. Since Bitcoin's launch in 2009, the longest orphan chain ever was seven blocks. There are, at the time of writing, no instances of a six-block orphan chain and only a couple of instances of five-block orphan chains.

Chapter 4

Bitcoin basics

So far, we have explained the concepts behind Blockchain.

By now, you should be aware that a blockchain is a sequential chain of blocks where each block is linked to the previous block. You should know that all these blocks are stored on every full node of the network and that it is impossible to delete a block. Finally, you should understand that Bitcoin blocks are created by miners through a concept called *proof-of-work*, and that one of the conditions for a block to be valid is to find a hash starting with a certain number of zeros.

To sum up:

- Blockchain, generically speaking, is a distributed database that stores information that is secured through a consensus mechanism. Unlike traditional databases, information can never be altered or removed.

If we make this more specific to the Bitcoin Blockchain, we can say that:

- The Bitcoin Blockchain is a distributed ledger storing a record of bitcoin transactions, which is secured by a proof-of-work consensus mechanism.

Let us now delve into some of the other rules used by Bitcoin.

BITCOIN ACHIEVES TRUST BY CONSENSUS

The Bitcoin protocol is open-source; it runs on the Bitcoin Blockchain and is a set of unchangeable rules accepted by the different nodes of the network. If you disrespect one of these rules, you will be stepping out of the network and the possible blocks you produce will be rejected.

The Bitcoin protocol incorporates a set of rules chosen when Satoshi Nakamoto launched the protocol for the first time. Each node that uses the Bitcoin protocol complies with this set of rules and will check that every block acts according to this set of rules. If the block does, it will be added to the chain. If not, it will be rejected.

Changing the rules is very difficult; it would require all nodes to agree on accepting blocks incorporating these new rules.

We have already discovered a few rules, like the fact that a valid block should always be linked to the previous block and start with a certain number of zeros.

In this chapter, we will study four other rules of the Bitcoin protocol: the supply of bitcoins, the divisibility of bitcoins, the average time per block, and the size of blocks. In the next two chapters, we will discover some additional rules related to the way transactions are built and settled.

SUPPLY

In the previous chapter, we saw that the process of generating a new block is based on computing power, which leads to a certain electricity cost. To incentivize people to maintain the system, the node that generates a valid hash can include one special transaction, called a *coinbase* transaction. This transaction allows the creator of a new block to reward himself with a fixed number of bitcoins. This is how new bitcoins are created in the system. The number of bitcoins created approximately every 10 minutes is fixed, and to prevent over-inflation in the monetary supply, this fixed reward is cut in half every 210,000 blocks (a period of almost four years). For example, in Bitcoin's early years (from January 3, 2009, to November 28, 2012), 50 bitcoins were created each time a block was solved. After the first halving occurred in November 2012, 25 bitcoins were created each time a block was solved. In July 2016, this amount was halved again, making the current reward for solving a block 12.5 bitcoins. The reward will continue to be halved every 210,000 subsequent blocks.

Halving is a rare event for the Bitcoin community. It is a bit like New Year's: Bitcoin believers around the globe gather to celebrate the halving.

Figure 7. Celebration of the second halving in Los Angeles
(Source: Rob Mitchell's twitter account @TheBTCGame)

From an economical point of view, all bitcoins created through mining can be considered an inflation of the monetary supply. As we can see on the chart below, the halving of newly generated bitcoins every 210,000 blocks decreases the inflation rate over time. In the end, inflation will be close to zero, and the total number of bitcoins will be around 21 million. Actually, when we take into account the fact that bitcoins can be lost (more on this later), the Bitcoin economy will ultimately become a deflationary economy, meaning that new bitcoins will no longer be created and the scarcity will increase—which should result in a price increase. In an economy where bitcoins become scarce, people will tend to hold on to their bitcoins instead of spending them.

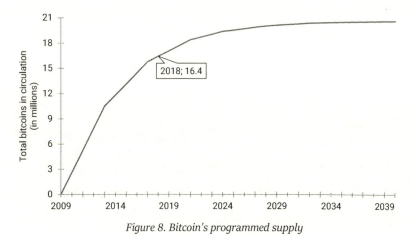

Figure 8. Bitcoin's programmed supply

One new and interesting thing about Bitcoin's monetary policy: the supply is programmed into the open-source protocol[8] and cannot be modified (unless consensus is achieved to do so). This is a key feature in safeguarding the scarcity of bitcoins, and it makes bitcoins unique when compared to fiat currencies, which can be printed or burned by the central bank whenever they want. In times of economic uncertainty, there is no doubt that having a predictable supply of currency is appealing.

Of course, the dwindling reward that miners receive for solving a block might cause many miners to drop out of the game. Who will validate blocks if there is little to no reward? Eighty percent of the bitcoin supply will be in circulation by 2020, leaving a comparatively small reward for miners. A few scenarios are possible:

- As bitcoins become scarcer, the value of each bitcoin will increase and make mining activities profitable even if the rewards are substantially less.
- Because people who own bitcoins have an interest in keeping the system afloat, they will continue to mine and validate new blocks in order to avoid a system collapse, which would render their bitcoins worthless.
- Transaction fees will increase and serve as a reward to the miners.

DIVISIBILITY

One bitcoin can be divided into 100,000,000 smaller units, called satoshis (named in tribute to Bitcoin's founder). One satoshi is the smallest unit possible. In this book, we will use the term bitcoin to refer to a group of bitcoins or parts of a bitcoin (satoshis).

Just as 100 dollar-cents ($0.01) make up one dollar ($1), 100 million satoshis (0.00000001฿) make up one bitcoin (1฿).

Unit	Smallest possible unit	Name of smallest unit
$1	$0.01	dollar-cent
1€	0.01€	eurocent
1฿	0.00000001฿	satoshi

Table 2. Currency units

Should it be necessary, the protocol can be extended to support more decimals in the future. Such an extension would require the network to agree on it. Currently, this seems unnecessary. If one bitcoin became worth 1 million dollars, one satoshi would be equal to $0.01, which is still manageable.

AVERAGE TIME PER BLOCK

In the Bitcoin Blockchain, the generation time of a block is set to 10 minutes. We saw in the previous chapter that the solving time of 10 minutes is set by adjusting the difficulty of solving a block to the computing power available on the network. This adjustment occurs every 2,016 blocks, or roughly every two weeks. By setting the average solving time to 10 minutes, blocks have enough time to spread over the network and reach consensus before the next one arrives.

SIZE OF BLOCKS

Each block has a maximum size of one megabyte (MB), which is good for 2,000 transactions. As the average time between the creation of blocks is 10 minutes, an average of three to four transactions can be processed per second. By contrast, Visa can handle up to 24,000 transactions per second.[9] This limited number of transactions makes Bitcoin not (yet) ready for mass adoption (more on the scalability of Bitcoin in Chapter 8). In May 2017, an agreement was reached to update the maximum block size to 2 MB, which should go in effect in November 2017. Subscribe to *The Reader's list* (see "I have more for you" at the end of book) to stay informed of this update when it sees daylight.

Chapter 5

Transacting in Bitcoin

BITCOIN WALLETS

To do a Bitcoin transaction, a user must own a wallet. A wallet is a place where you can store, send, and receive your bitcoins (or, to be more accurate, your wallet will store a set of digital keys that you will use to send and receive bitcoins).

Multiple types of wallets exist, with features that make them more or less secure and user-friendly. Your wallet might be a software on your computer, smartphone, or web application. There are even paper wallets. A list of downloadable wallets can be found at https://bitcoin.org/en/choose-your-wallet.

We will describe wallets in detail in Chapter 9. For now, all we need to know is that they hold our keys.

DIGITAL KEYS

Inside your wallet, you will be able to generate a private and a public key. Once your keys are generated, you can send and receive bitcoins.

The private key is secret, so only you, the owner of the wallet, know what it is. It is generated by the wallet or by the user, and it functions like a complex, very strong, and unchangeable password, forever linked to your account number. Keeping your private key safe is extremely important, not only to prevent bitcoin theft but also because you will not be able to sign transactions or spend your bitcoins without your private key.

The public key is generated from your private key. It is safe to share your public key and the Bitcoin address generated from your public key. The Bitcoin address is like a bank account number to which people send money. It looks like this:

1EqK7dw7jFmfFtWqAFw5UGeVALA4Q1iUeD

As mentioned earlier, private keys are used to generate public keys, which are then used to generate Bitcoin addresses. Let us take a closer look at how this process works.

Everything starts when you generate a private key. One-way cryptographic functions then take over to generate your public key and Bitcoin address. One-way cryptographic functions are mathematical puzzles that can be solved only in one direction. In this case, it is easy to derive a public key from a private key, but impossible to derive a private key from a public key because there is no known "reverse" function to the cryptographic function. The fastest way to guess a private key would be to generate multiple private keys, apply the same one-way function, and see if they correspond to the public key. This is known as "brute force attacking." In the case of Bitcoin, the length of the private key (256 bits[10]) makes it statistically near impossible to guess.

To go from a private key to a public key, the Bitcoin protocol uses a function called "elliptic curve multiplication." To generate the Bitcoin address from the public key, the protocol uses two hashing functions (SHA256 and RIPEMD-160) followed by functions called "Base58Encode" and "Base58Check." The idea is to make the public key shorter and easier to read by excluding characters such as capital i ("I"), lowercase L ("l"), zero ("0"), and capital o ("O"), which are frequently mistaken for other characters. The function checksum is included at the end of the process to detect typing errors.

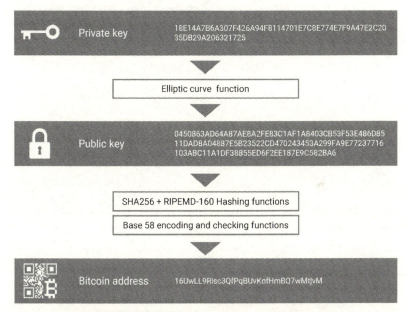

Figure 9. Cryptographic functions used to generate a Bitcoin address from a private key[11]

GETTING YOUR FIRST BITCOINS

Now that you know where to find wallets capable of generating a set of digital keys, how do you get your first bitcoins? You have several options:

Friends

Ask a friend to transfer bitcoins to your account and pay him or her in your local currency.

ATMs

Find a Bitcoin ATM near you. To use the ATM, you will need to enter cash and show the machine your Bitcoin address (via a QR code). The machine will transfer the equivalent number of bitcoins to your Bitcoin address (wallet). We will discuss ATMs in more detail in Chapter 10.

Local sellers

Websites like localbitcoins.com enable people to find Bitcoin traders nearby, so that they can meet up and exchange bitcoins for cash or via a wire transfer.

Exchanges

Exchanges are probably the most popular way to get bitcoins nowadays. They are online marketplaces where buyers and sellers of bitcoins come together to trade. Just as in the stock or foreign exchange market, the price (or in this case exchange rate) is set by supply and demand.

If you use an exchange, you will have to credit your exchange account with one of the accepted fiat currencies before buying bitcoins. These exchanges are often subject to know your customer (KYC) and anti-money laundering (AML) regulations, just like banks. In other words, you will have to prove your identity before trading your fiat currency for bitcoins. Once the amount of fiat currency is credited to your account, you will be able to exchange it for bitcoins. Notable exchanges that accept several fiat currencies (e.g., USD, EUR) via wire transfer are Bitstamp and Kraken.

The exchange will set up a Bitcoin wallet for you on their website. This is where your freshly traded bitcoins will be stored before you move them to another wallet. The wallet created by the website is also the one to which you can send bitcoins from outside the exchange before converting them back into a fiat currency.

SENDING BITCOINS

Now that you have a wallet and know how to fill it with your first bitcoins, let us take a look at how you can spend your bitcoins.

Once you are inside your wallet, you can send bitcoins to other addresses by entering the public Bitcoin address of the recipient. As we saw before, the addresses are quite long and complex to remember so usually the text is copy-pasted.

More user-friendly solutions also exist. The most popular example is the possibility of using your mobile phone to scan a QR Code, which prefills the Bitcoin address of the receiver.

For example, scanning the left QR code will prefill the receiver's address with my Bitcoin address: 1EqK7dw7jFmfFtWqAFw5UGeVALA4Q1iUeD

You, the sender, are now free to enter the amount you would like to send me! These will be used for the purposes stated on my website www.jeanlucverhelst.com.

QR codes are convenient for donations and money transfers. There are even QR codes designed especially for making purchases. Merchants can use these QR codes to prefill both the recipient's Bitcoin address and the number of bitcoins to be transferred (the exact price of the purchase).

For example, scanning this right QR code will prefill the transaction form with the address of the merchant (me again!) and the amount of 0.02 BTC. Note that this QR code is different from the previous one, even though they are both linked to the same address: 1EqK7dw7jFmfFtWqAFw5UGeVALA4Q1iUeD

After scanning the code, the sender only has to sign the transaction before the money is sent. Signing the transaction takes only a few seconds and can be done with one push of a button.

As soon as you press the send button, the transaction is signed with your private key, and it spreads across the nodes of the network. The receiver, as well as everyone else, can see the transaction via a Blockchain explorer. For example, if you send a transaction to one of the above QR codes, you will see your transaction appear at the following link: http://bit.ly/29vf6tv

Note that right after the payment is made, the transaction status remains unconfirmed until it is included in a block. Each new block built on top of that block will result in an additional confirmation and strengthen the irreversibility of the transaction.

Signing a transaction

As we saw earlier, the public key (P) is derived from the private key (p), but the real magic happens when someone uses their private key to sign transactions, thereby generating a digital signature. With a digital signature, it becomes possible to link transactions to the sender's public key without revealing his private key. This is possible because the public key is required to verify the digital signature. Let us look at an example:

To sign a message, a user (let us call him Bob) uses a signature function $S = f(p, M)$ requiring two inputs:

- Bob's private key (p)
- A message (M), i.e., the transaction itself

The signing function returns a unique signature (S). Only Bob's private key (p) can generate the signature (S) for the message (M). Note that the same message signed by someone else would result in a different signature, as it would be signed with a different private key (p).

Bob now sends the message, the signature, and his public key to the network.

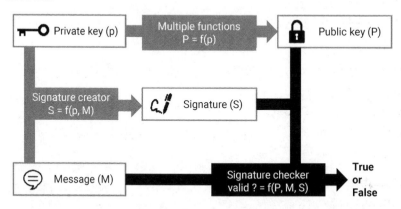

Figure 10. Signing of a message

To verify that this particular message has been signed by Bob, other users can use a signature verification algorithm f(P,M,S). This algorithm requires three inputs:

- The message (M)
- The signature (S)
- Bob's public identity, i.e., his public key (P)

With these three inputs, the signature checking function is capable of certifying that the message has been signed by Bob, using his private key (p), because Bob's public key (P) is a function of his private key (p).

Do you need to do all of this manually? Fortunately, no! Your wallets will use your private key and generate a signature upon your request. Some wallets will remember your private key for you, while others will ask you to provide your private key when you make a transaction. Either way, your wallet will sign your transaction[12] and broadcast it on the network, based on the information you provide. Full nodes check all signatures and ensure that every transaction is valid.

PSEUDO-ANONYMITY

Every Bitcoin account is identified by a Bitcoin address, and every transaction relating to that specific address can be found by anyone through a Blockchain explorer. Still, as you know, Bitcoin addresses do not reveal the account owner's identity. It is this combination of transparency and anonymity that has led many people to call Bitcoin "pseudonymous."

Obviously, your anonymity crumbles as soon as you communicate your Bitcoin address to someone, just like I have done in the pages above. As of the publication of this book, I am no longer anonymous.

Exchanges are one of the major breaking points in Bitcoin anonymity. Because they have to comply with KYC regulations, they are required to ask the identity of their users. This makes it easier for authorities to trace bitcoins back to a person who used an exchange. Occasionally, it is important for authorities to have this information. For example, a person might come into a large amount of cash by turning bitcoins into fiat currency. Because the person's identity is known by the exchange, authorities can verify that the person came into their cash legally. On the other hand, authorities might link a chain of Bitcoin transactions to illegal activities. If one of the criminals later uses an exchange, thereby linking his Bitcoin address to his identity, the authorities will be able to arrest him for his crime.

As soon as you interact with a third party requiring your ID information, your identity can be coupled with your Blockchain trail. This data can be used to better understand who you interact with and how you behave as a customer or to reveal illegal activities.

In response to this weakness in Bitcoin's anonymity, mixing services emerged. Mixing services are platforms where bitcoins from different people are pooled together, divided, mixed, and redistributed, thus making individual transactions less traceable. Using a mixing service involves some risk. For one thing, Bitcoin transactions are irreversible, so when you send your bitcoins to a mixing service, there is no way to force the service to return your coins (after mixing them). They could easily run away with your money! Additionally, mixing services are a perfect target for investigation by law enforcers. Better yet, law enforcers can operate mixing services themselves, which serve as a honeypot to attract people who have something to hide.

Chapter 6

The settlement of transactions

We have seen how user-friendly it is to send a transaction in less than a few seconds. Right after the transaction is sent, it is broadcasted on the network. However, it is not immediately included in a block of the Blockchain; it takes a few extra minutes before the transaction is settled in the Blockchain forever. This chapter will cover what happens from the moment you press send until the transaction is settled in the Blockchain.

POOL OF PENDING TRANSACTIONS

Immediately after a transaction is sent, it becomes part of a pool of pending transactions. The pool consists of all unconfirmed/unmined transactions, also called open-transactions. These transactions are waiting to be selected to become part of the next block. A miner collects transactions into a block and includes one extra transaction, called the coinbase transaction, which will reward him if he solves the block. If there are more transactions in the pending pool than the miner can fit into his block, he will probably pick the transactions with the highest fees. Transaction fees are not mandatory and are used at the discretion of the sender. The higher the transaction fee, the more likely a miner will include the transaction into a block, especially when many transactions are waiting to be processed.

Once the block is ready, the miner starts searching for a valid hash (see Chapter 3). As soon as he solves the block, he broadcasts it on the network to claim his reward.

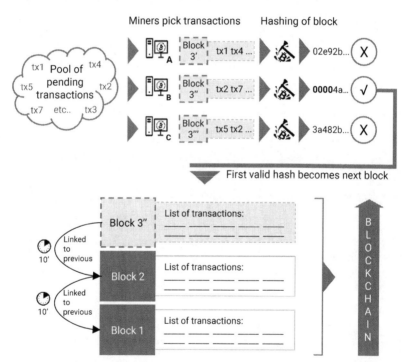

Figure 11. Miners pick transactions from the pool to form a block they will mine

In the Bitcoin system, much less time is needed to settle a transaction when compared to the settlement of a traditional banking payment, which can take days. The protocol sets approximately 10 minutes between the creation of each new block, so it takes about 10 minutes for a transaction to become part of a block in the Blockchain. At least, this is the case when the number of transactions in the pool of pending transactions is lower than the number of transactions that can fit into a block.

RECORD TRANSACTIONS IN THE BLOCKCHAIN

So far, we have seen that the Bitcoin Blockchain is a chain of blocks in which each block is linked to the previous one. We also know that each block contains a list of publicly visible and identifiable transactions. Fortunately, you do not have to store the entire Blockchain on your computer to search the records of Bitcoin transactions. Bitcoin enthusiasts have created online Blockchain explorers for that purpose!

Thanks to a Blockchain explorer, you can look into each block of the Blockchain, as illustrated by Figure 12 on the next page.

Block #317801

Summary

Number Of Transactions	403
Output Total	1,665.29398581 BTC
Estimated Transaction Volume	195.41416365
Transaction Fees	0.06244197 BTC
Height	317801 (Main Chain)
Timestamp	2014-08-27 22:15:15
Received Time	2014-08-27 22:15:15
Relayed By	F2Pool
Difficulty	23,844,670,038.8
Bits	405675096
Size	228.673 KB
Version	2
Nonce	1807217468
Block Reward	25 BTC

Hashes

Hash	00000000000000002739fcf0def76a7a4e3b4d43ac89...
Previous Block	00000000000000023ed8e1770d9626583ee0923dc9...
Next Block(s)	0000000000000000279895f50771246b6dbed293959...
Merkle Root	8fa6ebc9629d3c1dff49b65f214d5328f9953966ad6...

Transactions

5fe09d18a905de404c018a0a34cd557e2c054e7ee309f57bf4d0e3534c3e69ab   **2014-08-27 22:10:52**

1LSYTSbWyvPiVSMHtscQEou2kSwyNigMDj ➡ 1PFTEyZJ6DS6ivT77SeDMK868VBT4E7a8R

0.0749 BTC

81a77af40127b0456eb7d12890a29d0c7ab0bf67e2dd664b7d1d1eb41ed38ebe   **2014-08-27 22:09:59**

18mL2f4RdaaTXvo21qkPFEGE19s6cjhnB6 ➡ 19m1rmz1oic8xXwYBiPXfppGs4R4hvTsVG

0.05815242 BTC

Figure 12. Some information on block n317801 via the Blockchain explorer (Source: blockchain.info)

As you can see from the previous figure, each block has a list of transactions. For each transaction, you can look into more information. Let us take a look at the details of the first transaction (starting with "5feo") in the next figure.

Transactions

5fe09d18a905de404c018a0a34cd557e2c054e7ee309f57bf4d0e3534c3e69ab	**2014-08-27 22:10:52**
1LSYTSbWyvPiVSMHtscQEou2kSwyNigMDj ➡	1PFTEyZJ6DS6ivT77SeDMK868VBT4E7a8R
	0.0749 BTC

Summary

Size	191 (bytes)
Received Time	27/08/2014 22:10
Included in Blocks	317801 (2014-08-27 22:15:15 + 4 minutes)
Confirmations	155755 Confirmations
Relayed by IP	54.187.82.121 (whois)
Visualize	View Tree Chart

Inputs and Outputs

Total Input	0.075 BTC
Total Output	0.0749 BTC
Fees	0.0001 BTC
Fee per byte	52.356 sat/B
Estimated BTC Transacted	0.0749 BTC
Scripts	Show scripts & coinbase

Figure 13. Transaction detail in Blockchain explorer (Source: blockchain.info)

As you can see, each transaction has a unique identifier (in this case, it starts with "5feo" and ends with "69ab"). In the column on the left, you can see the Bitcoin address of the sender, and on the right, you can see the account of the receiver. You can also find some other information related to this transaction, such as the time it was sent, the ID of the block, the number of nodes confirming the transaction, etc.

In this case, there is a record in Block number 317801 indicating that 0.075 BTC was spent by the sender (address starting with "1LSY") and 0.0749 BTC now belongs to the receiver (address starting with "1PFT"). 0.0001 BTC is being spent as a fee. This transaction was sent at 10:10 pm on August 27, 2014. The block number 317801 was mined at 10:25 pm on August 27, 2014. Hence, this transaction took 15 minutes to settle.

DOUBLE SPENDING

In the Internet age, sharing information is actually copying information. Think of "sending" an email attachment. Not only does the recipient receive a copy of the attachment, you also retain a copy of the attachment on your computer. However, money would quickly become worthless if it was copied instead of being transferred. Finding a way to transfer, not copy, money was the biggest challenge in previous attempts to create a digital currency. How could they ensure that every transaction would be unique and that coins could only be spent once?

The Bitcoin Blockchain does more than just keep track of transactions; it is capable of tracing the ownership of each individual bitcoin all the way back to the moment it was generated by the system as a reward for a miner. This is possible because every transaction using bitcoins or satoshis can be identified, making them unique.

To ensure the bitcoins in a transaction were not spent previously, the protocol requires checking whether the sender has enough bitcoins to make the transaction and, consequently, include it in the Blockchain. Because every transaction is recorded in the Blockchain, it is easy to sum up all the bitcoins that have been spent and received by the sender. Subtract the number of bitcoins he has spent from the number of bitcoins he has received and you will find the number of bitcoins he owns. If he has enough bitcoins, the Blockchain will record the transfer of ownership of his bitcoins to the receiver and mark them as spent by the sender. The sender will no longer be able to spend the same bitcoins because they will be marked in the Blockchain as transferred to someone else and, therefore, no longer in his possession. In this light, the Blockchain can be seen as a chain of ownership. It can tell you who owned what, when they owned it, and who they transferred it to.

HOW BITCOINS ARE TRANSFERRED AND RECORDED IN THE BLOCKCHAIN

By now, you know that the Blockchain maintains a record of all bitcoin transactions, but the details of the record-keeping process get a bit gnarly. Let us take a closer look.

As you know, bitcoins are divisible into satoshis, where one bitcoin equals 100 million satoshis. Because every bitcoin is identifiable, you might ask yourself if for every bitcoin recorded in the network there are 100 million records of satoshis. The answer is no.

In the Blockchain, each record represents a transaction transferring a property (where the property is a given number of satoshis). Each record has the same size and structure—regardless of the number of satoshis it transfers. Think of each record as a paper note (or check) on which any value can be written.

Splitting and merging records

One of the challenges of Bitcoin's record-keeping system is that users might not always have a record that matches the price they want to pay in a new transaction. It is like having a check for $20 when you want to buy something that only costs $2.

Bitcoin gets around this problem by splitting and merging records and distributing change. If you think about it, you are already familiar with all three of these concepts:

- Splitting records is like trading a $10 bill for two $5 bills, so that you can pay two different people with a $5 note.

- Merging records is like using two $20 bills to buy something for $40.
- Receiving change is like using $10 to buy something for $9 and receiving $1 back in change.

During the process of a transaction, the Bitcoin protocol can (if needed) split or merge records belonging to the sender to create new records that are more convenient for the desired transaction.

In case you split an existing record to pay multiple people, you will use one existing record and create multiple new records, each having its own value. The sum of the new records has to be equal to or smaller than the existing record (you cannot spend $120 if you only have $100). Change can be returned to the initial owner and the remainder, if any, can be collected by the miner as a transaction fee.

Value of initial existing record =
Sum of value of each new record (including change) + transaction fee

In case you need multiple records to make a payment, the new record has a value equal to the sum of merged records minus the potential change that returns to the sender, minus a potential transaction fee. The "change" will be recorded as a new transaction, returning bitcoins to the sender, and the transaction fee will be added to the number of bitcoins awarded to the miner.

Value of new record =
Sum of initial records merged – change – transaction fee

Every merge or split of records is stored in the Blockchain. The information is linked to the transaction in which the merge or split occurred.

EXAMPLES OF BITCOIN OWNERSHIP TRANSFER

Single input for a single output

The simplest type of transaction is a single input, single output transaction, wherein one input is used to make a payment.

Transactions

5986f4b6a2458fceb395fdbeb7daf0888d53410b85f57958d3af84365aa2aefa	2014-08-27 22:15:15
36XR2X7qp85W2qo66GpKTEvT6Q2hmsGtaY	1LPJmkPJsMnLifinkJ5MSne3MiAxRhR3yw
	0.04899211 BTC

Figure 14. Single input for single output transaction (Source: blockchain.info)

The above transaction is a payment of 0.04899211 BTC made by the address that starts with "36XR" to the address that starts with "1LPJ." In this case, the sender has a record that is exactly equal to the amount he wants to transfer. It is like using a $20 check to pay for an item that costs $20.

Single input for multiple outputs

Probably the most common type of transaction is a single input, multiple outputs transaction. This type of transaction happens in two cases: when the sender transfers some change back to himself or when multiple payments are done by the same person at the same time.

Let us start with the case where the sender transfers some change back to himself.

3b6648fd6f18240e9a989e2e04aa40c05731d6715cd4522c8d2f28388e17b99d	2014-08-27 22:09:59
13AsooST91cmAfQPYCUVt511rdyWbgJodi	13qnEgPTxJW6mm88dLpnHX... (Richy_T)
	0.0175 BTC
	13AsooST91cmAfQPYCUVt511rdyWbgJodi
	0.3824 BTC
	0.3999 BTC

Figure 15. Single input for multiple outputs transaction (Source: blockchain.info)

The above transaction is a payment of 0.0175 BTC made by the address that starts with "13As" to the address that starts with "13qn." It may seem like a simple transaction, but there is a trick to it. Unless "13As" has received a payment of exactly 0.0175 BTC in the past, she does not have a record that matches the price she wants to pay. It is like trying to use a $20 check to pay for a $2 item.

Luckily, the Bitcoin protocol has a solution. To perform this transaction, the protocol splits an unspent record of 0.40 BTC belonging to "13As" into two: one record of 0.0175 BTC, which is sent to the address starting with "13qn," and another record of 0.3824 BTC, which is returned to "13As" as change. Note that 0.0001 BTC has been withheld as a transaction fee. The miner validating the block will receive the transaction fee on top of the block reward.

The second instance in which a single input, multiple output transaction occurs is when multiple payments are made by the same user. If the sum of the payments and fees is smaller or equal to one of the unspent records, that record can be used to make the different payments.

Let us say Alice is paying three people with an amount of 0.1 BTC, 0.2 BTC, and 0.4 BTC respectively. Alice also has a 1 BTC note. This single note will be split to pay for all three of the smaller transactions and the leftover change (0.3 BTC) will be returned to Alice via a fourth transaction.

Finally, you might have noticed "Richy_T" written next to the recipient's address in the last figure. This is the consequence of someone having linked his Bitcoin address to an online profile or website. By clicking on the name, we can find out whom this address belongs to. In this case, "Richy_T" is a user of a forum who advertised his Bitcoin address in his signature.

Multiple inputs for a single output

This occurs when multiple small records are summed up to make a large payment. It is like using two notes of $5 and one note of $10 to make a $20 payment.

Multiple inputs for multiple outputs

This is a common practice within bitcoin exchanges. The exchange accepts hundreds of bitcoin deposits from its clients daily. It records each deposit so that the client can request his bitcoins back whenever he wants to use them. However, exchanges do not store the bitcoins themselves. Instead, the exchange uses these bitcoins to fund bitcoin withdrawals made by other clients. This is the same procedure your bank uses when you deposit or withdraw money.

Of course, an exchange does not always have matching deposits and withdrawals. For example, the exchange might receive three deposits of 0.25 BTC, 0.15 BTC, and 0.30 BTC each and then receive three withdrawals of 0.20 BTC, 0.05 BTC, and 0.40 BTC.

To satisfy the withdrawals, the exchange will merge multiple deposits (to yield 0.70 BTC), then split that new record into three records that match the correct withdrawal amounts (0.20 BTC, 0.05 BTC, and 0.40 BTC).

Of course, there are other possible input and output combinations. You can see a more realistic picture of an exchange's activity below. Here, you can see transactions the exchange has received (on the right side) being merged to pay withdrawal requests (on the left side).

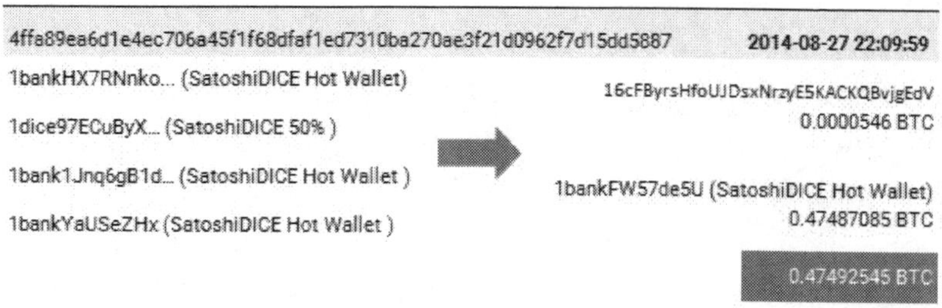

4ffa89ea6d1e4ec706a45f1f68dfaf1ed7310ba270ae3f21d0962f7d15dd5887	2014-08-27 22:09:59
1bankHX7RNnko... (SatoshiDICE Hot Wallet)	16cFByrsHfoUJDsxNrzyE5KACKQBvjgEdV
1dice97ECuByX... (SatoshiDICE 50%)	0.0000546 BTC
1bank1Jnq6gB1d... (SatoshiDICE Hot Wallet)	
1bankYaUSeZHx (SatoshiDICE Hot Wallet)	1bankFW57de5U (SatoshiDICE Hot Wallet)
	0.47487085 BTC
	0.47492545 BTC

Figure 16. Multiple inputs for multiple outputs transaction (Source: blockchain.info)

All of this is possible because the exchange acts as one single entity, receiving many small transactions from Bitcoin users and sending many small transactions to new Bitcoin users. Remember, the exchange is in possession of all the bitcoins it receives and can do anything it wants with them, just like the bank does with your money. Therefore, sending your bitcoins to an exchange requires some faith!

FULL TRANSPARENCY AND AUDITABILITY

Blockchain keeps track of every transaction ever performed with bitcoins. Because the Blockchain is pseudo-anonymous (with users creating addresses that cannot be linked back to their "real-world" personal information), everyone can see which Bitcoin address sent how much to another public address. The transparency provided by Blockchain accounts is one of its major breakthroughs. Never before has such transparency been possible in the context of online monetary transaction processing. Whether everyone wants such transparency is another question.

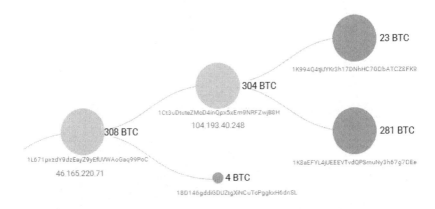

Figure 17. The full history of transactions is traceable (Source: blockchain.info)

IRREVERSIBILITY OF TRANSACTIONS

One of the dangers of transacting with bitcoins is its settlement irreversibility. Once a payment is executed, the transaction will take place. No one has the power to cancel it. A minor mistake, like typing an extra zero in the amount of your payment, will have consequences, and only the goodwill of the receiver can help you reclaim any bitcoins sent by mistake. It would take the agreement of all the nodes of the network to reverse a transaction by changing the Blockchain. In theory, a unanimous change in the Blockchain would be called a *hard fork* of the Blockchain (more on hard forks later). However, reversing a transaction has never happened on the Bitcoin Blockchain and, although not impossible, it will most likely never happen, as it would set a precedent that could endanger the network's trust in Bitcoin.

Chapter 7

Security

By now, you have assimilated a decent amount of technical information and gained an understanding of how Bitcoin operates. You know that it operates in a distributed way by consensus and that the security is backed by state-of-the-art cryptography. It is thanks to these two properties that Bitcoin has been up and running since 2009. For the first time in history, digital payments do not require a third party. Payments occur on an open-source and transparent system, which is accessible to everyone. Such a system is constantly exposed to hackers, and yet, no one has managed to hack it.

Bitcoin may seem like an impenetrable fortress, and it is true that its security is a modern marvel. Still, there are a few risks and theoretical scenarios that Bitcoin users should be aware of. You will learn about them in this chapter.

PRIVATE KEYS ARE EVERYTHING

From reading the previous chapters, you have learned that most of the information in the Bitcoin system is stored publicly. Your Bitcoin address and your transaction records are public information. You can access this information from wherever you want and spend your bitcoins anywhere in the world—provided you keep one piece of information secret: your private key.

Your private key gives you access to your wallet. It is *irreplaceable*. If you lose your private key, you will lose all your bitcoins. A lost smartphone, a misplaced USB-stick, or a fried hard-drive that had stored your private key could cost you all of your bitcoins.

To avoid this nightmarish scenario, it is recommended that you create multiple backups of your private keys in different places. However, be aware that the more backups or copies you create, the more likely it becomes that one of them will be exposed or stolen. So keep them safe.

Another strategy to manage the risk of losing one private key is to spread your bitcoins over multiple accounts. That way, if one private key gets lost, only part of your bitcoins will be lost.

HOT AND COLD STORAGE

Storing your private keys is of utmost importance. There are two main types of storage: hot storage and cold storage.

Hot storage refers to private keys stored online or on a device connected to the Internet. Hot storage is vulnerable to hacker attacks. A hacker in possession of your private keys could use them to steal your bitcoins by sending them to other addresses.

Cold storage, on the other hand, refers to any wallet disconnected from the web. Cold storage is more difficult to access, which means that it is also more secure. Note that if private keys are cold stored (offline), it is still possible to receive bitcoins to the account. Only the Bitcoin address needs to be disclosed to receive money. Think about it like a bank transfer; when someone is sending you money, they do not need your password; they only need your bank account number. The money sent will arrive in your bank account whether you are logged in or not. You only need your password or PIN code when you want to check your bank account balance or send money. The same goes for Bitcoin. You only need your private key when you want to send bitcoins. The difference with Bitcoin is that your transaction record and account balance can be checked without entering a private key. It is public information!

To limit the risk of hacking and stealing while maintaining a decent service level, most Bitcoin exchanges use both hot and cold storage. A provision of hot stored bitcoins is used to provide instant withdrawal to the users. At the same time, cold storage is used for the majority of their bitcoin reserve, which is only accessed when the hot storage reserve is not sufficient to cover an unusually high demand for withdrawals.

You can implement the same principles to your wallet management by using a hot wallet for daily operations and a cold wallet as reserve. With this setup, a user will usually have one or two hot wallets on his computer or smartphone to make payments on the go. Aside from his hot wallets, the user can keep his bitcoin reserve safe in one or multiple cold wallet(s), to which he can always send bitcoins. He only connects to the network when he needs to use his funds (and thus his private key). When compared to traditional bank accounts, hot wallets can be thought of as checking accounts used for daily transactions, while cold wallets can be thought of as savings accounts (except that they do not generate interest).

There are many options to store private keys: USB keys, offline hardware wallets, brain wallets, or paper wallets (more on this in Chapter 9).

51% ATTACK

In Chapter 3, we saw that the Bitcoin Blockchain is based on a consensus mechanism where miners use their computing power to find a valid hash before broadcasting the newly generated block. Other nodes then validate this block and add it to their chain.

In the unlikely event that someone with bad intentions takes possession of 51% of the computing power in the Bitcoin network, he would be able to mine blocks faster than anyone else and use those blocks to build a longer blockchain branch than anyone else in the same duration of time.

Let us represent the blockchain before the attack as PP, where P stands for blocks created by the Bitcoin network prior to someone launching a 51% attack. When someone gains 51% of Bitcoin's mining power, he will begin building his own branch of the blockchain: PPAAAA, where A stands for blocks created by the attacker.

Crucially, the attacker will not release his branch of the blockchain immediately. Instead, he will allow the network to continue adding blocks to their branch of the blockchain: PPHHH, where H stands for blocks created by honest miners.

Figure 18. Blockchain during a 51% attack (1/2)

Eventually, the attacker will release his branch of the Blockchain. Since it is longer than other branches, it will overrule the H blocks created by honest miners, effectively allowing the attacker to decide which transactions are stored in the blocks.

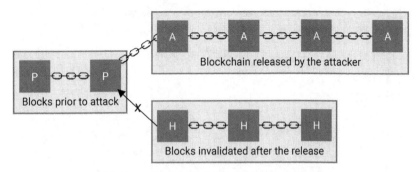

Figure 19. Blockchain during a 51% attack (2/2)

During the period in which the fraudster had control, he could:

- Prevent other people from creating blocks that will remain in the Blockchain (this is a condition to maintain control).
- Create empty blocks by selecting none of the transactions in the pool of pending transactions.
- Control which transactions are or are not included in his branch of the Blockchain.
- Mislead users about the transactions that are recorded in the blockchain. People who received a payment while the fraudster was producing a longer chain might see their transaction disappear once the longer blockchain is released. This opens the door for the attacker to make transactions that other users will not see until he releases the longer chain. Only when the attacker decides to spread his longer chain (which does not include his spent transactions), replacing the previous chain, will the receivers realize that they were misled.

The consequences would be limited to the duration of the fraudster's control over the Blockchain (i.e., the period during which he has over 50% of the computing power). His actions would only affect the transactions that occurred during this period. No bitcoins would be stolen or redirected since private keys are necessary to spend them, but recent transactions could be blocked.

More than practical damage to the Bitcoin economy, a 51% attack would damage Bitcoin's reputation. Bitcoin users might panic, weakening Bitcoin as a currency. The attacker could profit from this by monopolizing the mining revenue or by shorting[13] bitcoins before launching the attack.

It is worth mentioning that controlling over 50% of the network's hashing power would require massive investments in mining material. Currently, it seems impossible for an individual to gain that much computing power. Only big corporations or governments would have the required money to perform such an attack and take the Bitcoin system down.

In the event of a 51% attack, the price of Bitcoin would drop, as people would no longer trust the system. To counter the attack, more users might start mining activities to decrease the hashing-share of the attacker, bringing it below 50% and gaining back control of the network.

The rise of "mining pools" could possibly lead to an absolute control of the Blockchain by a mining pool with more than 50% of the total computing power available on the network. When two pools together represent over 50% of computing power, controlling coalitions become possible. This would threaten user trust in Bitcoin and the idea of a currency free from central authority.

The size of mining pools is continuously monitored. The pie chart in Figure 20 shows the repartition of hashing power on the network before publication.[14]

In January 2014, the two biggest pools together represented more than 50% of the hashing power, which placed a dangerous coalition within reach and threatened Bitcoin's ideal (see Figure 21).

The concerned pool "GHash.IO" decided to temporarily disallow new mining facilities from joining the pool and announced that it would implement a feature allowing its users to sell their computing power to other pools.[15] Many miners, aware that a 51% control could be a threat to the value of their bitcoins, left the pool. A few days later, GHash.IO's market share had dropped to 32%.[16]

On June 13, 2014, GHash.IO's market share reached new heights with a computing power representing 51% of the total power available on the network. The price of Bitcoin dropped by 12%. The website of the pool also became unavailable, probably due to a distributed denial-of-service (DDoS) attack.[17][18]

There are currently no regulations for mining pools, but common sense mandates that there should be a healthy distribution of the mining share between pools. As different pools have different reward systems and views on how the Blockchain should evolve, choosing a pool to mine for is not a trivial choice.

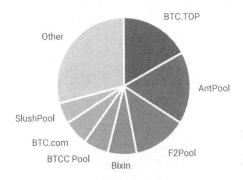

Figure 20. Hashing distribution – July 2017 (Source: blockchain.info)

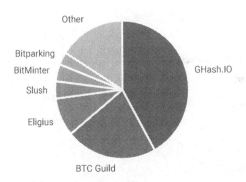

Figure 21. Hashing distribution – January 8, 2014 (Source: blockchain.info)

FINNEY ATTACK

A Finney attack could occur if a fraudster generated a valid block and this block included a bitcoin transaction made by the fraudster to himself. Let us say that he transfers the funds from his account A to his account B. So far, nothing is abnormal; this is perfectly legitimate.

Now let us imagine that, instead of broadcasting the valid block and collecting his mining reward immediately, the fraudster decides to wait. He runs to a shop as fast as possible. He makes a transaction with his account A to the account of the merchant. If the merchant decides to deliver the goods before receiving confirmation from the network (in other words, before seeing the transaction included in a block), the fraudster can run away from the merchant and quickly release the block he previously created.

In this case, the fraudster (1) succeeds in validating a block, (2) collects the goods for a transaction he has just made, and (3) spreads his valid block before anyone else broadcasts a valid block. If he succeeds, the transaction he made to the merchant will be considered invalid by the network. This is because the transaction to himself, which he included in his block, would have used the funds he was supposed to pay to the merchant.

In other words, the funds from account A will be marked as spent (sent to account B) in the block he released. The fraudster spreads this block across the network as soon as he walks out of the store, and the network starts accepting the block. The miners now start to create a new block, with the account-A-to-merchant transaction waiting in the pool of pending transactions. This transaction will be refused by the network because the funds from account A are marked as spent.

Note that, even if such a fraudulent transaction is possible, it is unlikely to occur for three reasons:

- The fraudster has a very limited time period to act (i.e., before someone else finds a block).
- He might prefer to have a guarantee on the mining reward instead of taking the risk that someone else might broadcast a valid block before him.
- He would need a significant amount of computing power to have a realistic chance of finding a valid block.

Therefore, the fraudster would have to buy something worth a significant number of bitcoins to make up for the risk of losing his mining reward. Still, it is easy for merchants to thwart Finney attacks. They only have to wait until new blocks are broadcasted before delivering goods. This is advisable in the event of large transactions.

In conclusion, the Finney attack is mainly a theoretical concept and is, in reality, unlikely and easily avoidable.

QUANTUM COMPUTERS AND CRYPTOGRAPHIC STANDARDS

In Chapter 5, we described how private keys, public keys, and Bitcoin addresses relate to each other by using different cryptographic functions. These cryptographic functions are secured by the mathematics behind them and the difficulty involved in finding the corresponding input given a certain output. With today's computers, the number of brute force guesses you would have to make to crack the cryptography is just too high.

What if, tomorrow, quantum computers, which are capable of solving certain algorithms faster than our current computers do, leave the labs? Will the cryptographic functions securing Bitcoin hold up?

According to Vitalik Buterin,[19] founder of Ethereum, the most vulnerable point would be situated at the elliptic curve function, the function that turns the private key into a public key. As a result, Bitcoin wallets could become more vulnerable to some algorithms that can only be performed by quantum computers (e.g. Shor's algorithm). Shor's algorithm would make it easier to derive the private key from a public key. As you may remember, the public key is only shared with the network when the signature of an outgoing transaction needs to be validated. Therefore, unless you decide to make an outgoing transaction, it is possible to share only your Bitcoin address with the network.

As long as someone only receives funds on a Bitcoin address without spending them, bitcoins are securely stored. This is possible since the public key behind a Bitcoin address remains safeguarded by a double hash function (SHA256 + RIPEMD-160). A simple solution to counter the risk of attack from a quantum computer is to spend all the funds in an account every time you make an outgoing transaction. This may sound extravagant, but it is actually very simple. All you have to do is make two simultaneous transactions: one sending the correct payment to the beneficiary and the other sending the remainder of your bitcoins to a new Bitcoin address, which you own.

Shor's algorithm could also be used by a fraudster to intercept and redirect transactions. This type of attack is also known as a "man-in-the-middle" attack, referring to a party changing the message between the sender and the receiver.

In this case, the fraudster would (1) intercept a transaction before it is validated by the network, (2) use a quantum computer to find the sender's private key, (3) create a new transaction, using the same funds, and send it to himself, and (4) sign the new transaction with the sender's private key. If he succeeds, the falsified transaction could be picked up by the miners, and the funds would be sent to the fraudster.

Luckily, there are quantum-resistant solutions (e.g., Lamport Signatures[20]) for generating digital signatures. In the event of quantum computers becoming an imminent threat, the network could implement these solutions without changing much of Bitcoin's functioning.[21]

It is unclear whether anti-quantum solutions would be easily accepted by the network's nodes, as some solutions would come at the cost of larger transaction messages. Assuming the block size remains the same, this would result in fewer transactions per block.[22]

Besides Bitcoin, many other institutions that rely on cryptography will have to upgrade their security measures in the age of mainstream quantum computers. This includes the entire Internet, a large portion of the banking infrastructure, identification cards and badges,[23] etc.

Chapter 8

Challenges

Bitcoin has been on the market for a couple of years, but it still has some challenges to overcome before it can reach mainstream adoption. Let us take a look at them.

VOLATILITY

Bitcoin's price has been bouncing up and down since 2009, but overall, Bitcoin's price has experienced a spectacular rise since its creation. One bitcoin was worth less than $1 before June 2011, reached $10 only a few months later, and then surged to over $1,000 at the end of 2013. This bubble was followed by a long price decline, all the way down to almost $200, where the price hovered for almost one year. However, at the end of 2015, the price started to rise again as the potential of the distributed ledger technology became more and more mainstream.

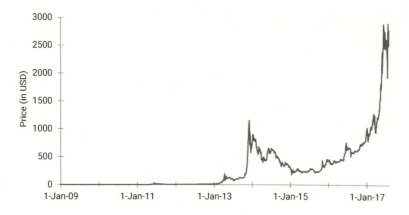

Figure 22. Evolution of Bitcoin's price (Source: blockchain.info)

Volatility is always computed against a reference (in this case the US dollar). The more the price of the asset (in this case, bitcoin) goes up and down over a period of time, the higher the volatility and riskier the asset. However, for every risky asset, the potential return on investment is higher. As such, high-volatility can be considered positive for an active investor and negative for a risk-averse person.

The chart below shows the 30-day historical volatility of daily returns of three assets against the US dollar: bitcoin, gold, and the euro.

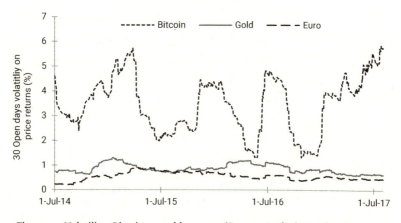

Figure 23. Volatility: Bitcoin vs. gold vs. euro (Source: Analysis on Bloomberg Data)

The chart below displays a similar analysis, performed by the author for his master thesis, this time based on price data taken every five minutes between June 9, 2013, and September 30, 2013. The data has been cleaned to keep only matching records (since not all assets are traded 24/7) and uses the three-month US treasury bill as a risk-free rate. As you can see, the results lead to a similar conclusion.

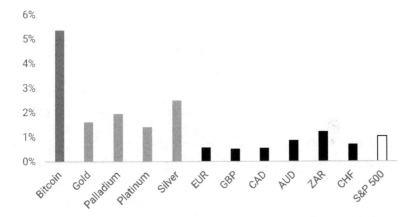

Figure 24. Volatility: Bitcoin vs. commodities vs. currencies (Source: Author's analysis)

From both graphs, you can conclude that Bitcoin's volatility is multiple times higher than the volatility of gold/commodities and the euro /currencies.

While high volatility can attract investors, Bitcoin needs low volatility to succeed as a currency. The average Joe does not want to check the trading markets 24/7 to make sure that his money holds its value.

Volatility is probably the main reason why merchants and businesses are reluctant to use Bitcoin as a currency. No merchant would like to adapt his prices multiple times per day, which, with Bitcoin's current volatility, would be necessary to ensure that all products were sold at the same value (relative to his fiat currency of choice). As we will see in Chapter 11, solutions exist to address these concerns for merchants.

ACCEPTANCE

By now, you have probably realized that Bitcoin is not easy to understand, let alone explain. It takes time to understand the system, and when money comes into play, people want to know what they are dealing with before they grant their trust. This understanding/trust barrier is one that Bitcoin must overcome.

People who do not have the skills to understand or use Bitcoin will likely avoid risking their savings in it, unless the brand becomes generally recognized as trustworthy. Moreover, in today's society, not everyone is digitally inclined enough to adopt such a system. Words like peer-to-peer network, cryptography, or digital currency can scare people off.

We could argue that understanding how fiat currencies are created is also complex, maybe even more complex than understanding Bitcoin. However, the fact is that fiat currencies have been imposed on civilization for centuries and that most people never question the use of fiat currencies because they are the standard. That being said, economic crises, bank haircuts (e.g., Cyprus in 2012), and limited bank withdrawals (e.g., Greece in 2015) have raised questions about the trustworthiness of fiat currencies, even in public sentiment. As we will see in Chapter 13, some of these events resulted in people turning to Bitcoin for its decentralized nature. In extreme circumstances, many people who are afraid of leaving their wealth in banks prefer to store it on the Blockchain.

Today, even though the trust in fiat currencies is decreasing, operating without them is practically impossible. The functioning of our entire society is based on the concept of a currency; wealth is captured and redistributed by means of currencies. People are working for a sum of money that they can exchange for goods and services such as transportation, entertainment, healthcare, and food. Governments incentivize behaviors and support healthcare systems with currencies.

A world without a common layer of trade, such as a currency, is difficult to imagine.

Another hurdle between Bitcoin and social acceptance is the reputation from which it suffers. A mysterious currency that has served criminal activities is difficult to consider trustworthy, but as you have already discovered in this book, Bitcoin's nefarious anonymity is a misconception since the transparency provided by the Bitcoin Blockchain makes it possible to trace every transaction back to its originator.

Finally, banks have a love-hate relationship with Bitcoin; they are continually making efforts to publicly distance themselves from the currency "Bitcoin," while at the same time adopting the distributed ledger technology, which backs Bitcoin.

SCALABILITY

Even if Bitcoin became widely accepted, it is unclear whether it would be able to operate as a currency. Currently, the size of a block is set to 1 MB, which enables the Blockchain to process approximately three to four transactions per second. Credit card companies are processing tens of thousands of transactions per second. If Bitcoin became widely accepted, it would, with the current block size of 1 MB, create huge queues in the pool of pending transactions and short processing time for all transactions could no longer be guaranteed.

As Bitcoin has gained users, the number of transactions per block has increased. Already, the Bitcoin community has reached the 1 MB block size limit, resulting in a saturated network with transactions taking hours to settle.

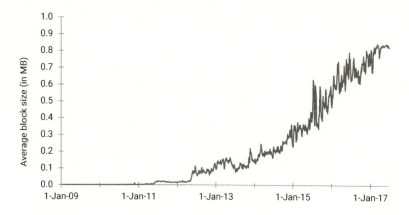

Figure 25. Evolution of the average block size in MB (Source: blockchain.info)

This problem could be solved by increasing the block size. Technically, changing the block size is possible, but it would require the consensus of the network to change any of the rules defining whether a block is valid. For years, no consensus could be reached about increasing the block size, so the validation rules remain the same. Two camps in the Bitcoin community have voiced their opinion. On one side, there are users who want to see Bitcoin scale fast and are willing to support a block size increase. On the other side, there are purists who believe that Bitcoin should remain, as much as possible, the way it was designed. What's more, there are mining pools that might see a drop in their profitability if the block size was increased (an increase in the block size would require more storage capacity, which represents a cost).

Another argument used by opponents of a block size increase is that, if the block size was increased to accommodate tens of thousands of transactions per second, the size of the blocks would be multiple gigabytes. Such large blocks would make it unaffordable for ordinary users to update the Blockchain on their computer, which would lead to a smaller number of nodes maintaining the ledger and a more centralized system. This would not only contradict Bitcoin's philosophy, it would also make it easier for governments to regulate Bitcoin, as they could exercise their power over the reduced number of nodes maintaining the Bitcoin Blockchain.

If Bitcoin keeps growing and the block size does not increase, payment senders might have to pay higher fees in order to tempt miners to choose their transactions out of the pool of pending transactions. Bitcoin would turn into a network where only people who can afford to pay high fees can get their transactions settled. This contradicts Bitcoin's early philosophy, namely that everyone can be part of the network and that transactions of any amount should be almost free.

In August 2015, a new version of the Bitcoin software was released, proposing to increase the maximum block size to 8 MB and to double the size every two years after that. The change was programmed in such a way that it would only go into effect if 75% of users agreed on the new software, but that percentage was never reached, so the block size increase did not happen. In May 2017, an agreement was reached to upgrade the block size to 2 MB during November 2017.

Multiple proposals exist to scale Bitcoin without increasing the block size. Below, we will explain the four most prominent propositions at the time of writing: segregated witness, payment channels, sidechains, and lightning networks. It is important to note that these proposals are currently animating many discussions in the community, but they might never be implemented or they might undergo significant changes before being implemented.

Segregated witness (SegWit)

If it were unacceptable for the network to create larger blocks, an alternative way to scale Bitcoin would be to store more transactions within a block. This is exactly what "segregated witness" does.

Segregated witness is one of the latest developments in the Bitcoin space. This proposal makes it possible to store transactions without their signatures. Remember that signatures are required for miners to verify that transactions are signed with the correct private key. This is only necessary at the moment when transactions are added to a new block and when this block is validated by other full nodes of the network. Once the block is accepted by consensus on the network, the signatures are, in essence, no longer needed.

Instead of storing both transactions and their signatures in a block, segregated witness removes signatures from the blocks and includes only transactions. As a result, less storage capacity is required and more transactions can be included in a block without having to increase the block size.

The signatures are stored outside of the chain in "the segregated witness," an add-on that carries the signatures and some other information. A Merkle tree (see Appendix 2 for more information) is then created with all the witnesses' signatures, and the hash of that Merkle tree is added to the coinbase transaction (the transaction rewarding miners who create a block) of the block of the Bitcoin Blockchain.[24] Consequently, the block's identifying hash links to the segregated witness tree, which is stored outside of the Blockchain. Every node is free to store a copy of the segregated witness if it wants.

Why do we need payment channels, sidechains, and lightning networks?

Bitcoin used to be a perfect payment method for small amounts and transactions without fees. However, as Bitcoin has gained popularity and users, this has changed.

As the value of Bitcoin rose and the number of transactions started to exceed the capacity a block could store, fees became more important, and it became more difficult to make micropayments of a few cents without paying considerable mining fees.

Moreover, let us imagine the case of someone who needs to make one large payment receiving hundreds of small payments across different blocks of the Blockchain. The large payment might need hundreds of these small transactions as input. (Remember that every transaction requires a list of past, unspent transactions as input to be valid). All of these small transactions will be written as input in the block storing the larger transaction. This uses lots of storage capacity while representing tiny amounts.

The following proposals try to resolve these issues by making more Bitcoin payments off-chain.[25]

Payment channels

Payment channels are useful for parties who make many transactions between each other, especially when the transactions represent tiny amounts.

A payment channel aims at reducing small, serial transactions on the Bitcoin Blockchain by opening a payment channel. Let us take a concrete example. John is translating a book for Johanna, who he has a working relationship with. Since the book has many pages, John translates one chapter at a time, and as soon as the chapter is finished, Johanna pays him for the number of words he translated before providing him with the next chapter.

Instead of sending a new transaction on the Bitcoin network each time a chapter is finished, Johanna and John open a unidirectional payment channel.

During the opening of the channel, Johanna (the payer) transfers a number of bitcoins to the channel. For each chapter John translates, Johanna gives part of the amount she owns on the channel to John.[26] When they decide to close the channel, the money collected by John is sent to his account on the Bitcoin Blockchain. The remaining bitcoins are sent to Johanna's account on the Bitcoin Blockchain. By working this way, the number of transactions occurring on the Bitcoin network is limited to the one transaction at the opening of the channel and the one transaction at the closing of the channel.

Johanna and John might also decide to open a bi-directional channel, which works in a very similar way. In this case, not only is Johanna capable of paying John, John is also capable of returning some of the money he receives from Johanna, in case he would like to do so for one reason or another.

Closing a channel can be done as soon as all parties agree on it. However, since parties might not always immediately agree on when to close a channel (or might even disappear before the work is finished), closing conditions are set in an agreement at the opening of the channel. For example, the agreement could state that the closing will occur at a certain date, after a certain period of inactivity, or a certain number of days after one party's request to close the channel is not accepted by the other party.

As long as the channel is open, the funds are blocked and cannot be used on the Bitcoin Blockchain. As a result, channels represent a tradeoff between the convenience of not having to revert to the Bitcoin Blockchain for small transactions and the convenience of always having enough funds on the Bitcoin network for spending.

The most interesting use of payment channels occurs when a party regularly consumes goods from another party. For example, you might pay a few cents for every 10 minutes you spend streaming a video. In this case, a couple of cents would flow to the streaming service as you watch the video, until all the bitcoins you had on the channel are consumed or you decide to terminate the contract.

Sidechains

Sidechains are connected blockchains that can receive bitcoins (think of it as a sub-chain of Bitcoin). Usually, the sidechain protocol states that the value of the coin on the connected blockchain is pegged to bitcoins (for example, 1 BTC = 10 coins on the sidechain). People can trade in bitcoins without actually using the Bitcoin Blockchain. Such a system does not resolve the fundamental scalability issue of Bitcoin's Blockchain protocol, but it does relieve Bitcoin's Blockchain of a certain number of transactions. Sidechains were designed to enable more permissionless innovation and testing of new features (e.g., more confidential transactions, more advanced contracts) before merging them to the main blockchain protocol.

In a white paper on pegged sidechain,[27] the authors[28] describe how the transfer from the Bitcoin Blockchain (parent blockchain) to the sidechain (child blockchain) can be enabled with a limited simplified payment verification (SPV) proof.

SPV is a system that provides proof that a transaction is included in a certain block of the Blockchain. This makes it possible to know how many blocks have been created since the transaction, giving us an indication of how likely it is that the block, and the transaction, will be overwritten by a longer chain.

In order to transfer bitcoins to a sidechain, these bitcoins are sent to a special transaction output and can only be spent with an SPV proof ensuring that you possess the coins on the sidechain. This transaction makes it impossible to spend the bitcoins on the Bitcoin Blockchain until they are unlocked in the future. The user can claim this transaction on the sidechain as soon as the locked transaction on the Bitcoin Blockchain has existed for a period of time long enough to ensure it will not be overwritten by a longer chain (confirmation period). Once claimed, the user receives the equivalent number of coins on the sidechain.

Before being able to transact on the sidechain, the user has to wait for an extra period of time (contest period), during which other users can provide proof that the coins were locked in a block that turned out not to be in the real blockchain.[29] This could happen in the event that, a longer chain invalidates the block containing the pegged coins.

Once both the confirmation and the contest period have passed, the coins are ready to be transferred on the sidechain. When moving around on the sidechain, the pegged coins are always backed by the underlying bitcoins, even as their ownership changes on the sidechain.

A few conditions are required to unlock the bitcoins on the Bitcoin Blockchain before they can be reclaimed. To meet these conditions, the owner of the sidechain coins can send them to a locked transaction and specify that their destination be on the parent blockchain. Once an SPV proof proves that the coins are sufficiently deep in the chain, the owner can claim these coins on the Bitcoin Blockchain.

Let us imagine Alice sends a transaction of 1 BTC on the Bitcoin Blockchain and is claiming 10 pegged coins on the sidechains. She sends three of the sidechain coins to someone else (Bob). What happens on the Bitcoin Blockchain when Bob claims 0.3 of the 1 BTC that is locked on the Bitcoin Blockchain? Depending on the sidechain, he would most likely get 0.3 BTC. The Bitcoin Blockchain would probably not even be aware of the transfer. It is only when the coins are claimed back on the Bitcoin Blockchain that the ownership on the sidechain might be checked to ensure the coins are locked.

Sidechains only make sense when transactions take place between people using the same sidechain. If different people use different sidechains that do not allow pegging between one another, they might increase the number of transactions on the Bitcoin Blockchain instead of decreasing it. For example, person A has coins on sidechain A and wants to pay person B, who is not using the sidechain. If person A pays person B, person A will have to transfer his coins back to the Bitcoin Blockchain (first transaction) before sending them to person B (second transaction). An alternative to avoid reverting to the Bitcoin Blockchain would be to pass through an intermediary, such as an exchange or a Lightning network.

Lightning networks

Lightning, as presented by Joseph Poon and Thaddeus Dryja at the Scaling Bitcoin conference in Hong Kong 2015 and at the Bitcoin Devs

Seminar in San Francisco in March 2015, involves opening multiple payment channels between users of a special "lightning" network.

Instead of having to create a separate, off-chain payment channel for every user with whom you regularly make transactions, the lightning network would allow you to use existing payment channels, which can link you to the person you want to pay without having to open a new payment channel.

For example, John has a payment channel open with both Claire and Marc. If Claire wants to pay Marc without opening a new payment channel, she can make a payment to Marc via the channel she has with John. John will then use his payment channel with Marc to forward the payment from Claire. The certainty that transactions will happen from one payment channel to another is secured by hashed timelock contracts.

The lightning setup requires users to know who has payment channels with whom, in order to find a possible route. This can be achieved by observing the network or by building a routing table,[30] which, according to the white paper,[31] is a current area of research.

Lightning networks could also facilitate the use of cross-chain applications, which allow a user who owns a certain cryptocurrency (e.g., Bitcoin) to use applications that accept a different cryptocurrency (e.g., ether). Suppose that Anne and Brittany have an open channel in bitcoin, while Brittany and Charles have an open channel in ether. In this scenario, Anne can pay Charles with bitcoins, even if Charles only accepts ether. In this case, Brittany would pay Charles in ether and claim a payment in bitcoins from Anne. In other words, Brittany would play a similar role to a money exchange.

Each intermediary, regardless of whether or not it acts as an exchange, might charge a predefined micro-fee, which would be negligible even for micropayments.

Overall, the lightning network is promising in its potential to scale Bitcoin up. It will be most useful for micropayments between people who do not transact on a regular basis and do not want to pay the higher fees on the Bitcoin Blockchain.

Lightning networks are currently widely discussed within the Bitcoin community, and they have begun early-stage testing. This proposal requires some changes to the Bitcoin protocol and may or may never be part of Bitcoin.

What is a hashed timelock contract? (HTLC)

Before explaining a hashed timelock contract, we have to understand what a hash locked contract is.

A hash locked contract is a script in which the receiver of the payment generates a hash, H, based on a random input, R. In order to unlock the funds, one has to prove that he knows R, the input that will lead to H, through the chosen hashing function. In the example above, Claire creates a contract with John, stating that if he is able to show R, he can receive the amount she is paying to Marc. The trick consists in giving R to the intermediary (in this case John) only after he makes the payment to Marc. As soon as John receives R, he can claim the payment from Claire.

To avoid the situation where one intermediary decides not to cooperate or is unable to receive his payment because the channel by which he is supposed to receive the payment has ceased to exist, Joseph Poon and Thaddeus Dryja propose to use hashed timelock contracts at each payment channel.

In a hashed timelock contract, both parties of one of the payment channels being used agree that the number of bitcoins equivalent to the payment can be claimed by: (1) the "forwarder of the payment" (i.e., John) when he shows R, or (2) the "sender" (i.e., Claire), if the forwarder (i.e., John) does not show R within a certain time.

In case an intermediary is not willing to cooperate and refuses to pay the person showing R, he can broadcast a transaction on the Bitcoin Blockchain to claim the funds he is eligible to receive because he is in possession of R.

Update before publication: SegWit2x

On May 23, 2017, an agreement was reached to scale Bitcoin at Consensus 2017 in New York—one of the world's most prominent blockchain conferences. The agreement consisted of two updates: adopt segregated witness and, at a later stage, allow a block size of 2 MB. The agreement was reached amongst 58 start-ups/businesses and miners representing 83% of the total hashing power. Soon after the agreement, a working group, called SegWit2x, was set up to develop the agreed-upon changes. On August 1, the Bitcoin network adopted segregated witness, which will be activated at block 481824, somewhere around August 21, 2017. It is expected that the network will accept 2 MB sized blocks as from block 494784, foreseen somewhere in November 2017.

FORKING

As you have seen, multiple solutions to Bitcoin's scalability issue have been proposed. However, changing one of the core rules of the Bitcoin protocol is not an easy task. A large percentage of the nodes must agree on any new validation criteria for it to become the new normal. In practice, finding consensus on a new rule is difficult; it requires all nodes to update their validation software.

When a new rule is proposed in the software, nodes are free to adopt the rule by downloading the new version. They can also refuse it and keep validating and rejecting blocks in the way they did before. This is a direct consequence of a decentralized network, where nodes have the power to decide on the course the Bitcoin Blockchain will take.

When new updates are proposed, they could lead to situations where some people are validating blocks based on new conditions while others keep validating them the old way. In such a case, the Blockchain might start to fork, and different branches could appear from the moment the update was proposed. Such branches are called forks on the Blockchain. There are two types of forks: soft forks and hard forks.

Soft-forking happens when the new software update includes stricter validation rules. As a result, every node with the new software will *only* accept blocks that satisfy the stricter rules. On the other hand, nodes that do not update to the new software will keep validating blocks in the old fashion and will keep accepting blocks that do not satisfy the stricter rules. This will result in the updated nodes rejecting some of the blocks created by nodes that did not update the software.

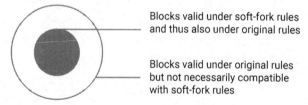

Blocks valid under soft-fork rules and thus also under original rules

Blocks valid under original rules but not necessarily compatible with soft-fork rules

Figure 26. In a soft fork, updated rules are always compliant with previous rules

Small forks might appear in the Blockchain, but as soon as old nodes encounter a longer branch produced by the updated nodes, they will accept it since the stricter rules are also considered valid by the old nodes. New nodes, on the other hand, will not accept longer chains from old nodes if the chain contains blocks that do not respect the new, stricter rules. Eventually, as the old nodes realize that their blocks are being rejected (because they do not necessarily comply with the new, stricter rules) and are being replaced by blocks mined by the new nodes, they will switch to the new update and consensus will be re-established. The key to success for a soft fork is having enough nodes switching to it.

Hard-forking is a bit more controversial and risky. Hard-forking occurs when a proposed update to the protocol validates blocks that were previously considered invalid or no longer validates blocks previously considered valid. Every node will have to choose its camp by deciding to either accept the update or reject it. On one side, you have the nodes using the old validation rules, which will reject blocks satisfying the new validation rules (as these blocks are considered invalid by old nodes). On the other side, you have the updated nodes doing the reverse; they reject new incoming blocks that are valid under the old rules but invalid under their rules. Both sides can refuse a longer branch under the pretext that the branch contains invalid blocks. As a result, the blockchain splits in two, resulting in two independent currencies, each having its own price valuation.

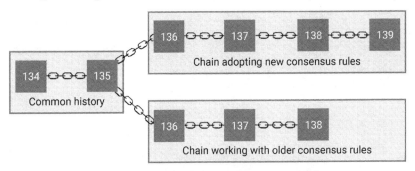

Figure 27. In a hard fork, rules are not compatible

Update before publication: Bitcoin Cash hard fork

On August 1, 2017, a group of miners initiated a hard fork of the Bitcoin Blockchain, known under the name of Bitcoin Cash. The hard fork refuses to adopt the SegWit2x proposal and aims at scaling Bitcoin by allowing an 8 MB block size. The hard fork also foresees rules to reduce the difficulty level should there be a limited amount of computing power available on the network. This change aims at keeping the hard fork viable for miners even when only a limited number of miners join the fork and the creation of a block takes a long time. This means that people who held Bitcoin before the hard fork was initiated now own the same amount of Bitcoin Cash as Bitcoin, both being valued independently.

Soon after the first block was created, Bitcoin cash briefly peaked to $700 before going down. As of August 15, 2017, the price of Bitcoin Cash is around $300 and the hashing power supporting the network is around 500 petahash per second, which is 13 times less than the nearly 6.5 exahash per second backing Bitcoin. On August 29, 2017, the price of Bitcoin Cash was around $600 after having bounced to $1,000 on August 19, 2017. More remarkably, between August 22 and August 26, 2017, Bitcoin Cash reached up to 3 exahash per second[32] of hashing power while Bitcoin knew unprecedented lows between 4 and 5 exahash per second.[33] This is partially explained by the fact that mining-returns for mining bitcoin cash compete with those for mining bitcoins.[34][35]

It is unclear how Bitcoin Cash will evolve, but it is interesting to see how, at the time of publishing,[36] Bitcoin Cash is gaining more traction that might have been initially expected. It is yet unclear to what degree the ecosystem will follow.

PART II

Bitcoin's ecosystem

Chapter 9

Wallets

The term "wallet" is a bit misleading when speaking about Bitcoin wallets. Unlike the wallets that we use to store our coins and bank notes, Bitcoin wallets do not store bitcoins. We have seen in Chapter 6 that the possession of bitcoins is only represented by unspent outputs of transactions on the Blockchain. Instead of coins, which are tracked on the Blockchain, Bitcoin wallets store the private keys that will give us access to our bitcoins.

In this chapter, we will often use the word "client." A client is an interface (software) between you and the Blockchain. Clients are equipped with wallets to store the keys that will enable you to send and receive bitcoins. Although it would technically be possible to transact bitcoins without a client, the purpose of a client is to make it easier for the user to make transactions on the Blockchain. Clients are open-source, which allows everyone to review the code behind them, an important feature designed to gain the trust of Bitcoin users. Wallet service providers can propose different types of clients and wallets, as well as services on different mediums (desktop, online, mobile, etc.).

Overall, wallets can be classified based on four major properties, namely (1) hot vs. cold stored wallets, (2) full node vs. non-full node clients, (3) non-deterministic vs. deterministic wallets, and (4) multi-signature vs. non-multi-signature wallets. Each wallet is a combination of these four properties.

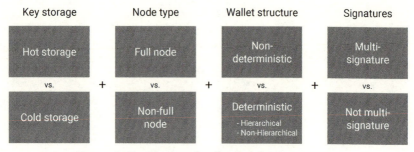

Figure 28. Classification of wallets based on key properties

Besides these four properties, wallets can also be classified by type, depending on the mediums supporting them. In this book, we will discuss six types of wallets.

Figure 29. Classification of wallets based on type

This chapter will explain the different properties and types of wallets.

FOUR PROPERTIES OF WALLETS

1. Hot vs. Cold wallets

Hot storage

Hot stored wallets are wallets stored online or on a device connected to the Internet. They are considered less secure than cold stored wallets, as their link to the Internet makes them subject to attacks, theft, etc. The most extreme example of a hot wallet is the one you use on your exchange, where you trust the exchange to correctly manage your funds.

Cold storage

Cold stored wallets are secluded from the Internet and, therefore, not subject to attacks. As we will see, precautionary measures need to be taken even for cold wallets. A typical example of a cold stored wallet is a private key stored on a hardware wallet or in a paper wallet.

Conclusion

Wallets that expose the private key to the Internet, for any length of time, are considered hot storage, while wallets that keep the private key offline for its entire lifespan are considered cold storage.

2. Full node vs. Non-full node clients

Full nodes

Full-node clients download and synchronize the full Bitcoin Blockchain as soon as the wallet connects to the Internet. The Blockchain is then maintained and continuously updated with the latest blocks.

Becoming a full node might take several hours, since downloading the full Bitcoin Blockchain takes time. As the Blockchain is becoming longer and the blocks are, today, often filled to maximum capacity, storing the complete Blockchain also takes space—a lot of space. At the time of writing,[37] the required storage is 110 GB, and this will continue to increase as blocks are added to the end of the chain. As we saw in Chapter 4, the current blocks cannot be larger than 1 MB, which limits the speed by which the storage requirements will increase.

As a full node, client wallets can consult every Bitcoin transaction that has ever occurred and verify the validity of incoming blocks by ensuring that they comply with the rules of the Bitcoin protocol (as defined in Chapter 4). A full-node client does not have to rely on a third party to verify previous transactions. Just like thousands of other full nodes, it can independently check the number of unspent bitcoins someone owns. A full-node client will verify that an incoming transaction is unspent and will update the Blockchain accordingly. It can go all the way back in time to trace where the funds constituting that transaction came from and ensure it has not been spent since then.

Finally, a full node can also be a mining node, but that is not mandatory. Today, most full nodes do not engage in mining activities.

Building a full node from space (and without Internet)

One major issue with full nodes is their size. Downloading over 130 GB is not easy, and this is especially true to those who might need Bitcoin the most. Countries where the monetary system is unstable are usually also plagued by poor Internet infrastructure. According to a 2016 report from the World Economic Forum and the consultancy firm Boston Consulting Group,[38] it is estimated that 4 billion people, mainly in developing countries, do not have access to the Internet. As a consequence, the number of full Blockchain nodes in Africa, for example, is limited. One man even claims to be the only one having a full node in West Africa.[39]

Blockchain company Blockstream aims at launching satellites that enable everyone to have a full Bitcoin node for a cost below $100. The satellites make Bitcoin independent from Internet connections that might be expensive, fail, or be inaccessible at certain times or in certain locations. According to their website, anyone in the coverage area with a small satellite antenna, such as a TV satellite, and a USB receiver can receive the blocks.[40] Ultimately, their plan is to cover 99.999996% of the world's population[41] by deploying the satellites in three phases.[42]

Non-full nodes

Non-full nodes do not download the full Blockchain. Wallets that do not require full nodes use either a simplified payment verification (SPV) system or a trusted third party.

Wallets using an SPV store the headers of each block and a cryptographic proof that an output belongs to a certain block. Unlike full nodes storing blocks of variable size, the required storage capacity for SPV nodes is linear and predictable.[43]

As a consequence of storing only the headers, the client cannot check the details of a transaction nor verify its history. However, an SPV wallet knows which block a transaction relates to and can verify if other networks have accepted it. The deeper the block is stored in the chain, the more confirmation it has (remember: a block receives an additional confirmation with every block built on top of it). In essence, an SPV client gives an indication of trustworthiness, based on the block's position in the Blockchain. It predicts the likelihood of a block being invalidated by a longer chain. The number of confirmations a client requires to consider a transaction valid varies from one client to another.

Wallets trusting a third party rely on a server, which is supposed to have a full copy of the Blockchain. The essential element here is trust. Indeed, the end user delegates the task of verifying and updating the Blockchain to a third party. The third party can provide incorrect and misleading information. It could, for example, pretend that spent transactions are unspent or tell the user he received transactions, which he did not.

Conclusion

By being a full node, you can be your own bank and independently verify what is going on in the Bitcoin network. Being a full node requires you to store the full Blockchain on your computer, but once it is installed, making and receiving payments can be done with a few clicks.

By being a non-full node, you win in convenience, as you are not required to store the full Blockchain. However, you lose in security, since you either have limited access to the information on the Blockchain or you trust a third party.

3. Non-deterministic vs. Deterministic wallets

Non-deterministic wallets

Non-deterministic wallets generate new private keys in a random way every time the user requires a new one. None of the generated private keys can be linked to one another. They are all independent. This is a great way to mitigate risks, but for someone managing multiple wallets, it is not the most convenient because the user needs to keep track of every private key he has generated. In the event that the user changes his device or client, he needs to import the private key of each wallet separately.

Deterministic wallets

Deterministic wallets are a set of wallets that can all be generated from one common seed. The seed can be a set of words or anything serving to generate a specific master private key. The master private key can also be randomly generated without the need for a seed. From this seed or master private key, multiple private keys can be generated through a specific method. For example, you can state that the next private key will be a hash from the previous one.

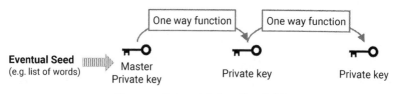

Figure 30. Deterministic wallets (1/3)

A public key and Bitcoin address can then be derived from each private key to receive transactions. This is convenient, as a user only has to remember the seed or master private key to backup and rebuild all his wallets.

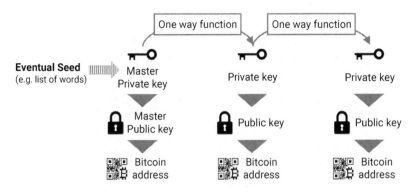

Figure 31. Deterministic wallets (2/3)

For additional security, some clients make it possible to generate the public keys of a deterministic wallet without requiring the master private key. In this case, a master public key is generated from the master private key. The client is then able to generate different public keys and addresses of wallets from the master public key. This way, the user can give his master public key to an online wallet provider and have an overview of all of his accounts while keeping the private key to himself.

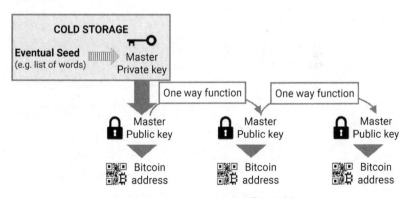

Figure 32. Deterministic wallets (3/3)

Going one step further, we can distinguish two types of deterministic wallets: non-hierarchical wallets and hierarchical wallets.

Non-hierarchical wallets are the ones we have been describing up until now, where each key is generated from the previous key and is required to generate the next key, forming a chain of keys. As a result, if someone has access to one of the private keys, he also has access to all the wallets generated downstream from that wallet. When sharing keys, this means that a person with a private key high in the chain of wallets can access the funds from every wallet down the chain.

Hierarchical wallets follow a tree structure and are composed of parent keys and child keys.

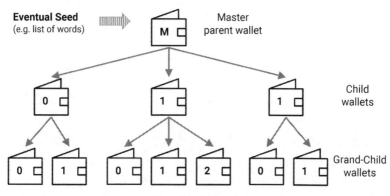

Figure 33. Hierarchical deterministic wallets

Each child key is generated from the parent key through a one-way function. The one-way function makes it impossible to know whether a given key has a parent or not. At the same time, none of the child keys are traceable to any of its siblings. However, the owner of the parent key can re-create the tree structure, assuming he is in possession of all elements necessary to re-create the child keys.

Parent keys can be either a parent *private* key or a parent *public* key. Both types of parent keys can generate multiple children of their type; a parent private key can generate a child private key (which can then generate the child public key) and a parent public key can generate a child public key.

In order to generate a child key, the client uses a function that has as input (1) the parent key, (2) a chaincode,[44] and (3) the index of the new wallet. Based on these elements, the one-way function generates a child key and a new chaincode, which the child will use to generate his own child keys.

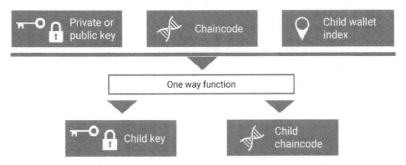

Figure 34. Key generation in hierarchical deterministic wallets

Only a person in possession of the parent private keys as well as the chaincode can regenerate the private keys of all children and spend their funds.[45] A person who is in possession of the parent public key as well as the chaincode can generate the public keys of the children, but because he does not have the parent private key, he cannot spend any funds.

The different branches of the tree can represent the different departments of a company, different accounts of an accounting system, different subsidiaries, or different entities of a governmental authority.

The use of hierarchical deterministic wallets offers a range of benefits linked to the efficiency, traceability, and transparency of the Bitcoin Blockchain. Budget allocations and spending could easily be traced, cash-pooling activities could be performed without the need for a bank, and the audit of accounting systems could be revolutionized.

Conclusion

Non-deterministic wallet clients generate a random and independent private key for each new wallet they create.

Deterministic wallet clients create multiple wallets from a single private key. Deterministic wallets can be broken down into two types: non-hierarchical wallets and hierarchical wallets. For both types, the number of wallets is infinite.

Non-hierarchical deterministic wallets are a chain of wallets in which each wallet is built upon the previous wallet. The owner of a private key can spend the funds of all wallets generated downstream but not those of the wallets generated upstream. This type of wallet is useful for a single user who wants to generate new addresses for each transaction he makes.

Hierarchical deterministic wallets are built in a tree structure, where the owner of a parent wallet can access the funds of its child wallets, but a child wallet cannot access the funds of its parents or sibling wallets. Each child wallet can have multiple children of its own.

4. Multi-signature vs. Non-multi-signature wallets

Some clients make it possible to create wallets that require signatures from multiple private keys before funds can be spent. This opens a new world of possibilities for shared Bitcoin accounts and can be of use for individuals and businesses. Such wallets are called multi-signature (aka multisig) wallets, while those that do not offer this feature are non-multi-signature wallets.

To mitigate the risk of stolen or lost keys, we could imagine that every transaction needs to be signed by multiple parties. An example could be that each transaction needs to be signed by two out of three keys, perhaps one key owned by you and another owned by a different party such as a bank or Facebook. A third key could be kept secret to be used to access the funds if one of the keys gets lost or stolen and to send them to a new two-out-of-three signature wallet.

SIX TYPES OF WALLETS

1. Desktop wallet

A desktop wallet is a software (a client) that can be installed on a computer to enable you to make payments in just a few clicks, using a user-friendly interface. As most desktops are connected to the Internet, we will consider them hot wallets. They come in the form of both full-node client wallets and non-full-node client wallets. Most of the full-node client wallets are desktop wallets, since computers are well suited to store the full blockchain due to their large storage capacity.

The most notable full-node desktop wallet is Bitcoin Core, probably used by Satoshi Nakamoto himself. MultiBitHD is an alternative desktop wallet. The Armory client provides enhanced security, while DarkWallet provides enhanced anonymity by providing features such as coin-mixing.[46] [47]

The most notable non-full-node desktop clients are Electrum and Copay, both of which use an SPV system.

In both full-node and non-full-node desktop clients, the end user remains responsible for his private key. Only he can spend the funds his wallet possesses. As the user is responsible for his keys, he should be aware of some of the risks this entails.

Losing the keys

If the computer storing your private key breaks down or gets stolen, you might lose access to your private key. It is therefore important to keep a backup of your key on another device or on paper. Backing up your key on a USB stick that you do not share with others is also a good option. However, you also do not want to have too many copies of your private key in different places, since one of them might fall into the wrong hands.

Infected computer

A second risk affects private keys stored on computers, and more broadly all keys stored on hot storage. If your computer is infected by malware, whether it is a virus, Trojan horse, or a key-logger, your private key might fall into the hands of a malicious person, who will then be able to spend your funds.

2. Mobile wallets

Using your computer for payments might be convenient compared to the time when we had to physically go to the bank to make transactions, but it is still not the most convenient method of payment that today's technology has to offer. When people are out on the street, they want to pay on the go. Fortunately, mobile Bitcoin wallets enable users to send and receive bitcoins by simply using their smartphones.

Mobile wallets are one of the most convenient wallets. Not only can you carry them with you, you can request and make payments with a few touches on the screen, using QR codes. Some mobile wallets even make it possible to pay via near-field communication[48] if the phone allows it.

This increased convenience comes at the cost of limited verification systems. Most handheld devices are not capable of storing the full Blockchain. Even if they do have enough storage space, downloading a new block every 10 minutes might quickly turn into an expensive invoice or data plan. Mobile wallets, therefore, often use simplified payment verification (SPV) or rely on other trusted nodes as a means to validate transactions.

The keys are encrypted on the phone and can be backed up on a web-based server, depending on the mobile wallet. In the event that the user does not want to back his keys up on the server of the mobile wallet provider, he is solely responsible for his private key. Losing the key might result in not being able to access his funds.

If the user prefers to store a copy of his private keys on the servers of the mobile wallet provider, he should be aware that any server can be corrupt or subject to an attack.

The user should make sure that, even if the keys are stored on the server of the wallet provider, no one else can read his private keys. This can be achieved by storing them inside an encrypted wallet on the server of the wallet provider. As the wallet is encrypted on the server, neither the owner of the server nor a potential hacker would be able to open the wallet. To decrypt the wallet, the user will use a password, which he will not store on the server.

Storing an encrypted version of your private key on a server has two main benefits. Firstly, in the event that you no longer have access to your phone and as such to your private key, you can still retrieve your private key from the server by using your password. Secondly, even if the server is attacked and someone steals your encrypted wallet, the thief will not be able to spend your funds, since the wallet is encrypted and only you can decrypt it with your password.

Notable mobile wallet clients are MyCelium and a wallet provider named Blockchain.info[49] working on both Android and iOS. Blackberry users can download the application Bitcoin Wallet. The Aegis Bitcoin wallet supports Android Smartwatches.

What if someone steals your phone?

We have seen that you can protect the access to your funds, even when you no longer have access to your phone, by having a backup copy of your keys stored in an encrypted wallet on a server. However, if someone steals your phone, he or she might be able to access the application containing your private key(s). To prevent the thief from spending the bitcoins stored in your mobile wallet, it is recommended to have at least one of the following two security measures in place.

PIN Code

By allowing the mobile wallet application to ask you for a pin code when opening it, the application adds an extra layer of authentication. It can also decide to block the application if too many incorrect pin codes have been entered.

Password confirmation

The application can also ask you to enter a password every time you want to sign a transaction, adding an extra layer of security before your private key is used to spend funds.

3. Online wallets

Online wallets, or web wallets, are online services that make it possible for someone to access his or her bitcoins from anywhere by simply logging into a website. To achieve this, the website provides the user with a set of keys, which are also stored on their server.

Online wallets are by far the most convenient type of wallets as they can be used anywhere there is an Internet connection, without having to install a client. The user trusts that the wallet provider will make all verifications for him on the Blockchain.

The convenience of online wallets comes at the price of security. Of all wallets, online wallets are the least secure. As you are allowing a third party to keep your private keys, you must trust that they will not spend your bitcoins themselves and will protect them from hackers and thieves. Still, by letting professionals take care of your private keys, you are also protecting yourself from losing them over time.

Some notable and trusted online wallets are Circle and Coinbase. Some online wallets, like BitGo and Greenaddress, enable multisig. Occasionally, online wallets can be duplicates of mobile wallets, making it possible to transact bitcoins via a web browser as well as a smartphone. Coinbase and Blockchain.info are two good examples of hybrid online/mobile wallets. Finally, bitcoins stored on exchanges can also be considered online wallets.

Online wallets have some security risks, namely account hacking, website hacking, and fraud. The following paragraphs will dig deeper into these risks and discuss potential solutions to mitigate them.

Account hacking

If, by any means, a hacker manages to log in to the wallet website with your credentials, he might be able to withdraw your bitcoins stored within that wallet.

To counter such attacks, websites, and in particular cryptocurrency exchanges, can put a few measures in place. Each of them decreases convenience but increases security.

Captcha

A captcha requires users to respond to a question that proves he is not a robot trying to make a brute force attack.[50]

Figure 35. Example of a captcha

Two-step authentication

With two-step authentication, the user provides a verification on top of the password to access his account. This can be done through an SMS sent to the user each time he logs in, but more often, the user will install an authentication app on his smartphone that provides a "random" number changing every few seconds. Such an app can then generate different codes for different websites connected to the app. Configuring a new website can be as simple as scanning a new QR code with the app.

Apart from downloading the app, using the app on a smartphone does not require a connection to the Internet.

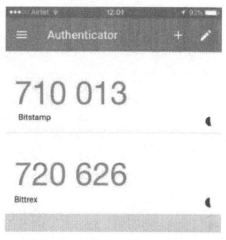

Figure 36. Two-step authentication app

When logging into the online wallet, the user will be asked to enter the verification code provided by the smartphone on top of his password. This step proves that you are in possession of your own smartphone.

During the installation process, the user receives a set of authentication keys to keep safe. In case the user loses his phone, these keys will be necessary to access the website. Some wallets, such as Bitstamp, provide customer support to people who lose their phone and authentication keys. When changing your phone, it is important to change the device registered on the website before you stop using your initial phone. The bottom line is: it is better to do some preventive work during the initial setup and safely store the authentication keys, in case you lose access to your phone.

Email confirmation

This feature can typically be enabled at exchanges. A link is sent to the user's email address to confirm his transactions. This proves that the user has access to his email account; a hacker must therefore also be in possession of the user's email password before he can spend any bitcoins.

Email encryption

Users can communicate with their online wallets or exchanges through encrypted emails. The user provides the exchange with the key with which he wants his email to be encrypted. The exchange will then communicate with the user by encrypting messages with that particular key. The message could, for example, be a request to validate a transaction. In this case, a hacker would require the login credentials to the website, the login credentials to the email address, and the key to decrypt the message.

Website hacking

Another weakness in having a third party storing your private keys lies in their ability to keep your keys safe. Unfortunately, websites are also subject to attacks. If attackers are able to pass through the security layers of the website, they may be able to access and steal keys. A solution to this could be encrypting the wallet by a password that only the user knows. When the wallet has its own independent encryption, the thief cannot access it, even if he has hacked the website.

Fraud

There are people behind any website. By trusting a website, you trust that the people behind the website are honest and will never become corrupt, but the truth is that a member of the organization could easily steal keys to which he or she has access. If the corruption is more widespread, websites can also "fake" a certain number of bitcoins on their interface, while they might already have spent them. To prevent this, websites can be audited by neutral third parties (more on this in the next chapter).

4. Brain wallets

A brain wallet is the concept of having the access to your wallets stored only in your mind. If you succeed in remembering your private key without recording it anywhere, you have yourself a brain wallet.

Private keys are a combination of 51 letters and numbers, in Base58 format, and are case sensitive. Ultimately, private keys can be compressed to 30 characters by using the "Mini private key format." Still, memorizing a private key, whether entire or compressed, requires an extraordinary memory. Only a few people can manage such a feat.

In the absence of a super memory, some people use tricks to help themselves remember their private keys. Passphrases are the most popular trick.

A passphrase is a set of words, numbers, special characters, and punctuation marks that, combined, is easy to remember because it relates to the user's personal life. Passphrases are different from passwords, as a password is too short and insecure for a network like Bitcoin.

The passphrase, a list of seemingly random words, is then used to generate a private key. This can be done through cryptographic algorithms. Therefore, the user does not have to memorize the private key itself, but only the set of words (also called seed) that will enable him to generate the private key. He should also remember which algorithm he used to get to the private key.

There are many tools to help you convert your passphrase into a private key. Still, it is important to remember which tool, or at least which algorithm, you used because you will have to use the same tool and algorithm to regenerate your private key and Bitcoin address from your passphrase in the future.

For security reasons, you should use your private key as rarely as possible. Ideally, you should use your private key only once to generate your Bitcoin address. Then you should write that Bitcoin address down, so that you do not have to regenerate it in the future and re-expose your private key to the algorithm in charge of converting your private key to a Bitcoin address.

Some wallets, like Electrum, brainwallet.org, and bitaddress.com, take care of converting passphrases into a private key. In order to log into one of these wallets and spend funds, the wallet owner must provide his passphrase.

It is important to mention that brain wallets have their own risks. In the event that the owner cannot remember his private key, loses his memory, gets incapacitated, or dies, the bitcoins are lost forever.

We mentioned that a passphrase is multiple times more secure than a password because of its length. It also gains in security by the algorithms transforming it. However, if a hacker is capable of guessing your passphrase and the algorithm, he will be capable of generating your private key. Unlike a website that freezes your account after a few failed attempts, the attempts to find your private key on the blockchain are unlimited. Thieves can launch "brute force" attacks, guessing phrase after phrase until they hit upon your private key. Hence, the length of your passphrase is very important. The difficulty to make a successful guess will increase with every word or character you add to your passphrase. You can add additional layers of security by hashing your passphrase several times (each hashing iteration being a new layer). For each layer the hacker has to guess, additional computing power is necessary to find your passphrase. Finally, it is recommended that you do not use names, dates, quotes, or references to your favorite entertainment in your passphrase, as these are easy to guess.

5. Hardware wallets

Hardware wallets are physical devices used to store private keys and generate signatures offline, before sending them to the network to which the device is connected (by a USB cable, for example). Hardware wallets are very secure because private keys are generated and kept inside the device. They are therefore protected from any external malware and safe to use even on an infected device.

The most notable hardware wallet is TREZOR, a deterministic wallet that can store multiple private keys. TREZOR also has a pin code serving as an extra security layer that keeps you safe from thieves. During the setup, the user is asked to create a "recovery seed," which is a list of words that can be written on paper and stored securely. The recovery seed can be used to recover the wallet in case the TREZOR gets lost. This is possible because the private keys are generated from hashes of this list of words. It is paramount to keep the recovery seed's words in a very secure place. Other hardware wallets include USB smart cards, which use chips like the ones in credit cards to sign transactions. Hardware wallets can be bought at various prices ranging from $30 to $300, depending on the wallet.

6. Paper wallets

Using paper wallets to store a digital currency might sound somewhat counter-intuitive. However, paper wallets are probably one of the simplest ways to store your private key.

Paper wallets come in multiple forms. In its most basic form, it is just a piece of paper with a string of characters representing the private key. However, most paper wallet designs are a bit more advanced. They include a QR Code to scan the private key, as well as the Bitcoin address and its corresponding QR Code.

Figure 37. Paper wallet

Paper wallets make it possible to store your bitcoins offline (cold storage). Since the private key is not stored digitally, it is not subject to any form of digital attack (i.e., viruses, key-loggers, hackings, etc.).

The great thing about paper wallets is that you can store them in a secure place, like a vault. As only the Bitcoin address is necessary to send funds to your wallet, you can send funds to your paper wallet even if you do not have physical access to it. You will only need to consult the paper wallet to spend the funds.

Before printing your wallet, you must generate a private key. This can be done by using a small piece of software that can generate a random private key for you and will compute the public key and Bitcoin address linked to your private key. To generate a random private key, some software will ask you to move your mouse around the screen. The movements you make will be translated into a private key.

Choose your wallet generator

We can make a distinction between two types of generators: those that generate your wallet online[51] and those that generate your wallet offline, after downloading the source code (software).

By now, you must be aware that generating your private key offline is the most secure option as it prevents the risk of your key being intercepted during the communication between you and the generator.

To generate your paper wallet offline, you must first download[52] the source code that will help you generate a random private key. You do not have to be a geek to run the source code. Actually, you just have to click on the generator and open it in your web browser. The user experience will be the same as surfing an Internet page.

Setting up an offline generator

Let us assume you decided to use an offline generator. The best thing you can do is run the software on a machine that is not connected to the Internet. This mitigates risks related to spyware.

However, even machines that are not connected to the Internet are subject to spyware. To be even safer, the generator should be run on a machine that has never been used and that was never connected to the Internet. Although this might sound unrealistic, it is quite easy to simulate such an environment without having to buy or reformat a computer. All you need is an operating system that starts running from a CD or USB stick. Typically, starting your computer with a live-boot of Ubuntu will do the job. You can download such a version on the Ubuntu website for free. You can also buy an Ubuntu live-boot disk, including a Bitcoin paper wallet generator, on bitcoinpaperwallet.com. The only thing you will have to ensure is that your computer starts from the CD or USB stick and not from the hard drive.

Generating your private keys and printing them

Whether you decide to use an online or offline generator, the procedure is very simple. You will easily be able to follow the steps provided by the generator. At the end, the generator will provide you with instructions to print your wallet.

The more basic the printer, the better. Some advanced printers store copies of what you print, and the most advanced printers, which connect directly to the Internet, could be hacked.[53] However, we are coming close to paranoia here.

Storing your paper wallets securely

Once you have created your own paper wallet, you possess one of the most secure wallets there is. (Congratulations!) However, there are still a few manageable risks related to your paper wallet.

Your private key is now on paper. That piece of paper gives access to all bitcoins stored at your Bitcoin address, so managing it carefully is paramount. If someone finds the paper and takes a picture or makes a copy of your private key, he or she can access your funds. If you lose the paper, you lose your funds.

Make sure you store your paper wallet somewhere safe, where no one else will look. Keeping your wallet somewhere inaccessible adds security, but of course, there is a trade-off with convenience. Your paper wallet should also be protected from fire, moisture, and animals that could damage it.[54]

Emptying your paper wallet after having used the funds

The key information stored on your paper wallet is your private key. You will use this private key to sign a transaction and spend funds. As a consequence, the private key gets exposed whenever a third party or connected computer is involved in the generation of the signature. Although the risk might be very limited, it is safer to empty the paper wallet of any remaining funds and send those funds to a new paper wallet, which has never been used to spend bitcoins and, therefore, has a completely secure private key.

Chapter 10

Exchanges and ATMs

EXCHANGES

The need for a platform to trade bitcoins easily at a market price gave birth to bitcoin exchanges and these exchanges play a vital role in facilitating the connection between the Bitcoin economy and the economies of the fiat currencies. Nowadays, they are the most common way to buy or sell bitcoins for fiat currencies.

Platforms to exchange fiat and digital currencies[55]

Bitcoin exchanges are platforms, usually websites, which provide a marketplace where buyers and sellers willing to trade fiat currencies for bitcoins or bitcoins for fiat currencies can meet. They fix the price of bitcoins (exchange rate with another currency) based on offer and demand, the same way other marketplaces do (i.e., stock exchange, foreign exchange, etc.).

All major exchanges now accept multiple currencies. The three fiat currencies representing the highest volume of transactions are the yuan, the dollar, and the euro (in that order).

As new cryptocurrencies have emerged, new exchanges specializing in the trade of bitcoins for other digital or cryptocurrencies have popped up. The most notable exchanges of this type in the western world are Poloniex and Bittrex, each of which lists hundreds of coins inspired by Bitcoin. Some exchanges make it possible to trade fiat currencies directly for some other digital currencies, but these are the exception rather than the rule.

Using an exchange

Exchanges are third parties that operate on top of the Bitcoin Blockchain. Yet, they are often necessary to enter or exit the Bitcoin economy.

Opening an account at an exchange is almost as simple as subscribing to a website, but getting your account ready to use might take a few extra steps. Most exchanges ask for identification documents to comply with know your customer (KYC) and anti-money laundering (AML) regulations. Going through these onboarding checks can take a few days.

In 2014, crediting an "account" at any of these exchanges with a credit card or PayPal was impossible and you had to do a SEPA payment or wire transfer. By 2017, the process has evolved, and platforms such as Bitstamp, CEX.io, and Coinbase are now accepting credit cards, although they charge a higher deposit fee. However, exchanges accepting credit cards represent a minority, and most exchanges rely mainly on wire transfers to receive new fiat deposits, which can also take a few days, during which the price of Bitcoin can change. Therefore, people are indirectly incentivized to park an amount of fiat currency in their exchange account, so they will be ready to trade whenever a buying opportunity arises. Once money is received by the exchange, it is credited to the user's online fiat currency balance. The user has one balance for each currency he can trade. The credit of his fiat currency balance can be exchanged for bitcoins. Those bitcoins can then be withdrawn to another Bitcoin address and stored in the wallet of the user's choice.

Most of the platforms operate as companies, but for some, such as BTC-e, we only know that money is sent to a Russian bank account. Otherwise, their management has decided to stay anonymous. At least, that was the case until July 25, 2017, when the US Justice Department closed the website and arrested its owner for money laundering.

Over time, exchanges have opened to multiple currencies, and some have started to provide more advanced trading tools such as stop-loss orders, shorting, and leverage trading. Some exchanges, such as Coinbase, are positioning themselves more as an "all-in" solution and offer wallet services and services to merchants.

Application Programming Interface (API)

Most exchanges provide application programming interfaces (APIs). APIs are interfaces that allow software to communicate with each other. APIs have multiple features. For example, they could allow a webmaster to display the price of certain cryptocurrencies on certain exchanges in real time. More advanced APIs allow users or software to make trading orders on the exchanges. This can be useful to trade cryptocurrencies from an application on the smartphone.

Links to the Blockchain

Exchanges are third parties that operate on top of the Bitcoin protocol and provide a service to Bitcoin users. Transactions that occur on an exchange are not recorded on the Bitcoin Blockchain. The exchanges are responsible for maintaining the balances of their users. Every time a transaction is executed on the marketplace, the balances of the two parties involved are updated, but there is no actual transfer of fiat currency or bitcoins outside the exchange until a user decides to deposit or withdraw bitcoins or fiat currencies.

As the Blockchain is not involved, it is paramount for Bitcoin users to trust the exchange. Storing fiat or cryptocurrencies in an exchange can be risky since the exchange can be hacked, mismanaged, or shut down at any time.

Mt. Gox

In February 2014, the Japanese exchange Mt. Gox closed its website and filed for bankruptcy, announcing that it had "lost" approximately 850,000 bitcoins belonging to its clients and to the company itself.[56] This represented 7% of all bitcoins and carried a loss of about $480 million at that time. Although authorities found 200,000 of the bitcoins in March 2014,[57] the rest of the bitcoins remain "lost" and their disappearance remains a mystery to date. Some analysis[58] suggests that bitcoins were gradually stolen from the hot wallet, starting in 2011.

Many Mt. Gox users who left their fiat currencies or bitcoins in the hands of the exchange might never see them again. Bitcoins that were bought on Mt. Gox and stored on wallets outside the exchange were not affected.

Audit of exchanges

Mt. Gox's collapse aroused doubts about whether other exchanges were solvent. It has since become good practice for exchanges to regularly let independent experts come in and audit their bitcoin reserves to prove that they possess all bitcoins they claim to possess (proof-of-reserve) and are capable of serving all withdrawal requests on their platform, both in bitcoins and in fiat currency (proof-of-liabilities). Finally, besides auditing the exchanges to make sure they are solvent, experts might also assess the security of the platform and provide recommendations. In June 2017, Joseph Poon and the OmiseGO team released a white paper[59] to build a decentralized exchange platform, aiming to make exchanges independent of a central party.

The Chinese take it all

This section will take a brief look at the market share evolution of volumes traded by different bitcoin exchanges.

Mt. Gox was one of the first exchanges to become popular and quickly found itself in a close to monopolistic position. In early 2013, Mt. Gox's trading volume market share was reduced as Bitstamp and Huobi appeared. In February 2014, it disappeared from the scene (see Figure 38).

From the chart in Figure 38, we observe that currently, the major market share of trading volumes is owned by Huobi, OKCoin, and BTCChina. All three of these platforms trade bitcoins for the Chinese yuan, leaving only a limited market share of the trading volume for platforms providing exchange services in other fiat currencies. Rumors persist that the Chinese exchanges' high trading volume is due to high-frequency trading bots.[60]

If we take a closer look at the players who provide services in yuan (see Figure 39), we see that BTCChina was once the only player in the field. BTCChina's market share started to decrease as new players emerged. On December 18, 2013, BTCChina temporarily suspended the acceptance of Chinese yuan deposits after the Chinese government issued a statement banning financial institutions from trading in bitcoin.[61] Ultimately, it resumed operations in January 2014.

For trades in US dollars (see Figure 40), the competitive landscape is more fragmented. After Mt. Gox collapsed, a few players took a more important position.

Just as the trades for U.S. dollars, the market share for trades in euros is also more fragmented (see Figure 41). In this segment of the market, Kraken is currently the leading exchange.

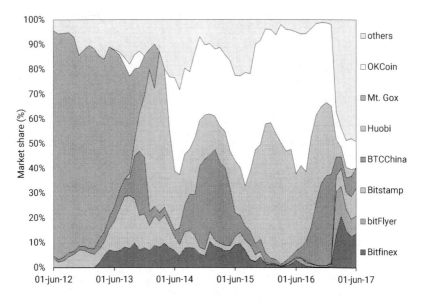

Figure 38. Global market share of trading volume in bitcoin (Source: data.bitcoinity.org)

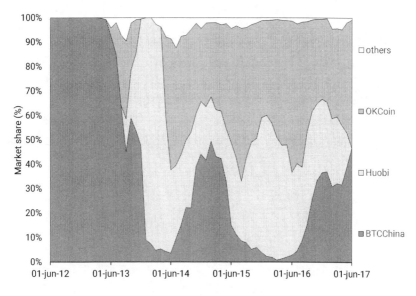

Figure 39. Market share of trading volume in bitcoin - CNY (Source: data.bitcoinity.org)

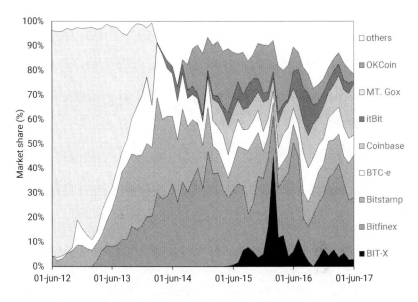

Figure 40. Market share of trading volume in bitcoin - USD (Source: data.bitcoinity.org)

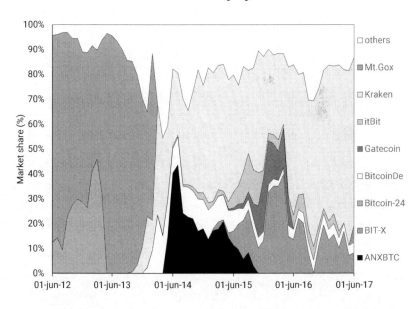

Figure 41. Market share of trading volume in bitcoin - EUR (Source: data.bitcoinity.org)

ATMS

Most Bitcoin ATMs[62] enable people to exchange cash-money of a fiat currency for bitcoins (unidirectional) while some ATMs also convert bitcoins into cash[63] (bi-directional). ATMs aim to provide a convenient and hands-on way to start using Bitcoin.

Bitcoin ATMs enable us to transfer and withdraw cash across the world, without having to pass through a bank. This is useful for people sending money to their family in other countries. Travelers can exchange their currency into bitcoins at the airport before boarding the plane and can convert the bitcoins back into the local currency of their destination upon arrival. The bitcoins/fiat currencies are received by showing your Bitcoin address to the machine. However, using ATMs comes at the expense of the fee they charge, which is usually between 2% and 15%, depending on the ATM.

The first Bitcoin ATM was installed in Vancouver, Canada. According to CoinATMRadar.com, there are close to 1,000 Bitcoin ATMs installed today. Still, it is difficult to know how up-to-date this information is, as Bitcoin ATMs are sometimes stolen, removed by the government, or simply shut down. The website CoinATMRadar.com keeps track of all the ATMs and their fees and is, at the time of writing, the best source to find an ATM near you (see Figure 42). Most of the ATMs are located in the US and Europe, despite regulations that are more sophisticated.[64]

According to Moe Adham, co-founder of BitAccess, a Bitcoin ATM manufacturer, ATMs target different users than exchanges. While many transactions on exchanges are speculative, ATM transactions are used to make real payments.

The user-friendliness of ATMs, relative to online exchanges and other platforms, remains debatable. Although the initial ambition was to appeal to new users by providing them with a machine they are familiar with, the user experience is quite different from that of traditional banks and their ATM networks. Even if, from a technical perspective, it is possible to create user-friendly Bitcoin ATMs, it is unclear how much they respect the laws and how long they can stay before being removed.

ATMs are not exempt from KYC and AML rules and, as such, an onboarding process. In many jurisdictions, ATMs sometimes operate in a gray zone, where no laws specific to cryptocurrencies are written or implemented. It is then up to the ATM operator to define the checks and balances that comply with existing laws, mitigate the risk of money laundering, and anticipate future legislation.[65]

Often, the solution is simply asking the user to identify himself when using the ATM. For example, Belgian ATMs provided by the firm EBTM require people to prove possession of their mobile phone number for amounts less than 1,000 EUR and require a full scan of the ID or passport for amounts above 1,000 EUR. EBTM caps the daily limit to 2,500 EUR.[66] In the US, daily limits tend to be higher. You can find them on CoinATMRadar.com.

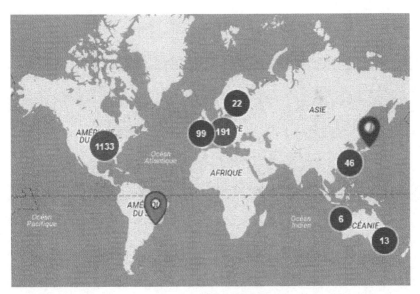

Figure 42. Map of locations having a Bitcoin ATM (Source: coinatmradar.com, August 2017)

EBTM performs an additional check when people try to exchange their bitcoins for cash. The ATM will trace the history of bitcoins through a service called Scorechain. Scorechain gives an index score to transactions based on their history and the likelihood that funds have been used in transactions on places like the dark web. If transactions exceed an index threshold, the ATM can decide not to dispense the money.[67] If the transaction has no suspect history, ATMs can decide to dispense the money after the block has received one confirmation by the network—that is, when one block has been created on top of the block, thus storing the transaction. When this measure is applied, there is an additional delay for the user.

Like many Bitcoin start-ups, ATM operators struggle to find banks willing to cooperate, mainly because Bitcoin has a reputation for attracting bad press.[68] [69]

Chapter 11

Merchants

One of the factors that will help Bitcoin reach a larger public is its acceptance by merchants as a means of payment. It is no surprise that a decentralized currency, lacking political authority, will not easily be accepted by many merchants. Nevertheless, we can see a growing number of businesses accepting payments in bitcoins.

BITCOIN IN COMMERCE

Silk Road

Silkroad.com was one of the first marketplaces that provided goods and services that could be purchased exclusively in bitcoins.[70] The website operated via the onion router (Tor) as a hidden service to assure surfer's anonymity while browsing. It allowed browsers to trade illegal substances and services, such as drugs and hitmen. Other legal categories of merchandise, such as hardware and books, could also be found. The website was seized by the US drug enforcement administration (DEA) in October 2013. The seizure of Silk Road had a negative impact on Bitcoin's price, going from $125 to $87 in one hour before being back at $110 one hour later. Two days later, the price was back to $120.

Bitcoin in mainstream commerce

Dell and Overstock are the most prominent websites currently accepting bitcoins. Overstock is a US-based online retailer that provides a large range of products, everything from furniture and electronics to jewelry. New websites, such as satoshidice.com and peerbet.org, have also emerged to propose gambling games paid for exclusively in bitcoins. Some VPN providers, banned by credit-card providers and PayPal, now use bitcoins exclusively.

Smaller retailers like Badoo, a dating website; Webjet, an online travel agency; Newegg, a retail giant; and airBaltic and Air Lithuania, two European airlines, also accept bitcoins. Richard Branson's "Virgin Galactic" accepts bitcoins from those who are interested in flying to space.[71] Bitcoins have even been used to buy a Tesla car.[72]

Even if you are not planning a European vacation or a space journey, you can still find more mundane ways to spend your bitcoins. Some pizza delivery services accept payments in bitcoins and so do some of the mobile-card providers (e.g., Mobile-Viking in Belgium). PayPal is also working on accepting bitcoins through its daughter company, Braintree. According to its website, Braintree has partnered with wallet provider Coinbase, and their bitcoin payment solution is available in beta.

Your bitcoins are not limited to online commerce. Local merchants, such as bars, restaurants, and coffee houses, are now accepting bitcoins too. Also, the MIT Bookstore has adopted Bitcoin.[73] To pay for items in a store, people send bitcoins from their digital wallet on their smartphone to the merchant by scanning the merchant's public Bitcoin address in the form of a QR code. Even if these businesses are the exception rather than the rule, they attract Bitcoin-tourists, and surrounding businesses are more likely to use bitcoins as well. The ultimate example is the creation of Bitcoin-friendly streets such as the "Bitcoin Boulevard" in Den Haag, Netherlands.[74]

Specialized websites, such as coinmap.org, have emerged to help people spend their coins by listing all merchants accepting bitcoins. In 2014, CoinMap provided statistics on the most common type of offline businesses accepting bitcoins. From this data, we can observe that Bitcoin is most welcomed by food establishments, probably thanks to the low fees.

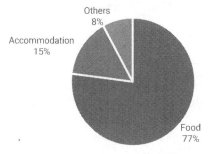

Figure 43. Merchant categories accepting bitcoins by number of businesses – April 2014 (Source: coinmap.org)

Updated data provided by SatoshiLabs (which is now operating CoinMap) shows an evolution. Food businesses (including grocery stores) remain a large portion of the offline businesses accepting bitcoins, but general shopping stores have also emerged as leaders in the Bitcoin economy, while accommodation remains a significant part of the pie.

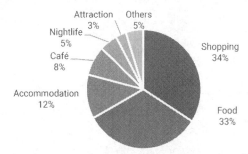

Figure 44. Merchant categories accepting bitcoin by number of businesses – January 2017 (Source: coinmap.org)

From a geographical point of view, we observe that bitcoins are mainly accepted in the western world. However, we should note that CoinMap is an English website, which might cause a bias.

Figure 45. Heat map of merchants accepting bitcoin – September 2017 (Source: coinmap.org)

As of today, it is estimated that over 100,000 global or local businesses accept bitcoins and the number is still rising. For most merchants, Bitcoin payments represent only a small part of their transactions.

PAYMENT PROCESSORS

Some of the above merchants do accept bitcoin payments to their Bitcoin accounts. However, most of them use a Bitcoin payment processor to convert the bitcoins back to their main currency immediately. Start-ups such as BitPay or BitKassa facilitate the adoption of Bitcoin by eliminating the exchange rate risk for merchants.[75]

It works like this: merchants set prices in their fiat currency. When the buyer decides to pay with bitcoins, the payment processors convert the fiat price into a bitcoin price. At the end of the day, the payment processor makes a fiat currency payment to the merchant. As the merchants receive the payment in their bookkeeping currency, they are not subject to regulations with regard to Bitcoin or to any extra bookkeeping costs. Some payment processors might apply a fee, while others do it for the sole purpose of widening the adoption of Bitcoin. However, most allow a certain number of transactions per month for free.

For the sake of this section, two players were interviewed: BitKassa, a smaller non-profit payment provider, active in the Netherlands, and BitPay, the world's leading Bitcoin payment processor. As you will see, their experience is quite different.

BitKassa started out of passion for Bitcoin. They started small, servicing 15 restaurants and bars in a specific neighborhood of The Hague in the Netherlands. Soon, retail shops and even dentists started to accept bitcoins.[76] The network effect created by this small, non-profit payment processor enabled bitcoin holders to spend their bitcoins quickly, which attracted Bitcoin enthusiasts from the Netherlands and neighboring countries to spend their bitcoins in the streets of The Hague. Today, the neighborhood is known as "Bitcoin Boulevard." It has received some media attention[77] and become a popular tourist spot for the community. There is sustainable growth in the number of merchants using BitKassa as a bitcoin payment processor, even though some of the small businesses have closed. BitKassa is proposing its services mainly to small businesses where the boss is also the one behind the counter. Big corporations are more difficult to contact, although BitKassa managed to convince a local Burger King to accept bitcoins.

BitPay is the world's leading Bitcoin payment processor. The company has seen a massive growth in Bitcoin transactions over the last couple of years. The number of monthly payments went from less than 10,000 in early 2013 to 50,000 in early 2014. It reached 100,000 at the end of 2015. In December 2016, the number of monthly payments exceeded 200,000 for the first time.

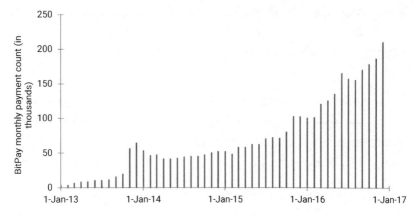

Figure 46. Monthly payments count at BitPay (Source: BitPay)

Initially, a large portion of the payments BitPay processed were high-value items like ASIC cards, which were specifically in demand in the Bitcoin community. Today, BitPay sees more transactions and more lower-value consumer purchases, such as gaming, electronics, web services, and e-wallet services.[78] Among BitPay's top merchants are industry leaders like gaming platform Steam, e-wallet NETELLER, and electronics dealer Newegg.com.

While processors like BitPay also encounter large transactions, such as $300,000 house purchases or $400,000 Lamborghini purchases,[79] BitPay's service shines most in online payments at e-commerce sites, particularly for international transactions. Bitcoin allows businesses to sell to consumers who have limited access to credit cards, and it allows businesses to transfer large payments inexpensively and with more speed and security than bank wire transfers do. For these reasons, Bitcoin is becoming increasingly popular with companies operating in emerging markets such as India and Brazil, where there is a strong demand for alternatives to local payment methods.[80]

Most Bitcoin payment processors provide detailed overviews of all transactions to their merchant users, denominating transactions in the chosen accounting currency. This makes it convenient for businesses to integrate Bitcoin transactions into their accounting processes. Patrick van der Meijde, from BitKassa, mentioned that around 20% of the company's merchants decide to keep the bitcoins in their account instead of transferring them to their accounting currency. For BitPay, this number is around 10%.[81]

Bitcoin debit cards

Xapo is a company devoted to making it possible to spend bitcoins at every shop that accepts Visa payments. After signing up on the website, you can send funds to your Xapo Bitcoin wallet and order a debit card to spend them. The interesting feature here is that you can pay in bitcoins even if the merchant does not accept them. He will not even notice!

When you want to spend your bitcoins, for example, in a restaurant that accepts euros and Visa, you will be able to do so even if the merchant only accepts euros. How? Here is what happens behind the scenes: as soon as you validate the payment denoted in the fiat currency at the merchant's terminal, the equivalent number of bitcoins will be deducted from your Xapo card. Xapo will then convert your bitcoins into the currency accepted by the merchant, in this case euros. Xapo will then pay the merchant in euros. The payment process is as smooth as any other payment with Visa, even though you are actually spending the bitcoins from your wallet.

BitPay launched a prepaid Visa debit card that could be loaded with dollars, using bitcoins, and used to withdraw cash at an ATM or to pay merchants who accept Visa. BitPay receives bitcoins from the customer, which are then converted to local funds at the exchange rate at the moment of the deposit.

According to BitPay,[82] many of the people using the BitPay card actually live off Bitcoin. For the most part, they are either early adopters or people who receive payments in bitcoins. Some users transfer money from their Bitcoin wallet to their BitPay card when they enter a shop. After a few minutes of browsing through the shop, the money should be deposited on the card and ready to use. Other users choose to fill their card when the value of Bitcoin is high, thus getting the most bang for their buck.

PART III

Bitcoin's nature

Chapter 12

What are money and currencies?

By now, you probably have a conceptual understanding of how Bitcoin operates under the hood. But what is the big picture? Where does Bitcoin fit into the world? Can it really work as a currency?

Throughout history, money has taken many forms, from cacao beans and salt to gold coins and paper notes. Political power created new forms of money, and banking evolution changed the way it was used. New inventions and technologies enabled people to transact in new ways, sometimes reducing money to bits[83] on a server. Then came Bitcoin, the most high-tech "money" of all time.

Before assessing Bitcoin's potential as money and/or currency in the next chapter, let us take a look at what money and currencies actually are, how they evolved over time, and what makes something qualify as money and/or currency.

MONEY

Money is nothing but the value people attach to something. It has three characteristics; it is a medium of exchange, a unit of account, and a way to store value.[84][85]

Let us examine what each of these features mean:

Medium of exchange: Money can be swapped for goods or services. It replaced the barter system, in which people exchanged goods and services for other goods and services. The barter system crumbled because exchanges were difficult to negotiate. Exchanging a cow for three pigs involved the not always easy task of finding someone in need of a cow, who owned three pigs and was willing to exchange them. Money was created to make these negotiations easier, to make the market more "liquid." Money, as a medium of exchange, allows a person to sell the cow to one person, collect money as payment, and then use that money to buy three pigs from someone else.

Unit of account: Money is such a strong reference that it can be used as a measure of wealth by economists.

Store of value: Money holds value over time, unlike the cow mentioned above, which might become less valuable as it ages.

CURRENCIES

Currencies are used for trade. Shells, salt, and gold coins were all once currencies. Today, notes issued by central banks are the mainstream currency. The dollar was backed by gold, but in 1971, US President Nixon announced the end of the convertibility to gold and as such, the end of the so-called gold standard. This is how our fiat currencies came to life—they are nothing more than paper backed by the trust we have in "the system."

For a full history on the different forms currencies have taken, refer to the following books:

- *The Ascent of Money* by Nail Ferguson
- *The History of Money* by Jack Weatherford

All currencies, from the ancient times to our modern times, have their pros and cons. History has taught us that good currencies must have the following seven characteristics:

Portable: To be seen as convenient, it must be easy to carry and transfer on a daily basis.

Acceptable: A large number of people must accept it as a medium of exchange. The more widely a currency is accepted, the more liquid it is.

Durable: It must be resistant and reliable. A dollar note is made not just from paper but also contains linen, silk, and wood pulp, which prevents it from disintegrating in the washing machine. In contrast, and as sad as the example might be, in ancient times, slaves were traded for goods or services. They were considered by some people as a currency, though not a very reliable one since they tried to escape and had a high mortality rate.[86]

Recognizable: In order to be widely accepted, the currency must be widely recognized as authentic. Between 640 and 630 BC, the Lydian king decided to stamp a lion's head on gold coins to make his currency recognizable,[87] thus standardizing them while making them difficult to counterfeit at the same time. This innovation enabled people without a scale to weigh gold to participate in trade.

Fungible: One unit must perfectly equal the value of a similar unit. For instance, one ounce of gold equals another ounce of gold; they both have the same value.

Divisible: In order to facilitate trade and negotiations, a currency must be transferable in a sufficiently small quantity. A unit must be divisible into smaller units of equal worth. One of history's most useful tools for this was the Arabic decimal system, imported into Europe by Fibonacci.[88]

Scarce: A currency available in a limited quantity, such as gold, will be more likely to keep its value over time. For instance, paper money that is not linked to gold or another commodity is exposed to an unlimited printing of notes. After World War I, currencies that had experienced hyperinflation, such as the German mark,[89] decided to either return to the gold standard or disappear. Nowadays, central banks try to keep monetary inflation (i.e., the emission of more of the currency) under control. Today, fiat currencies do not just exist in the form of banknotes; through fractional-reserve banking (a process by which banks issue more money by holding a fraction of it as deposits), most fiat currencies have a digital life. At the end of the day, it is scary to realize that no one really knows what the current supply of some fiat currencies is.

Most of our current fiat currencies also aim to fulfill the function of money, but not all of them succeed. Fiat currencies can be exposed to hyperinflation in its monetary supply. When that happens, a currency is no longer scarce and no longer holds value. The best thing a user of the currency can do, in such a case, is to convert it immediately to goods that store value in a better way.

The only value fiat currencies have is based on the trust people have in the monetary policy defined by the central bank.

Chapter 13

Is Bitcoin money? Currency?

Now that you know how Bitcoin works and what money and currencies are, it is time to answer some of the fundamental questions about Bitcoin: Is Bitcoin money? Is Bitcoin a currency? Or is it something else?

Before jumping into the assessment of Bitcoin as money and as currency, we will enrich our thinking by analyzing some remarkable events that might reveal more information about Bitcoin's role.

BITCOIN AS A SAFE HAVEN?

Cyprus

During 2012, some Cypriot banks were in serious trouble, and the state of Cyprus could not lend the required amount to save the banks from a bailout on the market, so it asked Europe for a loan.

On March 16, 2013, the European Union and the International Monetary Fund proposed a 10 billion euro deal with Cyprus and, for the first time, proposed a one-time levy on bank deposits (6.7% if the deposit was below 100,000€, 9.9% if above). This proposal would have made it impossible to transfer or withdraw large amounts of money from bank accounts. The Cypriot parliament rejected the deal on March 18, 2013. Many European citizens were worried, as this was the first time that bank deposits were attacked by political institutions.

On March 25, 2013, the following agreement emerged: all insured accounts with balances less than 100,000€ would remain untouched, but Laiki Bank, a major player in Cyprus, would be shut down.[90] All uninsured accounts with a balance above 100,000€ at Laiki Bank would be levied. Meanwhile, depositors at the Bank of Cyprus would lose 47.5% of their savings exceeding 100,000€.[91][92] According to western media coverage, most of the money in these bank accounts belonged to Russians and Russian companies that were using Cyprus as an offshore tax haven. The remaining Laiki Bank accounts with a balance below 100,000€ were transferred to the Bank of Cyprus. As a result, the Bank of Cyprus froze all uninsured accounts above 100,000€, in case an additional haircut was required. In July, the European Troika[93] agreed on a final levy of 47.5% on all accounts with a balance above 100,000€, with the first 100,000€ being exempted. For example, a person with 300,000€ in his account would pay 95,000€ ([300,000€ – 100,000€]*47.5%).[94]

Many users of the Cypriot system saw their tax haven disappear, and European citizens understood that their money might not be as safe at banks as they had first assumed. If the bank failed, their money might be subject to a haircut.

As a consequence of this uncertainty, Bitcoin's price doubled in those two weeks (from $46.95 on March 15 to $88.92 on March 26) as people were looking to put their money out of governmental hands. In the following days, Bitcoin peaked higher as it made its first strong appearance in mainstream media, and new people found their way to Bitcoin. In a matter of a few hours on April 9, the price reached a new, all-time high at $226 dollars, before dropping to $60 when a major exchange, Mt. Gox, started to process payments with delays and had problems due to the high amount of trades. Ultimately, they had to close for a few hours to upgrade servers.

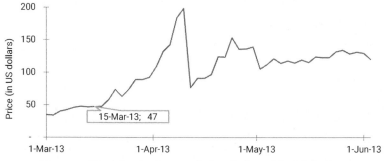

Figure 47. Bitcoin's price increase during the financial crisis in Cyprus

The Cyprus scare of 2013 illustrates that Bitcoin's uniqueness provides answers to some of the concerns about the current financial systems but also reveals the flaws of Bitcoin's still early ecosystem going through a test.

MH17 and Trump

Beginning in November 2013, a political crisis in Ukraine started gaining ground, and by 2014 the crisis had turned into civil conflict. The east of Ukraine is controlled by pro-Russians, aiming to be annexed by Russia, and the west of Ukraine is open to join Europe. On July 17, 2014, around 5:00 pm European time, shortly after the passenger flight MH17 from Amsterdam to Kuala Lumpur crashed in an area controlled by pro-Russians in the west of Ukraine. From Figures 48 to 50, it looks like investors, afraid of a new escalation of "The West vs. Russia" conflict, abandoned the stock market and flocked to alternative markets, causing Bitcoin and gold prices to increase by approximately 1.3% each.

A similar conclusion can be drawn during moments of uncertainty, like on the evening of November 8, 2016, American time, when it became clear that Trump would be announced as president of the United States (see Figures 51 to 53).

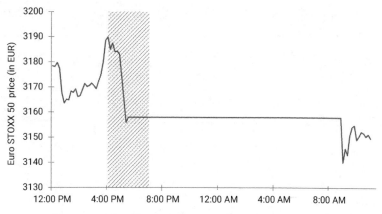

Figure 48. Price of Euro STOXX 50 – MH17 (Source: Bloomberg)

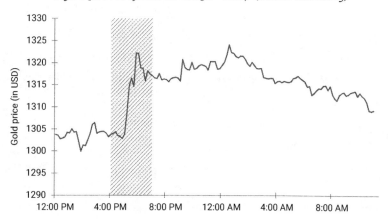

Figure 49. Price of gold – MH17 (Source: Bloomberg)

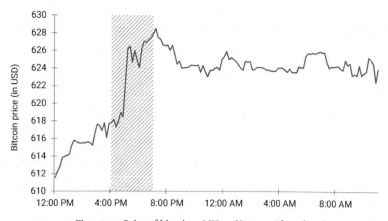

Figure 50. Price of bitcoin – MH17 (Source: Bloomberg)

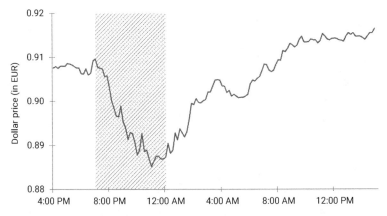

Figure 51. Price of the US dollar against euro - Trump's election (Source: Bloomberg)

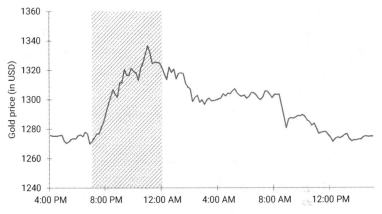

Figure 52. Price of gold - Trump's election (Source: Bloomberg)

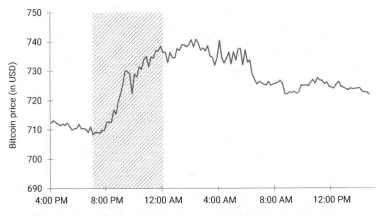

Figure 53. Price of bitcoin - Trump's election (Source: Bloomberg)

IS BITCOIN MONEY?

As you have seen, money is characterized by three features; it is a medium of exchange, a unit of account, and it stores value. This section will assess how Bitcoin performs against these three features.

Bitcoin as a medium of exchange

Bitcoin is highly competitive as a medium of exchange. It can be sent from one place to another without much delay. No central clearinghouse or settlement service is needed; Bitcoin's decentralized and robust protocol takes care of validating transactions. It is cheaper and faster than other electronic services, such as PayPal or credit cards, which might require extra information before processing a payment. In a matter of minutes, funds can move around the world. Finally, Bitcoin's pseudo-anonymity outside the mainstream financial system makes it ideal for those who prefer to keep their transactions outside the banking system.

On the cons side, if no one is willing to send bitcoins to a new user, he might be forced to exchange fiat currencies for bitcoins and thus to pass through an exchange. Passing through an exchange usually requires time, and most of them require an identification and residence validation process to comply with know your customer (KYC) regulations. Just like setting up a PayPal account, subscribing to a credit card, or even opening a bank account, the process can take days, but it is a one-time effort. This only applies if someone has zero bitcoins, so it should be seen more as a difficulty of swapping from one currency to another instead of a weakness in Bitcoin itself as a medium of exchange. If Bitcoin is widely adopted in your country, getting your first bitcoins should be as easy as getting the first units of your currency. You might not have to go through an exchange at all.

For all these reasons, Bitcoin can, without any doubt, be a good medium of exchange.

The big problem is scalability. As we saw earlier, the Bitcoin community is having a hard time reaching a consensus about the block size, and without a consensus, Bitcoin's small blocks can only handle a small percentage of worldwide transactions. If Bitcoin becomes widely adopted and transactions keep increasing, the block size limit will become a hurdle to Bitcoin as a medium of exchange and transaction fees might increase. Maybe, when the number of transactions reaches the maximum the block's size can handle efficiently, reluctant nodes will agree to increase the block size for the simple reason that it is in the general interest of Bitcoin's functioning. This casts a shadow on the future of Bitcoin as a medium of exchange—or, more precisely, as a medium of exchange capable of handling large volumes at a low price.

Finally, we might argue that, as Bitcoin gets closer to its fixed supply, a deflationary spiral might begin. As bitcoins become more and more scarce, people will withhold their bitcoins instead of spending them, and this might have a negative effect on Bitcoin as a medium of exchange.

To conclude, Bitcoin is currently a good medium of exchange, but its current scalability and programmed scarcity mean there is no guarantee that it will remain so in the future.

Bitcoin as a unit of account

Merchants who accept bitcoins usually do so in reference to another accounting unit, such as the fiat currency used for their bookkeeping. For example, if a merchant wants to set a price for an item, he will set the price as $25. Then, he will set another bitcoin price, which is equal to $25. In September 2015, that price was roughly 0.104 BTC. A year later, in September 2016, it was roughly 0.042 BTC, and in August 2017, it was roughly 0.006 BTC.

The value of a bitcoin fluctuates by its exchange rate, so bitcoin prices of an item can fluctuate widely. Like any other currency on a foreign exchange, the exchange rate is defined by offer and demand.

If bitcoin is to be considered a unit of account, people need to start "thinking" in bitcoins instead of thinking in other currencies. Today, only a minority of Bitcoin users are "thinking" in bitcoin as a unit of account. Besides this minority group, the mainstream population is currently not "thinking" in bitcoins when buying, selling, or doing business. This is also the case for the employees of Bitcoin's foundation, who receive their salary in bitcoin,[95] but the number of bitcoins depends on the exchange rate. People will probably not think in bitcoin as long as its price remains volatile, unless they live in an environment where the main currency is no longer trustworthy.

As Bitcoin gains acceptance, the volatility will keep decreasing as we come closer to Bitcoin's final supply of 21 million units. This future might form a more stable and fertile soil for Bitcoin as a unit of account. Still, uncertainties exist about how long the growth in acceptance will continue and about the transaction cost that will apply when miners are no longer rewarded for validating transactions. Until these elements are clear, Bitcoin cannot be considered a unit of account.

To conclude, Bitcoin cannot be seen as a unit of account today, and no certainty exists that it will be, some day.

Bitcoin as storage of value

Bitcoin can be stored safely in a variety of places (such as an encrypted USB drive or paper wallet) for an unlimited period of time, and can be used whenever a user decides to open his wallet. The coin itself is easily secured.

The coin's value, however, is more uncertain. Currently, Bitcoin is experiencing many highs and lows in its price and it is impossible to predict what value stored bitcoins will hold in the future.

From an economical perspective, Bitcoin's limited supply and decreasing emission will make them more and more scarce. Everything that is scarce holds value. As such, Bitcoin could enhance its function as a way to store value in the long term.

To conclude, Bitcoin is still in its early age and cannot, as of today, be seen as a reliable way to store value.

Conclusion

Bitcoin cannot be considered money. It performs best as a medium of exchange, but it cannot be considered as a reliable unit of account or a way to store value.

	Bitcoin
Medium of exchange	+
Unit of account	-
Storage of value	-

Table 3. Bitcoin's assessment as money

Concerning Bitcoin's long-term future, Bitcoin might remain a good medium of exchange, but the block size limit might remain a problem, and the possibility of a deflationary Bitcoin economy could impact Bitcoin's performance as a medium of exchange. Bitcoin might become a good unit of account and/or way to store value, but as of today, no clear trend can be detected.

	Future
Medium of exchange	?
Unit of account	?
Storage of value	?

Table 4. Bitcoin's assessment as money in the future

IS BITCOIN A CURRENCY?

Just as we did for money, we will now discuss Bitcoin's performance against the key factors of success for a currency. References to fiat currencies and gold, a commodity, might be made for the sake of a broader view and the ability to have a more nuanced opinion.

Portable

With today's increased access to technology, bitcoins can be considered portable. They can be stored on connected servers and transferred through QR codes. In developing countries, such as the Philippines[96] and Kenya,[97] mobile phones are used to make payments on a daily basis. However, smartphones in Africa might have limited storage capacity, and installing a proper Bitcoin wallet might require deleting other applications.[98]

Bitcoin performs better than gold, which is heavy to carry, and better than fiat money, which requires supply-chain strategies.[99] Therefore, we will conclude that bitcoins are portable.

Acceptable

Despite a sharp increase in acceptance by merchants and investments in platforms such as BitPay, which facilitate Bitcoin's use, Bitcoin is still only used by a minority of merchants and people.

Gold is not widely accepted, and fiat currencies, although often limited by political borders, are usually well-accepted inside the borders of a monetary system.

Durable

Bitcoin exists digitally, and its durability depends on the owner's caution. Every wallet can be duplicated with backup copies and stored in different ways. Similar to paper money, which is subject to being lost or burned, a digital file can be corrupted and a disk can be zero-fill formatted.[100] Moreover, if all copies of a wallet get lost, all bitcoins can be lost. Unlike fiat currencies, which can be printed by central banks, we can assume that bitcoins are lost forever, which increases its deflation. In conclusion, bitcoins are durable, as long as care is taken not to lose them.

Recognizable

We elaborated quite a bit on Bitcoin's inner workings in previous chapters. We saw that every bitcoin, or part of it, included in a transaction is a reference to a previous transaction in the Blockchain. It is therefore possible to verify a bitcoin's existence and spendability. Nevertheless, a bitcoin (or part of it) only exists through a series of abstract numbers and letters that form an address; it does not have a physical existence. It takes considerable technical skill for a human being to manually verify a bitcoin's authenticity in the Blockchain. However, the open-source Blockchain protocol does this automatically for you.

Because bitcoins have a traceable history, it is impossible to counterfeit bitcoins. On the other hand, physical currency is easier to counterfeit. As long as the counterfeit currency looks like regular currency, it is spendable. For example, two gold coins that are similar on the surface could be mistaken as having the same value, when, in reality, one of the gold coins could have copper mixed in it.[101] Closer to home, counterfeit paper money has been detected in a few cases,[102] leaving us to wonder how much counterfeit money may be circulating under the radar.

A threat to the reliability of the Bitcoin system is a 51% attack, which could occur if a single entity controlled the majority of the network's mining hash rate. In the case of a 51% attack, the perpetrator will work on a separate Blockchain branch, which he does not release immediately. When he decides to release the longer branch, he will be able to double-spend bitcoins by reversing transactions he made while working on his longer branch. However, the attack would be publicly known, bitcoins would still be recognizable, and private keys would still be secure. The attack would be short-lived, and the perpetrator would not be able to counterfeit bitcoins or steal bitcoins from other people's wallets—both of which are regular crimes in the world of paper money.

In conclusion, a bitcoin is recognizable and cannot be counterfeited. Even a 51% attack would not affect the recognizability of bitcoins and the information of someone possessing 51% of hashing power would be known.

Fungible

A bitcoin equals another bitcoin and a satoshi equals another satoshi. No matter the underlying combination of numbers and letters that defines the bitcoin or satoshi, a user could theoretically buy the same goods or services with it. It could be compared to notes of the same amount having different reference numbers, but who looks at the numbers when receiving a note? No one.

So is Bitcoin fungible? Not so fast.

As we saw earlier, a bitcoin's ownership can be traced from its previous transactions. As such, some transactions might represent a number of bitcoins that were, at one point in time, used for illegal activities. Today, Blockchain analytic tools, such as coinanalytics, claim to be capable of revealing entities in the network.[103] Scorechain also provides a trust-index based on the bitcoin's history. As a result, bitcoins that were once in the hands of a dark web user with a dirty past could be considered less valuable than freshly-mined bitcoins. This is good news for the traceability of money by governmental entities, but it is also an obstacle for Bitcoin to become a good fungible currency.

The non-fungibility of bitcoins could result in some bitcoins being refused by the network. For example, nodes could decide that bitcoins proven to be stolen or owned by an obscure organization are no longer valid. The nodes validating transactions could decide to consistently refuse them. In Chapter 10, we discussed how some ATMs perform these checks before providing cash.

Not knowing how valuable your bitcoins are and whether you will be able to exchange them in the future is a risk many users of a currency are not willing to take. No one wants to check the past of a coin every time he receives money.

As mentioned, fiat currency notes also have numbers on them, making them identifiable. In the seventeenth century, Scotland faced the same conflict; banks began seizing notes from their owners if it appeared that the notes had previously been stolen. The outraged owners then went to court, and the court ruled, "If notes could be returned to a previous owner after a theft, it could erode confidence in a currency."[104] This makes fiat currency fungible.

To conclude, we can say that even if bitcoins are exchanged in a fungible way today, they can be differentiated from each other, while fiat currencies and gold are fungible either by law or by nature.

Divisible

As discussed in Chapter 4, a bitcoin can be perfectly divided into 100,000,000 equal pieces, called satoshis. Further division is possible if needed in the future. Fiat currencies are perfectly divisible since they use the Arabic decimal system, and gold is also divisible even if this requires a less convenient process (smelting).

Scarce

A good currency should have sufficient and limited (or controlled) supply. Insufficient supply would make it impossible to trade, while an unlimited supply (think about the number of atoms in the universe) or an uncontrolled supply (think about the Zimbabwean dollar that was subject to hyperinflation) would make it worthless. A "trusted" central institution, such as the Federal Reserve, usually controls fiat currencies.

These institutions can decide to release more or less of the currency to balance shifts in their economy. Besides the creation of money by the centralized institution, fractional-reserve banking is currently used by different institutions. Simply explained, fractional-reserve banking is a mechanism that allows banks to loan out more money than people have deposited into their reserves. The amount of money a bank can "create" through fractional-reserve banking is regulated. These two elements make it difficult for people to have a grasp on the precise amount of money in circulation; it is difficult to truly know how scarce a fiat currency is.

Gold has a limited supply, but new reserves can be found at any time, thus reducing its scarcity. According to the rule of supply and demand, such an event would lead to a downward fluctuation in gold's price.

Bitcoin has a well-defined and limited supply of 21 million bitcoins. Since exchanges are considered as banks under certain legislations, fractional banking is technically possible, but no such system exists (yet?). Even if it did exist, one would know whether the coins he owned were created out of fractional banking or were present in the Blockchain. Thanks to the transparent supply, the exact number of bitcoins created is plainly visible. However, it is more difficult to estimate the number of bitcoins that are lost and have disappeared from the bitcoin economy (this is also the case for paper money, which can be burned).

In any case, Bitcoin's supply being fixed by an algorithm and backed by all nodes of the network, the number of storable bitcoins is programmed not to exceed 21 million (or 2.1 quadrillion[105] satoshis). We can, therefore, conclude that Bitcoin's scarcity is better than that of fiat currencies and commodities.

Conclusion

The following table summarizes the performance of fiat currencies, gold, and Bitcoin against the key success factors of a currency.

A "+" sign means that the "asset" successfully meets the criteria. A "+/-" sign means that either the criteria is theoretically possible but inconvenient (e.g., gold divisibility and recognizability), or that it affects only a marginal number of cases (e.g., authenticity of the dollar). A "-" sign means that the criteria is not met.

	Bitcoin	Fiat	Gold
Acceptance	-	+	-
Portability	+	+	+/-
Durability	+	+	+
Recognizability	+	+	+/-
Fungibility	-	+	+
Divisibility	+	+	+/-
Scarcity	+	+/-	+

Table 5. Bitcoin's evaluation against a currency's key factors of success

Bitcoin's performance as a currency can be seen as incomplete; it scores well in the way it has been designed and is sometimes even better than current fiat currencies; however, two flaws have been discovered.

The first flaw concerns Bitcoin's acceptance. Despite its global reach, Bitcoin has so far failed to go mainstream. This is because:

- Bitcoin is relatively new (compared to other mainstream currencies).
- Bitcoin's adopters can be seen as "more geeky" or "more greedy" than the mainstream population. Most of the interest in Bitcoin today emerges from investors or people with an IT or financial background, and not from the average John Doe.
- A limited number of merchants accept Bitcoin, and few people are aware that Bitcoin debit cards make it possible to pay anywhere.
- Exchange services can be seen as a barrier to entry.
- There is a lack of regulation for start-ups and companies dealing with Bitcoin.

- There is a lack of regulation on how to handle Bitcoin in standard bookkeeping.
- Bitcoin can be too complex and time-consuming to understand, which results in a lack of trust.
- Bitcoin has been a victim of bad press connected with several scandals: the dark web site Silk Road, the collapse of the exchange Mt. Gox, etc. These scandals foster the image of Bitcoin as a risky asset used for illegal activities.
- Currently, Bitcoin's value is subject to extreme volatility.

Many of these causes are not linked to the Bitcoin system itself but rather to the ecosystem in which it operates and which is still in development.

The second flaw is being fungible. In theory, except for freshly-mined bitcoins, one bitcoin cannot be considered exactly the same as another due to its historical trail in the Blockchain. Although the history does not truly affect Bitcoin's activity, the simple fact that these coins can be rejected by operators who connect the bitcoin with the real world makes us consider Bitcoin as non–fungible.

Overall, Bitcoin has some strengths and weaknesses compared to fiat currencies. The main strength against fiat currencies is the transparent supply. A second strength is the uniqueness and non-counterfeitability of each bitcoin. The flaws are the narrow acceptance and in some cases, the non-fungibility.

WHAT ABOUT THE FUTURE?

This section will reflect on Bitcoin's potential evolution as a currency.

Bitcoin's main flaw (acceptance) could disappear in the future. Recent and current evolution of the ecosystem shows that Bitcoin is aiming to become more convenient and "customer-friendly." It also shows an increasing number of transactions being processed in bitcoins. The trend toward a more widespread Bitcoin is clear, and as Bitcoin becomes more widespread, it might help people who are less "geeky" to trust and adopt the Bitcoin, helping it gain an even larger acceptance. Still, a decrease in volatility will be necessary to gain trust. In a less positive scenario, more bad press or failing services could endanger Bitcoin's credibility and change (slow down) the trend toward broader acceptance.

In the future, Bitcoin could become more widely accepted. The adoption of scalability solutions would then probably be required. It is unclear if the fungibility issue will be resolved and approved by the Bitcoin community.

	Bitcoin
Acceptance	?
Portability	+
Durability	+
Recognizability	+
Fungibility	?
Divisibility	+
Scarcity	+

Table 6. Bitcoin's potential future evaluation against a currency's key factors of success

Based on the previous reflection, Bitcoin has the potential to meet the key success factors of a currency at least as well, if not better, than our current mainstream fiat currencies do. However, some changes have to take place before this can happen.

Besides Bitcoin, a plentitude of new cryptocurrencies have emerged. Most of them are based on the same type of open-source codes, but their characteristics are different. Some do not have a limited supply, some have a larger block size, and others tend to be more fungible and anonymous. Some of these currencies learn from Bitcoin's flaws and operate on separate blockchains. These alternative currencies could one day be recognized as being better than Bitcoin and gain a larger acceptance, thus dethroning Bitcoin as the king of cryptocurrencies. We will discuss other cryptocurrencies in Chapter 15.

As such, the conclusion is that cryptocurrencies in general have the potential to meet the key success factors of a currency.

CONCLUSION ON BITCOIN'S NATURE

Conclusion: Bitcoin is not (yet) money and not (yet) a currency. It seems that Bitcoin behaves as a safe haven in short periods of heightened economic uncertainty. Cryptocurrencies, in general, have the potential to become currencies if widely accepted.

PART IV

Looking beyond Bitcoin

Chapter 14

The environment

To understand Bitcoin's innovative and disruptive nature, it is important to look beyond its core functioning and ecosystem. In the medium and long term, Bitcoin's success as a currency will depend on many elements outside the current Bitcoin landscape. If you want to know Bitcoin's chances of becoming a super-currency, you must look beyond the Bitcoin community and understand the much larger environment that might influence its future.

In this chapter, we will perform multiple qualitative analyses through the lens of strategic frameworks. We will perform four analyses (PESTEL, Hype Cycle, Adoption Cycle, and SWOT) that follow a top-down approach, focusing first on the macro-environment before moving on to the specific of Bitcoin and our conclusion.

PESTEL

The PESTEL framework focuses on the external environment and how external trends might impact Bitcoin. The framework is articulated around six dimensions: political, economic, social, technological, environmental, and legal. For each theme, we will discuss the different trends that could affect Bitcoin and cryptocurrencies in general.

Political

Trust issues

Trust in politics has decreased continually during the last decades.[106] While some central banks that issue currency are independent of governments, they still represent a centralized and institutionalized authority, of which the head is sometimes nominated by the government or president. In other cases, central banks are directly controlled by governments. Most fiat currencies rely on the trust we collectively have in the institutions safeguarding the value of our currencies.

The rise of anti-establishment political parties has taken off in the last couple of years. Instances such as the election of Donald Trump in the United States, anti-austerity movements in Europe, movements against the elected president, Duterte, in the Philippines, and the opposition to some African leaders who do not want to terminate their mandate are all concrete signs that people lack trust in the current authorities governing them.

Economic crises can lead to authorities taking extreme decisions. We discussed how the 2011 debt crisis in Europe resulted in haircuts on large bank deposits in Cyprus. It is unclear if this measure will be repeated in the event of a new crisis, but if it does happen, Bitcoin might serve as a safe haven to keep value safe (see Chapter 13).

When governance is disastrous

Sometimes, the governance of money is just dramatic. On November 8, 2016, 8:00 pm, Indian Prime Minister Narendra Modi announced that all 500- and 1,000-rupee notes would be invalid as of midnight the same day. The measure was announced as an attempt to stop the counterfeiting of rupee-notes and reduce corruption and the use of black money. All old banknotes needed to be handed to the Reserve Bank of

India before December 30. This resulted in a huge shortage of banknotes and endless lines of people trying to exchange their old banknotes on a daily basis. By December, cash withdrawals from ATMs were limited to 2,000 rupees per day.[107] As most ATMs were out of cash, lines started to form as soon as an ATM was refilled.[108] People died in queues[109] in front of the banks, and the same happened when hospitals refused to accept banknotes.[110] Trucks were stranded[111] on the highways because they were unable to pay road-tolls, and by November farmers could not purchase the goods they needed, like seeds, pesticides, etc.[112]

On the other hand, the Indian government's decision resulted in a boost in bitcoin demand by Indian consumers.[113]

Even more surreal was the ban of 100-bolivar notes in Venezuela a few weeks later. The 100-bolivar note was the largest and most commonly used banknote in Venezuela, representing 50% of all notes in circulation. Notes of 2, 5, 10, and 20 bolivares had become useless due to the hyperinflation of the preceding years.[114] Venezuelans had only 72 hours to exchange their 100-bolivar notes for new ones. This radical decision turned an already dire situation into a full-fledged disaster and left the poorest without any means to purchase the most basic supplies.[115]

These cases show how entire populations can suffer from human decisions about money. Money rules our lives, and the people who have experienced such dramatic situations will be the first ones in favor of a currency that is not controlled by governments or humans in general. A currency with clear and transparent rules. One that cannot be banned. A currency that allows anyone to make transactions, without having to rely on a third party to supply notes. In other words, they will be in favor of well-designed cryptocurrencies.

To the victims of geopolitics

Geopolitical conflicts can lead to everything from governmental cybercrime to deployment of military troops. As governments can use their power to block financing to certain causes, alternatives to the traditional financial system are useful to the people who believe in those causes.

In November 2010, Julian Assange, founder of WikiLeaks, released the diplomatic files of the United States. Soon, donations to WikiLeaks were banned by Bank of America, VISA, MasterCard, PayPal, and Western Union. A couple of months later, in June 2011,[116] WikiLeaks started to accept Bitcoin donations.

In 2014, after Russia annexed the Ukrainian territory of Crimea, the European Union sanctioned 149 individuals and 37 entities by freezing their assets in the European Union.[117] This meant that they could no longer access, move, or sell assets such as bank deposits, stocks, cash money, or real estate.[118]

The rise of geopolitical conflicts, such as the conflict at the Russian-European border, the conflict in Syria, or the spread of ISIS might lead to more "financial bans" and "asset freezes." Some of these restricted parties might find it easier to turn to bitcoins.[119] Despite some claims,[120] there is, until today, no supporting evidence that Bitcoin is used for these purposes.[121]

The return of nationalism and protectionism in various countries might lead to more national and local currencies. This is particularly true in the Eurozone, where popular extreme-right parties, such as "Le Front National" in France, are in favor of leaving the Eurozone and re-instituting a French national currency. Countries like Greece, who suffered from the Euro crisis in 2011, are already using the TEM as an alternative to the euro.[122] In the event that European countries restore national currencies, the lack of a single currency for the Eurozone will be a hurdle for international trade. Bitcoin might come forward as a solution to convert one currency to another, particularly during the transition period. We can also expect that the uncertainty created in the financial market by such bold switches of power will result in an increase in the demand for bitcoins.

Empower or combat fraud?

The increased exchange of financial information between countries makes it more difficult for individuals and corporations to embezzle money. In this regard, Bitcoin is not offering an ultimate solution; anti-money laundering rules affect most trading platforms, making it difficult for fraudsters to remain off the radar of governmental institutions.

Moreover, the non-fungibility and transparency provided by the Blockchain has demonstrated that every transaction can be traced. Still, the identification of the people behind the addresses might be difficult, especially when someone operates through networks such as Tor.

In conclusion, the art of transacting anonymously involves being able to transfer bitcoins to the "real economy" without being caught. Going to the "real economy" might involve exchanging bitcoins for fiat currencies or buying goods. For the latter, let us remember that asking a pizzeria to deliver a pizza requires the pizzeria to have your physical address. This makes a Bitcoin address traceable to a physical location.

The power of politics

Today, governments dictate the currency by which their countries should operate. To understand why, we need to go back a few centuries to a time when countries imposed standard currency so that they could: (1) certify the quality of a coin by stamping it and (2) capture seigniorage revenue (the difference between the value given to the money and its actual cost[123]) by issuing more currency. Standardizing currencies was also a way for governments to set the currency in which citizens should pay taxes to the country's administration. For the sake of pragmatism, people and businesses began operating with the same currency. Today, people have come to depend on standardized currencies. They are embraced as the norm.

It would take major changes in the government's monetary policies to see any country replace its tax-currency with Bitcoin. One of the reasons is that it is impossible to seize control of someone's funds, since they are protected by the owner himself, who has the private key. This is different from the current situation, where some administrations can cooperate with banks to seize unpaid taxes.

Finally, let us note that most countries' administrations express concerns about Bitcoin's high price volatility, but do not take a radical position against cryptocurrencies.

Economic

Empower the two billion unbanked

According to the World Bank, two billion adults worldwide, mainly located in developing countries, have no formal bank account.[124] Not having a trusted place to store money limits opportunities for saving and managing finances with a long-term vision. It also limits opportunities to receive governmental money or save for the education of children and limits access to financial products such as agricultural insurance against bad weather.

Cryptocurrencies give people the opportunity to be responsible for their own bank accounts. With advanced platforms such as Ethereum and oracles (more on this in Chapter 16), people could engage with insurance-based products more easily and independently, no matter where they are located in the world. This becomes more and more realistic as an ever-larger number of people are connected to mobile applications and have access to cashless payment systems. As we saw in Chapter 9, recent efforts aim at empowering people in developing countries to join the Bitcoin economy with the help of satellites.

Crisis and political responses

The 2008 financial crisis has reduced trust in the financial system and raised questions about the true value of currencies. In certain countries, we saw the value of real estate plummet, and people were confused by the rapid change in how much property they could afford to buy with their money. From one day to the next, the notion of what someone could afford with his money was distorted.

This resulted in a global financial crisis, which led to some severe changes in the way people look at the current financial system. The collapse of Lehman Brothers affected the trust in banks. Governmental bonds, which were once assumed to be risk-free, have defaulted in some countries, and the European debt crisis showed that bank deposits were no longer safe and could be subject to "haircuts" (e.g., Cyprus, see Chapter 13)

It is unclear whether similar decisions will be taken in the future, but those who fear the answer is yes find a solution in Bitcoin, where they have full control over their belongings, and their capital is not subject to haircuts imposed by third parties.

The long-lasting European economic slow-down has forced people to think about more extreme solutions to restore the economy. Concepts such as helicopter money (the direct distribution of money to the people) are sometimes discussed.[125] Some fear that this would result in disastrous consequences, like uncontrolled inflation, although this would probably depend on the amount of helicopter money that would be distributed.

Keeping inflation under control

It is unclear what course central banks will take to foster an economic recovery in the future. People who lose faith in the monetary policies of central banks and fear an increase of the monetary supply or hyperinflation might be in favor of a system like Bitcoin, where the monetary supply is well-defined and under control. Civilizations where the consequences of hyperinflation are well known understand the value of Bitcoin very well.

Inflation rate (%)

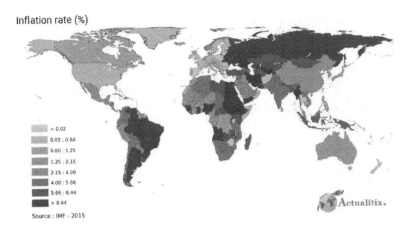

Figure 54. Inflation rate per country

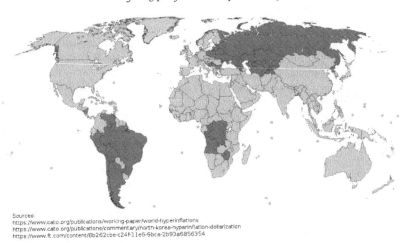

Figure 55. Countries with at least one episode of hyperinflation in the past 50 years

The reason why central banks are issuing new money is to slightly devaluate it over time. By doing so, people in the real economy tend to spend faster and transact more, which makes the economy turn. However, this practice does not always work as it should. For example, the low interest rate and even the quantitative easing program of the European Central Bank did not immediately result in the desired economic growth.[126]

Here again, Bitcoin's limited supply is attractive to people who want to safeguard their assets from hyperinflation. Unlike the fiat-based system, a person owning 1 BTC holds one 21-millionth of the Bitcoin economy and that proportion will not change over time. In this regard, holding bitcoins is similar to holding gold.

However, Bitcoin is not offering a solution for economic growth. On the contrary, Bitcoin's supply will decline over time and new bitcoins will become scarcer. As the number of bitcoins is limited, economic theory suggests that the number of bitcoins required to purchase goods should keep increasing, which is not good for economic growth, as it encourages people to hold on to their bitcoins instead of spending them.

We might imagine new cryptocurrencies embodying new monetary policies that would be more supportive of economic growth through inflation in the monetary supply. In such a case, these cryptocurrencies would more likely be used for daily trade, as their purchasing power would decrease over time, or as Gresham's law states: "bad money drives out good money." Bitcoin could then play the role of digital gold, with its price increasing relative to the other cryptocurrencies that embody a higher increase in monetary supply.

The difference between the described system and the fiat-based system would lie in the predictability of monetary policies. In the fiat-based system, the simple fact that centralized institutions can manipulate the money supply creates uncertainty, which would not exist in strong and collectively maintained cryptocurrencies. However, here again, cryptocurrencies are not the ultimate solution, as they would compete against each other. Moreover, unpredictability in human trading behavior might result in even more uncertainty when prices are denominated against another (crypto)currency.

A global currency for global trade

Today, economies are more interconnected than ever. Trading borders have vanished,[127] making trade and financial markets more globalized.

The need for trustworthy and fast-moving money transactions is higher than ever. When interoperability is ensured, satisfying centralized solutions exist, sometimes offering better services than Bitcoin.[128] The fundamental trust issue is not solved with Bitcoin itself, but the ease of transferring value from anywhere to anywhere is ground-breaking.

When it comes to large transactions between companies located in different regions, trust is enforced by an administrative process set up between the bank of the buyer and the bank of the seller.[129] Here again, the ultimate solution is not cryptocurrencies alone, but the combination of cryptocurrencies and smart contracts (which we will discuss in Chapter 16), which creates new ways to trade without trust and without trusted intermediaries.

So do we need a global currency like Bitcoin?

As we have seen in Chapter 11, Bitcoin helps international trade and allows people to buy online from other countries without encountering obstacles with currency exchange or credit card restrictions. It seems common sense that life would be easier and better off with one single currency. But is that really the case?

Different countries have different cultures, different values, and different productivity levels. Gilles Mitteau, Founder of Heu?reka, a French YouTube channel about macro-economics, uses the United States (with the US dollar) and France (with the euro) to demonstrate how two countries can have very different economies. He assumes, for the sake of the example, that investing in America is more favorable than investing in France because the workforce is more productive, opening a business is easier, and taxes are lower. With one single currency, investors would prefer to invest their money in the United States. However, the fact that America and France operate with different currencies makes it necessary for an investor willing to start a business in America to purchase US dollars first. As many people will be willing to invest in America because of its competitive advantage over France, the value of the US dollar will increase relative to the value of the euro.

For an investor, the US dollar becomes more expensive relative to the Euro, helping the latter to become more competitive. As the price of the dollar increases, an investor might start to consider investing in the cheaper Euro rather than in the expensive US dollar. Of course, this is a simple explanation. Many other factors come into play, but the general idea is that, in theory, having different currencies for different economies levels out differences and allows everyone to live more or less prosperously.

Using Bitcoin as a global currency while economies are still different in multiple aspects would create a situation similar to the one in Europe, where a country like Germany, which has a competitive economy relative to its neighbors, attracts more investments than other countries without seeing the price of its currency increasing compared to other countries attracting fewer investments. While euros can flow from one country to another, differences in culture and language make it difficult for people to move from one European country to another.[130] Overall, the different economies and social immobility create a larger gap between healthy and weak economies. The United States solves this problem by subsidizing the states with money from the federal budget, which is many times higher than the Eurozone's budget.

Therefore, having one global currency without global policies would not be beneficial to the global economy. When it comes down to currencies, the trend is to preserve local currencies, as we will discover in the next paragraphs.

Social

Back to authentic value

Aversion to politics and difficulty in understanding the complex banking and financial system are a breeding ground for libertarian movements. Bitcoin appeals to libertarians because it enables people to have "money of their own," of which they have full custody and a certain control over the rules. Moreover, understanding the current economics behind

Bitcoin is relatively straightforward compared to understanding the current, mainstream financial system.

Flying away from fiat currencies, some wealthy people tend to increase their investment in hard assets, such as land[131] or real estate, which has an intrinsic value and is less subject to monetary inflation or haircuts (although still subject to price bubbles). We mentioned that Bitcoin could be compared to digital gold and is safe from decisions by the establishment. However, the only intrinsic value the Bitcoin Blockchain provides is an immutable database backed by large amounts of mining material.[132] The rest is trust in the value people will give to bitcoins, just like any other currency.

Everybody plays the same game

Some people might think that virtual or privately controlled currencies do not have any credibility. However, there are many existing examples of such currencies. Most of the money that is created today is nothing more than mere numbers in the computers of our banks. Most of the currency in circulation is already virtual. Numerous websites, companies, and non-profits have their own private currency, like frequent flyer miles or gift cards.

More and more local community currencies are starting to emerge. These currencies are often limited to one specific region and are not legal tender. The idea behind local currencies is that they foster the local economy because they can only be spent in local stores, rather than online or at other national and international competitors. Multitudes of governances exist around these currencies. Some serve specific functions. Some are pegged to a national currency. Others are not. In California alone, dozens of these currencies exist.[133] One example is the Santa Barbara Missions tokens, which can be earned by helping out some local non-profits and can be used to buy organic food from farmers.[134]

Also, France has over 30 local currencies.[135] One of them is the eusko, active in the region of Basque. The ambition of the eusko is to support local merchants, the local economy, the environment, local employment, and the use of the Basque language.[136] This local currency is pegged to the euro, where one eusko is equal to one euro. Individuals cannot exchange euskos for euros—only merchants can, and they must pay a 5% fee to finance the system when they make exchanges.[137] Over 300 merchants[138] have joined the movement. There is even a eusko label; products can receive the eusko label when they are produced with local ingredients and involve reduced transportation.[139]

Private and local currencies are different from cryptocurrencies. They are often managed centrally (e.g., frequent flyer miles that are nominative) or are limited to a certain region (e.g., the eusko). In contrast, cryptocurrencies, in their current form, can be exchanged online between individuals from various regions. In essence, private and local currencies differ very much from Bitcoin; the major resemblance is the change of mindset needed to no longer see the imposed, legal currency as the only available option.

Technological

Machine humans

The relationship between humans and technology is reaching never-before-seen highs. Technology is becoming an extension of the human body, and people increasingly rely on the Internet and smart devices to manage their daily lives. People have even become enslaved to technology and their trust relies most often on the network adoption, rather than an understanding of the technology.

Everything at one touch on the screen

People are more and more virtually interconnected through the Internet. The Internet needs a currency, and Bitcoin is responding by being the "cash of the Internet." It facilitates the payment of Internet services between individuals who do not want to rely on or pay for more complex payment infrastructures. It operates in a more effective way than PayPal, credit cards, and other intermediaries, and the settlement of the payment is near real-time.

The Internet has made Bitcoin available across the globe, even when people are on the move. This supports Bitcoin as a payment method, since the required communication channel (i.e., the Internet) is broadly available.

Smartphones have integrated the functionalities of many different devices we used to carry. Examples include music players, cameras, and books. They are also a new way to synchronize agendas and get real-time news and information specific to your location—all in one single device. Only wallets and ID cards have not been fully integrated into smartphones yet, but it is only a matter of time before they will be.

Of all things the smartphone has integrated, customer experience has been at the center of the adoption. The customer experience of having a Bitcoin wallet on your phone is great, but the customer experience of registering at a Bitcoin exchange and moving money from fiat to a cryptocurrency is weak. To be user-friendly, the Bitcoin onboarding process needs a one-touch-on-the-screen solution.

Cashless

Countries such as Belgium, France, Canada, and the United Kingdom report that over 90% of the value of their consumer payments is cashless.[140] [141] In some countries, such as Sweden, even homeless people receive money through a device.[142]

In some African and Asia-Pacific countries, payments through mobile devices are a familiar practice. The most explicit example is M-Pesa, a mobile payment service launched by Vodafone, where people can use their mobile phone as a wallet and make transactions by SMS. M-Pesa allows people to deposit and withdraw money, pay bills, and make transactions. It has been widely adopted in African countries.

As the entire world's population becomes familiar with cashless money, the bridge toward Bitcoin, a purely cashless currency, is only one small step away.

Banking nerves under attack

Cybercrime is becoming a hot topic among companies, governments, and other central institutions. In the banking world, central payment processors, such as SWIFT, have been subject to cyberattacks.[143] SWIFT's former CEO, Leonard Schrank, openly admitted to his company's failure to pay attention to cybersecurity for years.[144] Relying on such a central point, which could fail, threatens the financial system as a whole.

Unlike centralized points of failure, we have seen in Chapter 3 that the decentralized nature of the Bitcoin Blockchain makes it one of the most secure networks in the world.

Environmental

Green, Greener, Greenest

We can observe a growing trend to a "greener" planet with less pollution. Bitcoin is often criticized for the large amounts of power consumed by mining activities. Other consensus mechanisms (see next chapter) have been tested and adopted by other cryptocurrencies. These alternative consensus mechanisms are more eco-friendly, and if Bitcoin adopted them one day, they could reduce Bitcoin's impact on the environment.

Legal

By challenging governmental and institutionalized currencies in a decentralized fashion, Bitcoin disobeys the rules of monetary policies and financial systems, and it has not failed to draw the attention of politicians and regulators. The legal landscape surrounding Bitcoin is different from one country to another and might change rapidly. This section provides an overview of how laws might affect Bitcoin, but changes in laws and regulations could make this section outdated or inaccurate soon.

A shady past

Like many new technologies, Bitcoin's past is full of examples where it was used for illegal purposes. Through the Silk Road website, it facilitated the anonymous purchase of drugs and other criminal goods. Bitcoin has also been used by "hacktivists" and WikiLeaks for receiving donations, when other services such as PayPal and credit cards made that impossible. Other presumed usages of Bitcoin are money laundering and criminal activities, such as child pornography and terrorism, through Tor. A Europol report, however, notes that there is little evidence that the Blockchain itself is being used for illegal purposes and points out that Bitcoin is only pseudonymous, meaning that there is potentially traceable data that could be used to link transactions to individuals. Therefore, other anonymous virtual currencies deserve closer watch, as they continue to gain momentum among criminals.[145]

In jurisdictions such as China, where access to the Internet is subject to censorship, Bitcoin has been used to pay VPN services that allow Internet users to surf websites otherwise banned by public authorities.

Bitcoin challenges the rules and even the laws, while also empowering libertarian activities. This is not always pleasing to governments, and we might expect them to be resistant and opposed to Bitcoin. But are they?

For what it is worth

It is clear that digital, decentralized currencies can be used for purposes that defy the government. These features, however, make it impossible for a country to, de facto, ban Bitcoin. Countries can incriminate possession and/or use of bitcoins, but most countries choose to regulate them instead.

Bitcoin users and start-ups are subject to different regulations, depending on where they operate. Since Bitcoin has been proven to create employment and is a breeding ground for entrepreneurs, it is important not to legislate too hard against using bitcoins, at the risk of making similar start-ups located in other countries more competitive.[146] Businesses are demanding clear legislation and frameworks in which they can operate legally. Over the past few years, these demands have been met by many regulators who have shown more and more interest in incorporating bitcoins into the legal system.

Current status

The legal environment has never been very hostile to Bitcoin. Today, legislators are mainly investigating the cryptocurrency, looking to find or develop a suitable legal framework for it. It is important to note that regulation changes continuously and this section will very rapidly be outdated; we decided to leave it in, however, as it gives an overview of the possible reactions toward Bitcoin.

Most of the western world and Latin American countries are permissive of Bitcoin, while Russia and Asian countries are more contentious toward Bitcoin. African countries do not take a position. Few countries take a hostile approach.

Hostile countries

In Iceland, Bitcoin is considered a foreign currency, and the purchase of foreign currencies has been prohibited since the financial collapse of 2008. However, Bitcoin mining facilities are allowed in Iceland.

The central bank of Bolivia stated that it is "illegal to use any currency that is not issued and controlled by a government or an authorized entity," which, of course, includes Bitcoin. At the end of May 2017, Bolivian authorities arrested 60 people for carrying out Bitcoin-related "training activities."[147][148]

Contentious countries

On December 17 and 18, 2013, the People's Bank of China (PBoC) ruled that Bitcoin is not a currency and cannot be used by financial institutions and third-party settlement services.[149] However, it is considered legal to mine bitcoins and trade them between individuals. China's position toward Bitcoin has taken many turns and has often been uncertain. The latest development occurred in early 2017, when the PBoC increased regulatory pressure and asked exchanges to comply with anti-money laundering rules. Exchanges froze withdrawals of cryptocurrencies for several months until they became compliant with AML rules.[150]

In Russia, a legal draft proposed to make Bitcoin illegal, but this draft has never been implemented.[151] The latest developments propose to regulate Bitcoin, but they still do not see it as a currency.[152]

The central bank of Jordan prohibits businesses from using Bitcoin but does not prohibit the use of bitcoins by individuals.[153]

The Venezuelan authorities did not make any statement against the use of bitcoins, despite widespread use of bitcoins as an alternative currency.[154] However, in 2017, the Venezuelan authorities began arresting Bitcoin miners and destroying their equipment, accusing them of stealing energy.[155] At the same time, Venezuela's main Bitcoin exchange, Surbitcoin, stopped operations after their bank account was closed[156] before resuming operations one month later.[157]

Permissive countries

Most permissive countries are aware of the cryptocurrency phenomenon but have decided not to legislate against Bitcoin.

Some countries have stated that Bitcoin is not regulated, and they have not adopted a position on how it should eventually be regulated. Often, permissive countries emit warnings on the risk of using Bitcoin, with the European Banking Authority (EBA) identifying over 70 risks related to virtual currencies.[158] Most of the existing regulation applies to businesses operating with bitcoins rather than to individuals using them.

The EBA has advised banks to stay away from virtual currencies until a regulatory regime is in place, and has recommended legislators to find solutions for businesses working with virtual currencies.[159] In December 2016, a proposal[160] from the European commission stated that exchanges and wallet providers should report suspicious activities.

Some countries believe that financial regulations do not apply to Bitcoin, while others have extended current rules to cryptocurrencies and start-ups. France, for example, regulates the operations of exchanges. In 2017, Japan, Korea, and Switzerland adapted their regulation to become more Bitcoin friendly.[161]

Germany considers bitcoins as a "unit of account" that falls under the same regulations as "financial instruments in the meaning of the German Banking Act."[162] This implies that they can be used for trade, tax purposes, and in multilateral clearing circles[163] and that businesses operating with Bitcoin should investigate how this regulation applies to them.

Note that, although some countries have recognized Bitcoin as a payment method, none have recognized it as legal tender.

For countries that will start legislating Bitcoin soon, two major areas of concern emerge: anti-money laundering and taxation.

Anti-money laundering laws

Money laundering is "the process of making illegally-gained proceeds (i.e., 'dirty money') appear legal (i.e., 'clean')."[164] Anti-money laundering (AML) laws typically involve bookkeeping requirements, the obligation to report transactions over a certain amount, ID and residence verification for users who want to join an exchange, and the obligation to report suspicious transactions or behaviors, etc.

174 | BITCOIN, THE BLOCKCHAIN AND BEYOND

Taxation

With regard to taxation, Bitcoin has been subject to different treatments, sometimes even within the same jurisdiction. An example is the United States, where the SEC (Securities & Exchange Commission) thinks of bitcoins as a security or money, the FinCEN (The Financial Crimes Enforcement Network) considers bitcoins a currency,[165] and the Internal Revenue Service (IRS) considers bitcoins property.

In the United States, taxation is a bit complex. The IRS states[166] that bitcoins are considered property and fall under those general tax principles. As such, it is not recognized as a currency than can generate foreign capital gains or losses. Just as for property the IRS states: "A taxpayer who receives virtual currency as a payment for goods or services must, in computing gross income, include the fair market value of the virtual currency."[167] In the event that the bitcoins are sold, a gain or loss will be reported based on the difference between the fair market value at the date of acquisition and the fair market value at the date of selling. If the bitcoins are held as a capital asset (similar to bonds and stocks) they will be reported as a capital gain or loss. If they are held as inventory for sale, they will be reported as an ordinary gain or loss.

The drawback of the United States' ruling is that capital gains have to be calculated on everyday transactions. As stated by Bloomberg journalists Richard Rubin and Carter Dougherty,[168] "Purchasing a $2 cup of coffee with bitcoins bought for $1 would trigger $1 in capital gains for the coffee drinker and $2 of gross income for the coffee shop." Indeed, bitcoins are acquired at different dates and thus almost certainly at different exchange rates. This creates numerous capital gain computations and a practical obstacle in the everyday use of bitcoins by US citizens.

Since August 2013, bitcoins have been classified as an "accounting unit" in Germany, and they are treated as a financial instrument for general tax purposes. It is expected that the total Bitcoin-related value creation will be added to the general income.

In October 2015, the European Court of Justice (ECJ) ruled that Bitcoin is a contractual means of payment and a direct means of payment between operators that accept it. The ECJ further considers that, provided that bitcoins are used and accepted as a means of payment, they should qualify as such and be treated just like other means of payment, such as regular money. This implies that in the EU, no value-added tax (VAT) is due on the mere transaction with bitcoins.[169]

Services relating to Bitcoin within the EU are, according to the ECJ, regarded as financial services. As financial services by "regular" currency exchanges are regarded to be exempt from VAT, the ECJ states that this should also be the case for Bitcoin exchanges.[170]

HYPE CYCLE

An often-regarded cycle in technology adoption is the "Hype Cycle," used by advisory firm Gartner. The cycle details a number of stages that every new technology passes through before it is adopted on a massive scale.

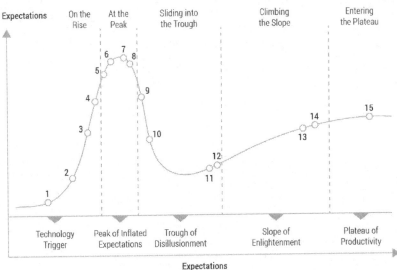

1: R&D

2: Start-up compagnies' first round of venture capital funding

3: First-generation products, high price, lots of customization needed

4: Early adopters investigate

5: Mass media hype begins

6: Supplier proliferation

7: Activity beyond early adopters

8: Negative press begins

9: Supplier consolidation and failures

10: Second/third rounds of venture capital funding

11: Less than 5% of the potential audience has adopted fully

12: Second-generation products,

some services

13: Methodologies and best practices developing

14: Third-generation products, out of the box, product suites

15: High-growth adoption phase starts: 20% to 30% of the potential audience has adopted the innovation

Figure 56. Gartner's hype cycle (Source: Gartner.com)

Today, Bitcoin has passed the stages of "Technology Trigger" and "Peak of Inflated Expectations." Indeed, a lot of money has been invested, and mass media attention was at an all-time high at the end of 2013. Quickly after having reached its peak, a flow of bad news occurred: stolen bitcoins, tentative proposal to ban Bitcoin in certain countries, the bankruptcy of Mt. Gox, and more.

In 2014, some start-ups were in their second round of funding. At that point in time, Bitcoin was close to the bottom of the "Trough of Disillusionment." According to Gartner, this means that less than 5% of the final audience had adopted Bitcoin.

Between 2014 and 2017, we can observe many efforts made by the Bitcoin community to provide a better understanding of Bitcoin. The ecosystem has stabilized, and conferences such as "Scaling Bitcoin" aim to gather people who have invented new concepts to improve Bitcoin's protocol and reach consensus. We can say that cryptocurrencies are slowly coming out of the trough of disillusionment and moving on to the slope of enlightenment with second-generation products. These products might provide a better user-experience for Bitcoin, but they might also give birth to new cryptocurrencies with different features. More on this in the next chapter.

If you are interested, the full 2017 hype cycle can be found in Appendix 3.

Does Bitcoin's price reflect the adoption stage or is it the other way around?

Bitcoin's price is determined by supply and demand. It is, in its very nature, not a reflection of the adoption stage. However, the price factors in the appetite for the solution and the belief in Bitcoin as a sustainable system. This can be illustrated by looking back to the end of 2013, when Bitcoin made headlines in the media, and people believed that it could be worth many times more than its current value. Demand increased and so did the price—until Mt. Gox collapsed, and people began believing that Bitcoin was hacked and unstable. Then, demand decreased and so did the price.

Today, people's understanding and the ecosystem has matured, and the price probably incorporates some belief that Bitcoin will see sustainable usage.

Unlike other technologies, for which production cost decreases and supply increases as the technology matures, Bitcoin's supply decreases as the ecosystem matures. Common sense would suggest that if Bitcoin matures and becomes more widely adopted, the price will be supported by the increased demand.

ADOPTION CYCLE

Having discussed the macro-environmental factors and the evolutionary cycle for technologies, it is time to deep-dive into the adoption of Bitcoin.

The hype cycle leads us to think that Bitcoin is in its early adoption phase. We will further discuss this assertion by using the more relevant adoption cycle framework. The adoption cycle for technological innovations is largely discussed by Geoffrey A. Moore in his book *Crossing the Chasm* (1991).

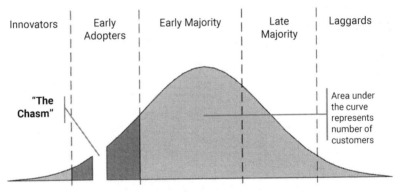

Figure 57. Technology Adoption Lifecycle (Source: Geoffrey A. Moore, Crossing the Chasm)

Geoffrey A. Moore distinguishes the following types of customers:[171]

Innovators are people continuously in search of new technologies; people who are proud to be the first among their peers to use them. Some will call them "the techies."

Early adopters are similar to innovators, but they come after innovators. They are not as interested in being the first ones to use the technology as they are in the potential benefits of a specific technology or the problems it could solve. Some will call them "the visionaries."

The early majority are those adopting the technology to solve problems or because it makes life easier. It is the practical side that appeals to them. They have less patience to understand how things work and are risk-averse. They want something that is stable, well-established, and long-lasting. They represent around one-third of the total adopters. Some will call them "the pragmatists."

The late majority are those who are more risk-averse to new technologies and wait until large masses and renowned organizations adopt the product before they make the leap. They also represent one-third of the market.

Finally, the laggards are those who do not feel accustomed to technology and will use it only if they are forced to.

The chasm is the gap between the visionaries and the pragmatists. This is what Bitcoin is trying, slowly but surely, to cross. Indeed, Bitcoin has benefited from wide media attention and has passed the stage of innovators. Many Bitcoin believers (the visionaries) are now in possession of some bitcoins. Many start-ups are working around Bitcoin. Still, today, Bitcoin is used by a limited number of customers and is not fully ready to be used by the pragmatists. As mentioned in Chapter 11, the number of merchants who accept bitcoins is marginal. Nevertheless, there is space for improvement over time. One point that needs to be improved is the entry process; as we discussed in Chapter 10, switching from fiat currencies to bitcoins requires a few steps. Pragmatists will need a one-click solution, like purchasing bitcoins with a credit card or PayPal. ATMs and exchanges will not provide the desired customer experience.

To reach a mainstream audience, Bitcoin will have to be adopted by the early majority (aka the pragmatists). We know that Bitcoin has shown itself very useful for cross-border payments (see Chapter 11), which can be seen as the first signs of an early majority. Also, the number of Bitcoin transactions is growing due to the availability of new services, like BitPay.

To conclude, Bitcoin has come a long way since its birth and has gained enough attention to reach visionaries, but the immaturity of the ecosystem is the reason why Bitcoin failed to reach an early majority despite its phenomenal rise in 2013. Bitcoin is still living in an ecosystem that is not pragmatic and mature enough to convince the mainstream, even if we start to see some promising services and applications of Bitcoin making the bridge to the real world. Today, in 2017, the ecosystem is much more mature and "the chasm" is closing.

SWOT

During the previous chapters, you acquired an understanding of Bitcoin's functioning and its ecosystem. We also analyzed whether Bitcoin could be considered money or currency. In this chapter, we have discussed different happenings outside of Bitcoin's universe, to better understand the bigger picture in which it plays out. We are now ready to build on these elements to further understand what Bitcoin is today, and what it can and cannot become in the future.

We will discuss this under the format of a "Strengths, Weaknesses, Opportunities and Threats" (SWOT) analysis, which can serve as a pre-conclusion of the book. The strengths and weaknesses focus mainly on the current core aspects of Bitcoin: its functioning and its ecosystem. The opportunities and threats are more related to external or futuristic factors.

Strengths

Trust through stable rules

Since 2009, the network has changed through Bitcoin improvement proposals that were developed and accepted by the network. These improvements were more frequent in the early days, and Bitcoin has now gained a good level of stability and maturity. We know that no sudden change will happen in the way Bitcoin operates, unless these changes are largely discussed and accepted by Bitcoin users.

Trust through transparency

Bitcoin's protocol being open-source, every rule is visible to anyone who wants to look into it. People trust Bitcoin because everyone can review how it operates and everyone understands that it is impossible to change these rules without a consensus on the network.

One of the key rules of Bitcoin's protocol is the pre-programmed monetary supply of bitcoins. This clear and transparent rule is an additional value compared to other financial systems.

Not only are the rules transparent, the transactions are as well, which makes it impossible to counterfeit bitcoins.

Trust through security

All these immutable rules are safeguarded by the massive computing power that is distributed across thousands of nodes on the network.

Bitcoin was the first virtual currency to successfully make peer-to-peer payments on the Internet possible. It has been acknowledged for this achievement and benefits from its first-mover advantage.

Being the first-mover resulted in a massive amount of computing power joining the network. Today, Bitcoin's security is backed by 7 billion Gigahashes[172] per second of computing power, all of which is devoted to performing proof-of-work. This power is many times larger than that of any other cryptocurrency or, for that matter, the hashing power of any other entity.

A certain level of anonymity

Bitcoin users are identified by their public key and their Bitcoin address. As you know by now, this is nothing more than a bunch of letters and numbers. We consider Bitcoin to be a pseudo-anonymous system; it is not fully anonymous, but it offers a stronger anonymity than other online payment alternatives, which are subject to investigations by authorities.

However, every Bitcoin transaction leaves a trail visible to everyone, and that trail cannot be erased. This trail certainly reduces the opportunities for fraud and makes it impossible to counterfeit bitcoins. However, it also reduces the un-traceability of coins, which would be useful in a more anonymous system. Coin mixing services and wallets that continuously generate new addresses make it more difficult, but still not impossible, to trace bitcoins. We will discuss how Bitcoin's traceability can also be considered a weakness later on.

Community of enthusiasts

Bitcoin has a strong community of users who work on its development and want to see Bitcoin succeed. Everyone who has adopted Bitcoin has an interest in seeing it succeed. The support and enthusiasm of the Bitcoin community has been a constant, and there is no reason to believe that will change.

Global

Bitcoins can be transferred from one side of the globe to another without middlemen or long delays at a limited transaction cost. We can, however, notice a trend toward higher transaction costs as the network grows while the scaling debate lasts; micro-transactions can no longer be processed in a few minutes without paying a considerable transaction fee. Hopefully, fees will decrease once scalability solutions are adopted.

Growth

With over 250,000 transactions daily, Bitcoin has established itself as a growing network that can serve the purpose of online transactions.

Born for immortality

Bitcoin is a currency of the Internet and the protocol cannot be subject to regulation thanks to its decentralized nature. As long as the Internet exists, Bitcoin will exist. In fact, with satellites connecting Bitcoin nodes, even the Internet will no longer be necessary.

Weaknesses

Niche and customer experience

Although Bitcoin accounts for over 250,000 transactions a day, it represents a tiny portion of the total number of transactions that occur every day. Bitcoin is still a niche; it is not a mainstream currency and only a limited number of merchants accept it.

One of the reasons for this limited acceptance could lie in the rather unfriendly onboarding process. Getting educated, setting up a wallet, going through an exchange, and passing the AML checks demands some motivation.

Scalability and consensus

Even if it was more widely accepted, Bitcoin would not be able to cope with its success. This brings us to Bitcoin's major weakness: its non-scalability. As seen in Chapter 8, the number of transactions on the Bitcoin network is currently limited and can under no circumstances compete with other players of the mainstream financial system. Even if the block size increases to 2 MB, this will not be enough to come anywhere close to the capacity of the mainstream financial system.

Even if a solution to improve Bitcoin's scalability exists, reaching a consensus to accept the improvement would be difficult, but not impossible. An alignment is needed between the developers, the miners validating the blocks, and the players of the ecosystem who provide services on top of the Bitcoin protocol. These groups do not necessarily have the same interests, so striking an agreement between them could be complicated. For example, miners might reject the idea of increasing the number of transactions per block because the "mining fees" that they charge to include transactions on a block might drop. Service providers, on the other hand, might object because they would have to adapt their system to keep providing the same services to their users.

Greed as a source of instability

Bitcoin has a justifiable reputation for being a volatile currency. Even if its volatility decreases, the current volatility makes it impossible for bitcoins to qualify as a unit of account. Since bitcoins are not a unit of account and are not accepted as legal tender, many businesses are unwilling to set their prices in bitcoins. This makes bitcoin holders subject to the exchange rate with fiat currencies, which is made of peaks and drops. The instable price remains an obstacle to bitcoins being considered a safe way to store value.

Gresham's Law

The limited monetary supply will ultimately lead to bitcoins being more scarce, and as a currency becomes scarce and the value goes up, people tend to use other, less valuable currencies to make daily transactions. This principle is also known as Gresham's Law.

Non-fungibility

Bitcoin's transparent traceability might be a problem in the long term, as it can make one bitcoin with a certain past different from a bitcoin with a different past. In Chapter 12, we explained the importance of currencies being fungible and in Chapter 13, we came to the conclusion that, in certain instances, bitcoins are refused by certain parties because of their shady past. Hence, its non-fungibility.

Opportunities

Lack of trust in the system

Instability in the mainstream financial system might lead to new bankruptcies and financial uncertainty. If major players in the current financial system fail to operate securely and reliably, the financial system might be paralyzed for a certain period of time. These situations would create distrust, and sometimes chaos, in the system underpinning the flow and stability of our fiat currencies. People might then consider alternative currencies, such as cryptocurrencies, which are transparent, robust, and secure.

Lack of trust in governance

The previous point addressed how Bitcoin and alternative currencies could benefit from a lack of trust in "the system." Alternative currencies, and cryptocurrencies in particular, could also benefit from a lack of trust in the people managing the fiat currencies and by extension, the financial system.

In the event of a new debt crisis, central banks might take more drastic measures to relaunch the economy. These measures sometimes include a *de facto* devaluation of the existing money. People might see the value of holding an asset with a pre-programmed and transparent monetary supply instead.

Powerful players might impose new haircuts and withdrawal limits, limiting the amount of money people can access. Your money should belong to you and not be in the control of banks or powerful players that can restrict your access to it. Bitcoin puts you in control of your money. Because you alone know your private key, you are 100% master of your own funds. You are your own bank.

Bad governance decisions, like India banning the 500- and 1,000-rupee notes or Venezuela banning the 100-bolivar note, show once more how fiat currencies are subject to drastic human decisions. Bitcoin is not subject to one-sided human decisions, and unpopular decisions would not be accepted by the network. If faced with more bad governance in the fiat currency system, people might see the value of Bitcoin's decentralized nature and get on board.

Safe haven

Bitcoin has slowly started to get the reputation of a safe haven. This trend might continue, especially if the above-mentioned events repeat themselves.

It is too soon to conclude that Bitcoin is a safe way to store value. The high volatility clearly argues in the opposite direction. Nonetheless, we can observe that, at specific events creating uncertainty, Bitcoin's price peaks and shows a correlation with gold, which is often considered a safe haven. If similar events occur, Bitcoin might become the digital equivalent of gold, namely a safe way to store value.

Understanding leading to credibility

Increased interest from central banks in researching and understanding Bitcoin's technology gives an extra boost to Bitcoin's credibility. In 2016, major central banks showed an interest in Bitcoin and the distributed ledger technology. Examples include the Federal Reserve, the European central bank, the Central Bank of England, and the People's Bank of China.[173][174] Some even admitted that bitcoins could replace cash.[175]

We see more and more banks partnering with Bitcoin and start-ups using distributed ledgers. The different partnership announcements and their collaboration prove that the technology is reliable and could be a catalyst for adoption.

Threats

Fighting the unstoppable

Legal measures cannot ban Bitcoin, break the network,[176] or make it *de facto* impossible to transact with bitcoins. Heavy regulation can, however, slow down the adoption of Bitcoin, create a negative perception and increase the bureaucratic obstacles around Bitcoin, or even make it illegal to transact with bitcoins. While this might make it difficult to exchange fiat currencies for cryptocurrencies (and vice versa), it would not stop Bitcoin from operating. Fortunately, very few countries are hostile toward Bitcoin; most are open to the innovation Bitcoin brings.

Transaction fees

The pre-programmed supply of bitcoins foretells that mining rewards will slowly disappear, and it is unclear how miners will be compensated for their efforts. One scenario could be that transaction fees will increase. If transaction fees are no longer competitive with alternative payment methods, people might begin to abandon Bitcoin in favor of cheaper alternatives.

The new kids

The emergence of alternative cryptocurrencies inspired by Bitcoin is spectacular and has led to new entrants and substitutes. Given the availability of open-source code, the entry-barrier to create a new cryptocurrency is low, and today, over 1,000 cryptocurrencies exist. Moreover, that number keeps increasing. However, all alternative cryptocurrencies together represent a market capitalization that is relatively small, when compared to Bitcoin's market capitalization.[177] In other words, Bitcoin is in a strong leader position, capturing +/- 90% of the cryptocurrency market. At least, this was the case until the summer of 2017, when money floated into both Bitcoin and altcoins to such a level that, by July 2017, Bitcoin owned roughly 50% of the cryptocurrency market.

The threat of a new and improved cryptocurrency overtaking Bitcoin could become acute at a rather fast pace, since users can switch between cryptocurrencies as fast and as often as they want to. Such a threat will most likely become real if Bitcoin keeps struggling to solve the challenges we discussed in Chapter 8. An alternative cryptocurrency that adds new and improved features to Bitcoin's security, user-experience, scalability, and credible monetary supply might take over.

Humans and their egos

Even if Bitcoin's functioning relies on its protocol and the mining material, the evolution of Bitcoin relies on the ability of humans to agree on how Bitcoin should evolve. An inability to find consensus when Bitcoin's protocol is in serious need of improvement could endanger the whole project.

The evolutionary cycles of innovation

Every innovation is eventually made obsolete by new innovations. The arrival of new mining equipment could make the risk of a 51% attack more real and threaten the trust and resilience of Bitcoin's network. Quantum computers could weaken the security of private keys as soon as public keys are shared. It is, however, rather unlikely that quantum computers will become available to everyone soon (see Chapter 7). When they do, many of our current institutions will have to adapt as well.

As Woody Allen mentions in an interview on the meaninglessness of life,[178] everything is vain and everything will be washed away sooner or later. Bitcoin is one evolution in the way we consider money. It might replace the way we currently operate and might one day be replaced by another form of money.

Conclusion

As we can conclude from the SWOT analysis, to be successful as a currency, further Bitcoin research should focus on its weaknesses, and Bitcoin should be ready to scale and become accepted by a larger audience.

More importantly, Bitcoin's future will most likely be affected by external factors. Slowly but surely, the different opportunities will give credibility and momentum to Bitcoin. Even so, the threats related to failure to reach a consensus and higher fees might very well make Bitcoin unfit for mainstream adoption, and other cryptocurrencies could rise to take its place as the most prominent cryptocurrency.

CONCLUSION

During the PESTEL analysis, we learned that trust in authorities and institutions is not always justified and that monetary policies dictated by humans can be mismanaged, leading to entire civilizations suffering. We also learned that the emergence of alternative currencies is a growing trend, and that technological advancement has placed us in a more virtual world where we rely on electronic devices for essential, everyday tasks. Finally, we learned that the legal framework does not currently pose a major problem to Bitcoin.

The more industry-oriented Hype Cycle framework taught us that Bitcoin has reached its peak of expectation and is slowly coming out of its "trough of disillusionment" phase.

The technological adoption cycle analysis allows us to assert that Bitcoin is currently crossing the "chasm" and must improve customer experience and stability before it can reach majority consumers. Bitcoins are, however, particularly relevant when other payment systems are banned or do not provide the desired customer experience.

Finally, the SWOT analysis highlights that Bitcoin has many benefits and weaknesses. Bitcoin could mainly benefit from uncertainty in the mainstream financial system, but it could suffer from failure to agree on protocol improvements and from other cryptocurrencies taking on a more important role in the future.

Chapter 15

Alternative cryptocurrencies

Since its birth in early 2009, Bitcoin has inspired many alternative, decentralized cryptocurrencies that are often referred to as "altcoins." Coders have reused Bitcoin's open-source code and tweaked it to change some properties, such as the time between the generation of blocks, reward systems, monetary supply policies, block size, and anonymity. Some coders try to create a better cryptocurrency. Some claim to serve a particular purpose. Others have no purpose at all. Altcoins can either use their own blockchain, which is sometimes referred to as "altchain," or use another blockchain, such as Ethereum, that allows the creation of multiple coins.

In 2011, more than two years after the launch of Bitcoin, the first altcoin appeared under the name of Namecoin. It was soon followed by others, including Litecoin and Peercoin, and the rate of new altcoins kept rising. At the time of publishing,[179] more than 1,000 cryptocurrencies coexist. The total cryptocurrency market capitalization is over 140 billion dollars, with Bitcoin representing approximately 70 billion USD (~50%).[180] The second largest market capitalization belongs to the Ethereum coin, representing approximately 28 billion USD (~20% of market capitalization). The rest of the altcoins are quite fragmented, and market shares change regularly.

Altcoins can be acquired through mining, through exchanges, or by fulfilling certain actions. Unlike bitcoins, which can be bought with fiat currencies, most altcoins on exchanges are bought with bitcoins. For that reason, the exchange rate of altcoins is often expressed in bitcoin.

The emergence of hundreds of cryptocurrencies has led to active trading communities, with traders seeking high returns in short time frames. Since altcoins have smaller market capitalization and are many times more volatile than Bitcoin, these traders also take huge risks. Bubbles and bursts are frequent when hundreds of new cryptocurrencies are subject to sudden attention from traders, who are willing to pump and dump[181] them.

This chapter will cover the different purposes of altcoins, the technical innovations they bring, and the different ways in which they are issued. We will also discuss some events and pitfalls associated with altcoins. Keep in mind that the cryptocurrency market is much larger than the few coins that we will mention, and new coins are popping up every week, each more original than the last. As a result, some parts of this chapter might be outdated by the time of publishing.

DIFFERENT PURPOSES AND INNOVATIONS

As we already mentioned, altcoins can have specific purposes. This section will describe some altcoins that have gained traction because of the purposes they serve or the innovation they bring to the cryptocurrency space. These descriptions will be short, giving only a general idea of the coin's potential. These descriptions will not provide enough information to fully understand the mechanisms or potential of a specific project and should not be considered as investment advice.

Ether (ETH) has the second largest market-capitalization at the time of writing.[182] The cryptocurrency behind Ethereum is used by writers of smart contracts (more on this in the next chapter), to buy "fuel" that will maintain and execute the self-enforceable smart contracts stored on the Ethereum blockchain. Hence, it also serves as a reward to compensate the computers that execute smart contracts. More insights on Ethereum and smart contracts will be provided in the next section. Thanks to its large market capitalization, Ethereum is one of the few altcoins that can be bought with fiat currency.

Dogecoin (DOGE), famously known for its logo representing the face of a dog, is a cryptocurrency introduced as a "joke currency." The makers of DOGE openly announced that it should not be taken seriously; it only promotes the fun aspects of cryptocurrencies. The Dogecoin protocol distributes random rewards to anyone who is willing to mine it. Despite its clear lack of purpose and seriousness, the coin had a market capitalization of 60 million dollars in early 2014, making it the third largest cryptocurrency in the world.

Peercoin (PPC) was released in 2012 by Scott Nadal and Sunny King.[183] Unlike Bitcoin, Peercoin has an unlimited supply of coins that is designed to eventually stabilize around an annual rate of 1% in new money supply.

Peercoin's major breakthrough is its proof-of-stake mechanism designed to address some of the issues faced by Bitcoin's proof-of-work mechanism. Peercoin's proof-of-stake mechanism eliminates high-energy consumption and the race for ever-faster mining equipment, which has led to more centralization of mining power in the Bitcoin community.

As we will discover in more detail in the next section on consensus mechanisms, proof-of-stake rewards people who own a stake in the cryptocurrency and actively maintain the network. In Peercoin's case, the proof-of-stake reward is a 1% annual monetary inflation rate. Peercoin also has a deflationary aspect because 0.01 PPC is destroyed for every kilobyte of transactions. The combination of these elements encourages Peercoin users to keep their assets.

Peercoin's invention of proof-of-stake contributed to the cryptocurrency community and opened the door for others to think about alternative consensus mechanisms, rather than defaulting to Bitcoin's proof-of-work.

Solarcoin (SLR) aims to encourage the production of solar energy for the next 40 years by granting one solarcoin to solar energy producers for each verified MWh of solar electricity produced.

A total of 98 billion solarcoins have been created:

- 500 million (~0.5%) solarcoins were allocated to a genesis pool, which aims to support the Solarcoin network in terms of infrastructure, early volunteers, advisers, and environmental charities.
- 97.5 billion (~99.4%) solarcoins have been pre-mined and are in the hands of the Solarcoin Foundation. The founders of Solarcoin predict that this amount is enough to cover the next 40 years of global solar energy production. The Solarcoin foundation is in charge of distributing solarcoins to people who can prove that they have produced solar energy. Today this is a manual, centralized process executed by the foundation. All granted and issued solarcoins are transparent and can be viewed on the Solarcoin blockchain explorer.[184] Each transaction that issues solarcoins from the publicly visible, pre-mined pool comes with metadata such as the country where the coins were claimed, the ID of the generator, etc.[185] The goal of the Solarcoin foundation is to move away from this centralized verification and distribution process and delegate the issuance and circulation of the Solarcoin rewards to the community of participants, using smart contracts.
- 33.7 million (~0.1%) solarcoins were mined through proof-of-work at the beginning of Solarcoin. Since then, the blockchain has hard-forked and adopted the more energy efficient proof-of-stake-of-time (PoST) consensus mechanism (more on proof-of-stake-of-time later).

All circulating solarcoins may generate up to 2% annual return for people who run full software nodes that support the network. For example, someone who owns 100 solarcoins will, after one year, receive roughly two newly-minted solarcoins.[186]

Dash (DASH), formerly known as Darkcoin, is a cryptocurrency that aims to improve user experience with cryptocurrencies. Dash has already released a number of enhancements, like instant confirmation of transaction time by a service called InstantSend, which confirms transactions instantly,[187] and a mixing service integrated directly into the protocol, which reduces the traceability of funds.

Services such as InstantSend and mixing are provided by masternodes. These masternodes must prove that they own at least 1,000 dash. Unlike most other protocols, Dash's block reward is distributed between miners, masternode operators, and a "treasury" used to finance ongoing operations and projects.

Projects are vetted by a Decentralized Autonomous Organization (DAO), where each masternode has one vote regarding each governance proposal. Any person or entity can submit proposals and receive funding for their projects, should the masternode owners approve. For example, individuals or teams often submit proposals to promote Dash or provide technical contributions. If the masternodes are not satisfied with an entity's performance, they can simply discontinue funding that entity.[188] Dash's core team, which includes management, developers, and support, is also appointed and funded by the blockchain.[189] By adopting this governance system, Dash is able to ensure accountability for performance, introduce new features quickly, and determine its future direction. Everything is governed in full transparency.

Dash recently upgraded to a Turing complete object-oriented programmable system with a relational database. In plain English, the new system will allow the creation of new types of governance, like unbreakable contracts, term modifications, assigned roles, accomplishment-based payments, etc. This increased flexibility will lead to new changes in the coming months.

Nxt (NXT) does not aim to be a cryptocurrency in itself. Rather, it aims to become the underlying infrastructure for multiple blockchain utilizations. It is limited to 1 billion tokens, but these tokens can serve as voting tokens, cryptocurrencies, bonds, commodities, shares, patents, or other digital assets. It has several interesting features, including one-minute block generation; a pure proof-of-stake consensus mechanism, where the collected transaction fees are the only reward; and extended multi-sig transactions, which enable a transaction system based on conditions.[190]

Monero (XMR) is a proof-of-work cryptocurrency that provides more fungibility, privacy, and anonymity than Bitcoin. These achievements made the currency popular in mid-2016 among users on the dark web, who might have used it to pay for activities or services deemed illegal in some countries. However, many Monero users are not interested in activities on the dark web but simply want to enjoy the privacy and anonymity features that Monero offers.[191]

Particular to Monero is the fact that a large amount of the currency (approximately 18.4 million XMR coins) will be issued in the first eight years. The supply will then follow a linear emission of 0.6 XMR per block with the block generation time being set at two minutes.

Besides its use of cryptography to increase fungibility, privacy, and anonymity, Monero has another original feature; there is no limit on the block size, but there is an incentive to keep the growth of the block size under control.[192] When the block size exceeds the median block size of the last 100 blocks, the reward is reduced. When the block size is slightly higher, the reward penalty is negligible, but if the block size is much larger, the reward penalty becomes significant,[193] possibly costing up to the entire block reward.

Zcash (ZEC) improves the anonymity of Bitcoin but with a vastly different method. Unlike Bitcoin, where the sender and the receiver of a transaction are identified by their addresses, the Zcash protocol allows users to encrypt the sending and receiving addresses, the value transacted, and a memo field. In order to verify these transactions, Zcash uses a cryptographic method called zk-SNARKs. This algorithm generates a proof that allows nodes to efficiently verify transactions without knowing the actual amount or addresses. The initial Zcash protocol provides two address types: shielded addresses (beginning with "z"), which are fully private and encrypt transaction data before storing it in the Zcash blockchain, and transparent addresses (beginning with "t"), which are similar to Bitcoin addresses in that the address and value are visible on the Zcash blockchain. The "selective disclosure" feature allows users to selectively disclose the contents of transactions sent to shielded addresses to specific third parties, without revealing them to the public.

Ripple (XRP) is a company that provides the financial services industry with "instant, certain, and low-cost international payments."[194] Ripple's clients are mainly banks looking for a faster and secure way to send payments across countries, without intermediaries. Thanks to the real-time information available on the network, Ripple is able to rapidly exchange currencies by using a bridge currency when necessary. Ripple is, in its current form, a quite centralized system.

From a cryptocurrency point of view, Ripple has created 100 billion XRP that are divisible to six decimals. Ripple's consensus method does not require mining,[195] since all coins were distributed when Ripple was founded. Initially, 20% of the 100 billion XRP were distributed to the founders while 80% were given to Ripple. The fact that Ripple is responsible for managing XRP and that a large proportion of XRP were allocated to the founders raised some controversy in the cryptocurrency community—at least, it caused controversy until the founders decided to sell part of their XRP in the coming years and donate a part of them to Ripple.[196] Ripple publicly discloses the amount of XRP in their possession and states that their goal "in distributing XRP is to incentivize actions that build trust, utility, and liquidity in the network" and that they "will engage in distribution strategies that [...] will result in a stable and strengthening XRP exchange rate against other currencies."[197]

Namecoin (NMC) is the first altcoin that appeared after Bitcoin. It allows for censorship-resistant and decentralized name/value storage. The first and most prominent use of Namecoin is a decentralized and censorship-resistant domain names system (DNS),[198] which creates domain names (ending in .bit) that are independent of centralized authority, unlike other domain names (ending in .com or .net). Namecoin also makes other applications possible, such as the registration of names in a completely decentralized and secure fashion.[199] It uses merged mining as a consensus mechanism. We will describe this innovation in the next section.

DIFFERENT CONSENSUS MECHANISMS

Nothing determines the security of a distributed ledger more than the consensus mechanism, which ensures consensus on the validation of the blocks. Simply put, the consensus mechanism is a set of rules to which a block must comply for it to be valid.

We know that Bitcoin uses a consensus mechanism called proof-of-work, which involves guessing a hash of a certain difficulty level (see Chapter 3).

Nevertheless, the proof-of-work algorithm is often criticized because of the large amount of electricity consumed in the competition to generate valid hashes. Many mining farms have even relocated to places where electricity is cheap such as China. In this section, we will discover that other, greener alternatives exist.

Proof-of-Work (PoW)

Proof-of-work is a consensus mechanism where blocks are validated by solving a difficult mathematical puzzle. In the case of Bitcoin, "work" refers to the large amount of computing power required to find a valid hash. Valid hashes prove that work (computer power) went into the generation of the hash, and by extension, into the validation of the block. The newly created block is linked to the previous block, and breaking this link is impossible. Only the creation of a longer chain could cause the block to be replaced in the chain (see Chapter 3).

The security of a distributed ledger that uses proof-of-work as a consensus mechanism is backed by the amount of computing power required to prove the work. The more computing power required, the more secure the ledger. In this regard, Bitcoin greatly benefits from its first-mover advantage and has by far the most secure distributed ledger of all.

Building an altcoin with a distributed ledger that uses proof-of-work can be risky, especially if the equipment used to mine bitcoins is compatible with the proof-of-work algorithm for the new altcoin's distributed ledger.

When a new altcoin is launched with a proof-of-work algorithm identical to Bitcoin's, Bitcoin miners can easily transfer part of their computing power to the altcoin. This in itself is not a problem, since Bitcoin miners are free to stop mining bitcoins and mine altcoins instead. Problems arise when the computing power on the Bitcoin network is many times higher than the computing power on the altcoin. When this happens, a Bitcoin miner might bring an overwhelming amount of mining power to the altcoin. If he possesses more than 50% of the mining power of the altcoin, he could easily launch a 51% attack (see Chapter 7) on the new altcoin.

Auxiliary PoW (Merged Mining)

In some cases, altcoins allow Bitcoin miners to use their equipment to mine the new altcoin while mining bitcoins at the same time. Both the altcoin and Bitcoin benefit from the same mining activities. Every Bitcoin miner or mining pool is free to choose if they want to engage in mining the altchain at the same time. It works like this:

- The two blockchains are fully independent.
- Nothing significant changes for the Bitcoin Blockchain. A small hash, representing the altchain block, is inserted into the coinbase transaction.
- The altchain stores extra information about the Bitcoin block that was used to generate the altchain block.

Let us have a detailed look

By now, you know how Bitcoin mining works; miners hash a combination of fixed elements and variable elements until they produce a valid hash (see Chapter 3). But how is it possible to generate a hash for two distributed ledgers when they have different fixed elements?

To understand this, let us look at an example: Bitcoin and Namecoin. Bitcoin is the parent chain, and Namecoin is the auxiliary altchain, which accepts PoW performed on the parent chain (Bitcoin Blockchain). Each of the distributed ledgers has its own difficulty level. We will take a look at how the blocks of both distributed ledgers are created.[200]

First, the miner creates the Namecoin block that contains all selected transactions and some additional information.

Second, the miner creates the Bitcoin block, the same way as he usually does, but with one critical difference: he adds the fingerprint (hash) of the Namecoin block in the coinbase transaction[201] description. The miner now has (1) a Namecoin block without information on the Bitcoin block and (2) a Bitcoin block with a hash referencing the Namecoin block.

Third, the miner will start looking for a valid hash for the Bitcoin block. After every guess, three scenarios are possible:

Scenario A: The generated hash does not meet either of the difficulty levels. In this case, the miner continues generating hashes, hoping the next one will meet at least one of the difficulty levels.

Scenario B: The generated hash meets the difficulty level of the auxiliary chain (Namecoin) but not the difficulty level of the parent chain (Bitcoin). In this case, the Namecoin block is sent to the Namecoin network together with (1) the Bitcoin block header including the transaction Merkle root (2) the Bitcoin coinbase transaction referring to the Namecoin block (even if this Bitcoin block will never be part of the Bitcoin Blockchain). All this information is necessary for the other nodes of the Namecoin network to verify the proof-of-work behind the Namecoin block. Indeed, as the hash of the Bitcoin block was generated from the Namecoin block, the nodes need the elements that led to the generation of both blocks in order to verify it. Given all this information, Namecoin nodes can validate the Namecoin block, regardless of whether or not the Bitcoin block is ever created.

Scenario C: The generated hash meets the difficulty level of the parent chain (Bitcoin). In this case, both the Bitcoin block and the Namecoin block are sent out to the network and accepted by the other nodes. Every Namecoin node will accept the block as the fingerprint (hash) of the Namecoin block is included in a valid Bitcoin block. The Bitcoin nodes will validate the Bitcoin block as they would validate any other Bitcoin block. Note that no Namecoin transactions or other information from the auxiliary chain, besides the small hash in the coinbase transaction, is incorporated into the Bitcoin block. Therefore, no additional space is required on the Bitcoin Blockchain.

This assumes that Bitcoin's difficulty level is higher than the difficult level of the auxiliary chain. If that were not the case, the second scenario would be dismissed.

In conclusion, merged mining makes it possible for Bitcoin miners to keep participating in the Bitcoin Blockchain and collect rewards for mining altcoins. There is no lost opportunity, only additional benefit. This makes Bitcoin miners more likely to mine the altchain. As a result, the altchain will benefit from more proof-of-work and will be less subject to a 51% attack.

How can an altcoin avoid a 51% PoW attack?

Altcoins using the same PoW algorithm as Bitcoin[202] are exposed to the risk of a 51% attack because Bitcoin miners, who have access to huge amounts of computer power, can easily dominate the new altcoin's mining activity. This is especially true if the altcoin has lower difficulty requirements than Bitcoin.

The cryptocurrency community received a startling example of this vulnerability when an altcoin, called Coiledcoin, suffered from a major 51% attack. The leader of a Bitcoin mining pool, called Eligius, focused his pool's computing power on mining coiledcoins, without informing other members of the pool what he was doing. He easily dominated Coiledcoin's mining activity and became the main producer of blocks, but instead of filling his blocks with transactions, he left them empty.[203] Coiledcoin was rendered unusable. The attacker claimed that he launched his attack because he believed Coiledcoin was a pyramid scheme (not true) and that altcoins, which enable pump-and-dump schemes, hurt the reputation of cryptocurrencies in general.[204]

The Coiledcoin attack sparked a new wave of security measures. Many altcoins adopted new features that would help prevent them from becoming the next Coiledcoin.

The easiest solution is to create a proof-of-work algorithm that is resistant to existing PoW validation algorithms. By using a different algorithm, altcoins can prevent miners with advanced ASIC cards and massive amounts of computing power from entering their network.

ASIC cards are designed to perform one very specific type of operation in a very efficient way. If the proof-of-work consensus mechanism uses a different validation algorithm, the ASIC card will not be able to perform it. Miners will have to use their CPUs or GPUs, which have much less computing power, to solve the algorithm. Ultimately, when an altcoin gains in popularity, more specialized mining materials, such as brand-specific ASIC cards, begin to appear. However, this is a gradual process, which will give multiple players the time to equip themselves with ASIC cards, so that the computing power is distributed.

Another way to avoid a 51% attack is to use a different consensus mechanism, such as proof-of-stake.

Proof-of-Stake (PoS)

Proof-of-stake is a consensus mechanism that can take multiple forms. The basic principle is that miners need to own coins to own mining power (or minting power, as it is sometimes called in PoS algorithms). In other words, miners need to have a stake in the coin. The idea is that the more coins a miner owns, the more stake he has in the market and the more mining power he should have.

Similar to proof-of-work, the nodes of the network receive newly mined blocks and ensure that everything is valid, as dictated by the consensus mechanism. If so, the block is added to the chain. After a certain number of minutes, a new block is added and so on.

In a proof-of-stake consensus mechanism, unlike proof-of-work, miners are selected to mine the next block.

The consensus mechanism defines the selection process. A pure proof-of-stake mechanism would assign odds to every miner depending on his stake in the coin. For example, if John owns 3% of all coins and is willing to mine a block, he will have at least a 3% chance of mining the next block. Note that we mentioned "at least" since some people might not be interested in mining. In any case, the more coins a miner has, the higher the probability he mines the next block and the more likely he is to collect the mining rewards and transactions fees (if any), making him even richer. However, in order to avoid the rich getting richer by default, some proof-of-stake consensus mechanisms are tweaked a bit.

The miner selection process varies from one proof-of-stake protocol to another. Here are a few examples of how the consensus mechanism can define the selection process:

- Every mining node needs to hold at least 0.00001% of the total number of coins in circulation but no more than 1% of all coins in circulation. All mining nodes satisfying these two conditions have an equal chance of being picked to be the next mining node. This assumes that every node has only one identity.
- The probability of a miner being selected is computed by multiplying his stake by the number of days the coins did not move from his wallet.[205] The consensus mechanism can define both the stake percentage and the number of days with an upper limit.
- Once a miner has been selected to mine a block, he cannot be re-selected for any of the next 100 blocks.
- All miners who have 99% uptime in the last 24 hours (i.e., they have been connected to the network 99% of the time) have an equal chance of being selected.

The options and combinations are limitless.

Most adjustments to the proof-of-stake mechanism are designed to prevent the rich from getting richer—and possibly even gaining enough mining power to launch a 51% attack. Nevertheless, even if someone did manage to gain more than 50% of the mining power, he would probably behave honestly as he would not want to attack a network in which he had invested many coins.

Unlike proof-of-work, which is backed by computing power, and thus large amounts of electrical power, proof-of-stake is a cheaper and more eco-friendly algorithm that can be run on smartphones and other small devices.

The cheapness of proof-of-stake mining is, however, causing another challenge: the "nothing-at-stake problem." Since miners do not have to spend money to mine, they can easily work on multiple forks at the same time. In extreme situations, this leads to no consensus at all. Therefore, some altcoins that wish to use proof-of-stake are looking into mechanisms to penalize miners who are active on more than one chain.[206] Another idea is bonded proof-of-stake, where miners have to deposit a certain stake[207] to be a mining node. This way there is always something at stake.

Two examples of altcoins using proof-of-stake are NXT and ShadowCash. Ethereum is also planning to move from proof-of-work to proof-of-stake.

Proof-of-Burn (PoB)

A Proof-of-burn (PoB) consensus mechanism requires miners to burn coins in a competition to validate a block and claim a reward. Burning coins means sending them to a burn address, with a denomination so particular that it is statistically infeasible that it was randomly generated by someone possessing the private key. An example of a burning address would be BTCburnBTCburnBTCburnBTCburn7eS4Rf. By assuming that no one has the private key to spend the funds belonging to that address, we can assert that all coins sent to that address are lost forever. In other words, they are burned.

Slimcoin is an altcoin combining PoB, PoW, and PoS. Each miner can decide what type he is. In the PoB consensus mechanism of Slimcoin, a miner sends his coins to the Slimcoin burning address. This transaction is used to generate a burn hash in the competition to mine a block. The burn hash is the combination of two elements: (1) an internal hash that changes every time a new PoW block is generated and (2) a multiplier that changes based on the number of blocks mined since the burned transaction happened.

From all burned hashes, the protocol will accept burn hashes that are smaller than a burn target. Hashes that are smaller than the burn target will receive a reward, as defined by the protocol. If multiple burn hashes are smaller than the target, the chain might have a fork on its last block. If none of the burn hashes are smaller than the burn target, PoB miners have to wait until a PoW block is mined. As soon as a PoW block is mined, the internal hash will change and generate a new burn hash, in the hope that it is, this time, smaller than the burn target. This process continues until the burned transactions mine a block.

We mentioned that Slimcoin is using PoB in combination with PoW. In fact, the Slimcoin protocol states that every PoB block needs to be preceded by a PoW block to avoid blocks being mined one after another at a fast pace. The added value of PoB lies in the fact that only one hash needs to be generated for a PoB block to be mined. Indeed, since the PoB hash is dependent on the preceding PoW, hashing it multiple times is useless as it would generate the same result.

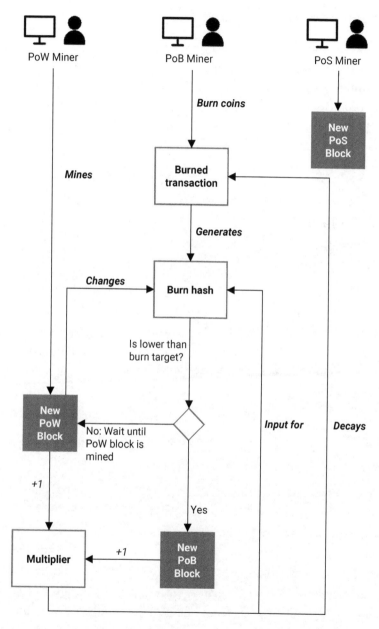

Figure 58. Slimcoin's Proof-of-Burn consensus mechanism

Other consensus mechanisms

Proof-of-work and proof-of-stake are the two most widely adopted consensus mechanisms, but altcoins are a real breeding ground for experiments and innovations. Variants and new ideas emerge continuously. Many altcoins propose new rules and are governed by new consensus mechanisms. Covering all possibilities would be an endless exercise. We will, however, take a look at some of these innovations.

Proof-of-Stake-of-Time (PoST) is a consensus mechanism similar to proof-of-stake but with a weighted factor of time. People receive decision-making power by holding a certain stake of the cryptocurrency over a certain amount of time. Blocks are solved and a reward is given that targets a certain annualized rate.

An example of proof-of-stake-of-time is Solarcoin, where people are rewarded with a targeted 2% annualized return rate for being a proof-of-stake mining node.[208] However, due to only partial user participation, the overall monetary inflation rate can be much lower. For Solarcoin, the inflation in monetary supply through PoST is estimated to have been 0.7% in 2016.[209]

Delegated Proof-of-Stake (DPoS) is a consensus mechanism where everyone who owns tokens can delegate their vote to someone else. Votes can be redeemed and changed at any point in time.

In the case of BitShares,[210] an altcoin using DPoS, the shareholders (people who have a stake in BitShares) appoint a "board of validators." This board consists of block producers who will also validate new blocks. The number of members in the "board of validators" is defined by the shareholders, through voting. A vote to define this number happens at every "maintenance interval," which is currently every 24 hours. The maintenance interval can also be changed by voting. Finally, the members of the board are also chosen by the shareholders, based on the number of votes they collect.

Members of the board sign blocks on a rotational basis and receive a small fee as compensation for campaigning and being online to validate the blocks. After a round is completed (i.e., when each member of the board of validators has produced a block), a new round begins with a newly appointed board of validators. The board might be very similar to the previous one, if votes do not change significantly.

Proof-of-Importance (PoI) was introduced by the altcoin NEM in its white paper with the ambition to reward reputation[211] instead of stake only.[212] The importance of a node can be defined through a number of parameters, such as the amount at stake, the number and spread of transactions, the contribution to the network, and other relevant signals that can be found in their white paper.

Proof-of-Activity[213] (PoA) is a combination of proof-of-work and proof-of-stake. Blocks are created through proof-of-work mining, just like Bitcoin. However, when a valid block is found, it is not yet a "real block." Instead, it is considered a "template block" and sent out to the network. Multiple template blocks might circulate the network. For each template block to become a real block, it needs to be signed by a certain number of nodes, which are randomly selected based on the number of coins they own.[214] The more coins a shareholder owns, the more likely he is to be a signer. Hence, the proof-of-stake part of proof-of-activity. The first template block to be signed by all of its assigned nodes becomes a real block. The block rewards are then distributed between the miner and the signers.

The power of proof-of-activity lies in the fact that an honest majority of the stake is more likely than an honest majority of the hash power. Therefore, it makes sense to utilize stakeholders to create the longest chain. Since proof-of-activity requires both proof-of-work and proof-of-stake to mine a block, it is not subject to the "nothing-at-stake problem," which plagues altcoins that only use the proof-of-stake consensus mechanism.

Proof-of-Capacity[215] (PoC) (also called *Proof-of-Space*[216]) is a concept where each unit of hard drive space dedicated to mining gives miners a better chance to mine the block. This means using the hard drive to generate proof-of-capacity instead of a CPU to generate proof-of-work, which should be more eco-friendly.

Social-proof requires users to trust other nodes to validate transactions. Each validating node has a "Unique Node List" (UNL) with a list of other nodes it trusts. In case of a conflict over a transaction on the network, each node will define its opinion based on what the other nodes in its list are doing. If the node itself features on the UNL of other validating nodes, its decision to accept or decline a transaction will be a signal to other nodes. However, nodes cannot agree that an invalid transaction is valid. They can only weigh in on conflicting transactions or choose when to accept a valid transaction. Ultimately, a consensus is reached through the network effect. Ripple is the most well-known altcoin that relies on social-proof.

Hybrid consensus mechanisms

It is not rare to see altcoins combining multiple consensus mechanisms to secure their distributed ledgers. In such a case, a combination of different consensus mechanisms work together in building the distributed ledger. For example, Peercoin uses proof-of-work, proof-of-stake, and centrally validated checkpoints. Another example is Slimcoin, which combines proof-of-work, proof-of-stake, and proof-of-burn.

DIFFERENT WAYS TO SUPPLY NEW COINS

Once a coin has a purpose and is designed, the time has come to issue the coin. The initial distribution of a coin is a critical factor for success, as it enables people to experience the coin and fosters the involvement of the stakeholders. The number of coins in circulation in the beginning should be sufficient to meet the initial demand and enable a liquid circulation of coins. However, having an unjustifiably large number of coins in circulation too early might affect the credibility of the altcoin. Finally, the allocation of coins to the founders and early adopters is sometimes a controversial topic. If it is too high, people might be skeptical about the true intentions of the people behind the coin. In this section, we will briefly describe a few ways to issue the first coins of a new cryptocurrency.

Pre-sale (aka Initial Coin Offering [ICO])

Pre-sales, also known as "Crowdsales" or "ICOs," happen before a coin is launched. During the pre-sale phase, the coins are given to people in exchange for other cryptocurrencies or fiat currencies. This is a way to collect funds to develop the project and to create a community of stakeholders.

When the ICO is launched, it typically proposes a plan and a timeline for the project, the required funds, the accepted cryptocurrencies to fund it, and the period during which people can invest in the project. If the minimum funds are not collected in the defined period, funds can be returned to the investors.

When the project successfully comes to life, the early investors can make big money by having acquired the coins at a very low price.

In 2017, we have seen an explosive growth of ICOs collecting money. With some good marketing, many start-ups have managed to collect a couple million dollars.

In a system where everyone can start his crowdsales and collect money, it is difficult for most investors, especially those who are new to the cryptocurrency world, to assess the seriousness, viability, and technical integrity of the project proposed. Many ICO scams have appeared and investors are left to do their own due diligence on the chance of a project to succeed.

Pre-mined

Pre-mined coins are coins that are created by the protocol during the creation of the first block. They can be allocated to the founders, used to further develop the project, or claimed when certain conditions are met.

When the project began, Solarcoin awarded pre-mined coins to a group of founders. These coins are stored in large, publicly visible, pre-mined pools. Normally, awarding pre-mined coins to a single person or entity raises eyebrows because the coins might be used for personal gain. Solarcoin aims to get around this by dictating that transactions with pre-mined coins entering general circulation follow certain rules. They require specific signatures of approval and transaction messages confirming that the receiver produced a certain amount of Megawatts per hour (MWh).[217]

Airdrop

In an airdrop, pre-mined coins are distributed for free. This strategy is a great way to create a larger community, in hopes that the coin will be widely adopted. Sometimes the distribution is limited to specific people or done under certain conditions.

Auroracoin used an airdrop in 2014. Auroracoin was supposed to be an alternative currency for Iceland, so everyone in possession of a national Icelandic ID could claim 31.8 of the 10.5 million auroracoins. Unfortunately, as soon as people received their auroracoins, they started selling them. The initial price fell and never really recovered.

Burning coins

A more radical way to generate new coins of a cryptocurrency is by requiring people to burn coins from other currencies. For example, an altcoin could require people to burn their bitcoins in order to get coins on the altchain. Burning bitcoins is done by sending them to a public address, of which no one has the private key. After the coins are sent, the altcoin protocol allocates coins to the owner of the burned bitcoins. The coins will be credited to an address identical to the one on the Bitcoin Blockchain, but it will be on the new altchain.[218][219] Some altcoins have specific periods at the beginning of the project during which people can burn coins.

Mining

Most commonly, new coins are created to reward the mining activities that process and validate transactions, while also ensuring the security of the network.

Bitcoin creates new coins through coinbase transactions that are added to every newly mined Bitcoin block, to reward the miner who created the block. Mining rewards can be offered through proof-of-work, proof-of-stake, and other consensus mechanisms.

CRYPTOCURRENCIES AT WAR

We already discussed how a distributed ledger backed by the same mining equipment as another distributed ledger can be subject to a 51% attack. Coiledcoin is the perfect example of a cryptocurrency that was destroyed that way. In order to avoid such an attack, we explained that the consensus mechanism should use unique consensus algorithms that cannot be attacked by pre-existing mining equipment. However, even with a unique consensus algorithm, a distributed ledger application is not protected from failure.

As the name states, consensus mechanisms are built to ensure consensus. We saw in Chapter 8 that, when the consensus rules are changed, soft forks and hard forks are possible. While soft forks are not really an issue, hard forks result in two incompatible branches of the distributed ledger; both branches have a common history preceding the fork, but they will follow their own path after the fork.

For the sake of the stability and credibility of cryptocurrencies, consensus should be maintained and hard forks avoided. Consensus is achieved by the adoption of the consensus mechanism and the acceptance, by the network, of any change to the consensus mechanism.

In the summer of 2016, the Ethereum community was faced with the decision to take a controversial measure, requiring a hard fork of the underlying distributed ledger. They were unable to reach consensus in the short period of time they were given, and they decided to move forward with proposing the hard fork. Although a large portion of the network initially switched to the hard fork, miners supporting the status quo decided to switch their mining equipment back to the previous version of the chain. This resulted in two forked chains and two currencies. One was the Ethereum chain that hard-forked and the other one was the chain without the hard fork, which became known as Ethereum Classic. Exchanges that initially followed the hard fork started to accept both coins after some miners switched back to the non-hard-forked chain. People having ether coins before the hard fork now possessed the same number of coins on both chains. The coins were traded for different prices fixed by the bids and asks on the exchange platforms.

The above example shows that when the consensus mechanism is backed by the same mining algorithms, miners can use their validation power as voting power, which helps to achieve the network effect and reshape the currency.

Beyond similar consensus mechanisms, we have seen that multiple altcoins present themselves as more anonymous and fungible than their competitors. In such a constellation, grasping what differentiates one coin from another can be difficult.

Finally, the multitude of cryptocurrencies has created volatile competition and free-floating exchange rates that move continuously. People can move from one altcoin to another very easily, around the clock, 24/7. This creates a world of competing currencies similar to what was imagined by Nobel Prize winning economist, Friedrich August Hayek, in his book, *The Denationalization of Money*.

CONCLUSION

The proliferation of cryptocurrencies is probably excessive, and it is unclear what the leading cryptocurrencies of tomorrow will be.

Some serve a specific purpose, like encouraging the production of solar energy or masking black market transactions. Some of them are created for the single purpose of enriching their early adopters.

Others get innovative with new technical features. They help the whole cryptocurrency community figure out what works and what does not. These experiments will help in the creation of better designed cryptocurrencies in the future.

Some of these new features might even, one day, be integrated into Bitcoin, making Bitcoin a better cryptocurrency. On the other hand, if Bitcoin ignores valuable new features, they might contribute to the rise of a new altcoin, which will dethrone Bitcoin as the king of cryptocurrencies.

Chapter 16

Blockchain beyond cryptocurrencies

So far, we have discovered how Bitcoin and other cryptocurrencies are using distributed ledger technology (DLT) to make transactions without the need of a third party. In fact, DLT enables much more than only the use of cryptocurrencies. The world has realized that Bitcoin was only the first application of a technology that can be used to serve many purposes.

To better understand the different applications DLT could serve, let us take a look at what DLT has made possible for Bitcoin and other cryptocurrencies.

- The decentralized nature can make trusted third-party intermediaries obsolete
- The consensus mechanism ensures a general agreement on the validity of records.
- Records are time-stamped.
- Records are immutable.
- The system is secured by cryptographic functions.

We also saw that cryptocurrencies face some risks and challenges such as losing private keys, scalability issues, a 51% attack, etc. Depending on how new applications are built, they could face the same challenges.

PURELY PRIVATE, PERMISSIONED, AND PUBLIC DISTRIBUTED LEDGERS

The Bitcoin Blockchain is a publicly distributed ledger. Recently, distributed ledgers have been deployed inside closed environments, and new kinds of ledgers have emerged to support the needs of these closed environments. Today, we can distinguish three types of distributed ledgers:

Purely private: These ledgers are fully managed by one entity, such as a corporation. Because control over the blockchain is centralized, the value of the distributed ledger is often questionable. If a single entity is controlling and maintaining the ledger, this entity could easily modify past records. Often, a database is a better solution than a distributed ledger when information is managed by one single party.

Permissioned (also named private or hybrid): These ledgers are shared and maintained by various parties that have been granted access to the ledger. Permissioned ledgers can be useful when different players have a common interest in transacting and sharing information but have trust issues or different interests overall. These players are often part of the same industry. For example, banks have started to form partnerships with each other to create platforms that eliminate some of their middlemen who traditionally oversee transactions. Eventually, business models could be incorporated within the consensus mechanism. Compared to publicly distributed ledgers, permissioned distributed ledgers provide more flexibility in terms of user access, scalability, and data privacy.

Public (also named permissionless): These ledgers can be accessed and maintained by everyone. Everyone is free to join and maintain the distributed ledger. The most prominent examples are Bitcoin and Ethereum.

Describing the full potential of distributed ledgers in multiple industries could easily result in another book. We will just briefly mention the potential applications and, when appropriate, provide examples. Some of these applications are more concrete and easy to achieve while other more advanced applications exist purely on a theoretical level, at least for now.

DATA STORAGE

Because they are immutable, time-stamped, and decentralized, distributed ledgers are a reliable place to store data without the need for a trusted third party to certify the data.

The data can be stored in full when it is not too lengthy, but data can also be hashed. Hashes allow users to store a fingerprint of the data without the data itself being revealed. However, users should always keep an exact copy of the hashed document to prove that this document is the one that generated the hash stored on the distributed ledger.

In both cases, the data or hash of data is stored through a signed message on the distributed ledger. This message is signed with the user's private key, which demonstrates ownership of the message. In a permissionless distributed ledger, every message is publicly available.

A few examples include the hashing of a patent, a picture, an ID document, research data, or a book.

TRACEABILITY OF OWNERSHIP

In Chapter 6, we illustrated how bitcoins pass from one person to another and how the Blockchain provides a transparent record of the number of bitcoins each Bitcoin address has owned over time.

Other assets—like bonds, shares, land titles, and domain names—could also be passed and tracked through distributed ledgers without an intermediary. Using a distributed ledger would improve transparency and enable near real-time auditability, making it easy to know who owns what when.

The benefits of real-time auditability become clear when we think about shareholder meetings, where the exercise of determining who owns how many shares of a company can take weeks.

The history of ownership provided by a distributed ledger also ensures the traceability of goods. For this to be effective, it is better to have a good that can be identified as unique by nature. These natural characteristics can then be used to identify a unique token, making the link between the physical asset and its digital record complete.

Everledger is an emerging technology start-up that secures certified diamonds on the Blockchain. Each diamond is uniquely identifiable by using 40 data-points, which serve as the fingerprint of the stone.[220] Beyond diamonds, the start-up aims to improve the traceability of multiple luxury goods.[221] By doing so, the start-up hopes to reduce theft, fraudulent insurance claims, and blood-diamond sales by improving the supply chain integrity.

SMART CONTRACTS

In 2015, Ethereum introduced a new and exciting development in DLT. They made it possible to run code through distributed ledgers by creating smart contracts. Smart contracts offer a wide range of new possibilities and are regarded as a key enabler to reach the potential of blockchain technologies.

Smart contracts enable users to code a set of rules and have it signed by multiple parties. A smart contract cannot be altered and is executed by nodes of the distributed ledger. This is particularly useful when (1) there is a lack of trust between parties and (2) future events may trigger various outcomes. In the second case, the user proactively programs actions into the code, to take place if/when certain events occur in the future. One user can store a smart contract in the distributed ledger and others can start interacting with the smart contract according to the rules specified in the smart contract.

Through pre-programmed rules, smart contracts can automate payments. Ethereum has its own cryptocurrency, named ether, that can be converted to "gas." Every smart contract running on the Ethereum blockchain is fueled by a balance of gas to compensate the miners of the distributed ledger for maintaining the contract. The heavier the contract, the more processing power is required to execute the code and the more gas the contract will consume. Prices for each type of operation are fixed. The simplest operations, such as adding, will cost a small amount of gas while more complex operations, such as multiplying, will cost more gas. The most expensive operations are the ones that result in permanent state change such as storing a piece of data within a contract. To sum up: the heavier the code, the more expensive it is.

If the contract runs out of gas before the code is finished, the transaction is canceled and the contract rolls back (meaning that we go back to the state before the contract started executing), but the miner, who executed the contract, keeps the gas.

A simple bet

The simplest example to illustrate how a smart contract operates is one of two friends (John and James) placing a bet on tomorrow's weather. John believes that the temperature will reach 25°C in Bengaluru. James, on the other hand, believes it will not reach 25°C. They are both willing to bet 10 ether and agree that whoever was right receives 10 ether from the other. Although they are friends, neither of them trusts that the other will honor his bet. To solve this, they write a smart contract in which they specify a source of information they both trust for the weather in Bengaluru. John writes the contract and deploys it on the blockchain by depositing his stake; James reviews the code in the smart contract and engages in the smart contract by depositing his stake. Both of them have now given custody of 10 ether each to the smart contract. The day after, one of them calls the contract that will check the source to see who won the bet and the contract will execute a transfer of 20 ether to the winner. Every time someone interacts with the smart contract, a small amount of gas is used to run it and compensate the miners. Because every interaction has a cost, it dis-incentivizes spam transactions and useless usage of the network.

Delayed flight insurance

Delayed flight insurance is another example that illustrates the potential benefits of smart contracts.

Here is how delayed flight insurance works today:

When booking his flight, the passenger gets insurance to protect himself against a flight delay or cancellation. If his flight is either delayed or canceled, he is entitled to a refund. Let us say the flight was delayed or canceled. Now, the passenger has to submit an insurance claim. The claim will be handled by humans, and if it is approved, it will be forwarded to the payment department. Only after the payment department processes the payment will the passenger get his refund.

Here is how delayed flight insurance could work with smart contracts:

When booking his flight, the passenger and the airline company sign a smart contract, agreeing that if the flight is either delayed or canceled, a refund payment will be executed automatically. The smart contract monitors flight delay and cancellation information, which is publicly available online. If the flight is delayed or canceled, a payment is sent to the passenger.

It is that simple. No manual checking or payment processing by the office managing the claims is necessary. The contract can be executed and paid immediately, and the passenger does not have to fear that an unwillingness to pay the policy or an unforeseen interpretation of a clause in the fine print would make the policy void. Both parties save time and energy and avoid human errors. This use-case has been coded during a Hackathon by InsurETH.

Oracles

An oracle is a "bridge" between a smart contract and a third party providing data that you cannot or do not want to provide yourself.[222] This data can be used by the smart contract to make decisions, automate payments, etc. Using oracles involves trusting a third party, so all parties who engage with the smart contract should assess the trustworthiness of this third party. Will it provide the real information when the contract asks for it? Can it be corrupted? Can it be hacked to provide false information? Typically, when a smart contract relies on an external source to check the weather or flight departures, it will use an oracle.

Limitations

That being said, smart contracts are not applicable to everything. Their immutable nature and algorithmic working might be a problem when new elements appear that were not or could not be foreseen at the time when the smart contract was written. With smart contracts, every foreseeable outcome should be encoded because smart contracts cannot integrate unforeseen elements after they are written. In such a system, the code is law and whatever is stated within the smart contract will be executed.

An analogy can be made with the current legal system, which has the concepts of the "letter of the law" and the "spirit of the law." The current legal system deals with legal misinterpretation and new and unique cases by allowing courts to clarify the law and make decisions on a case-by-case basis. With smart contracts, this is not possible. Whatever is encoded will happen. Code is law. Period.

Updating and canceling smart contracts

There is, however, one way to update a smart contract after all the different parties have signed it. When the contract is made, certain conditions can be programmed into it, so that the contract can be changed if the conditions are met. A smart contract could state, for example, that if all participants of the smart contract agree and sign an updated version of this smart contract, the updated version overrules the previous version of the smart contract.

A smart contract can also have an encoded "suicide function" that makes the contract void when certain conditions are met—for example, if 80% of the users of the contract agree to void it.

Of course, you can create your smart contract without including either of these two features, but remember, if they are not integrated from the start, the smart contract cannot be changed later.

DECENTRALIZED APPLICATIONS (DAPPS)

Decentralized applications (Dapps) are applications based on a set of smart contracts that are typically supplemented by web applications and a complete user interface[223] to provide a user experience comparable to the applications we use every day. Just as the Bitcoin Blockchain differs from a centralized database, Dapps differ from apps in the sense that there is no central party providing the IT infrastructure to run the software. Instead, the software runs across multiple nodes of the network. The users of a Dapp can interact directly with each other on the shared infrastructure. As a result, everyone is free to join the network, and there is no single entity managing the information or capturing the value of the service.

Dapps are still in their early days, and there is no consensus on the criteria a decentralized application should fulfill to be recognized as a Dapp. However, the following features are common to Dapps:[224] [225]

- The code is 100% open-source.
- Improvements to the code can be proposed but changes should be validated by a majority consensus of its users.
- Data must be cryptographically stored in a shared distributed ledger; the Dapp can use its own blockchain or leverage an existing blockchain.
- Tokens can be generated by an algorithm and can be used to reward contributing users. No entity controls a majority of tokens.

A full list of Dapps in progress can be found at dapps.ethercasts.com. We present two examples.

Uberizing Uber

Uber is often regarded as an example of disruptive technology and the birth of the sharing economy. However, when you take a closer look, there is not much that adheres to the principles of a sharing economy. Uber is, in fact, one big multinational company connecting Uber drivers with people who are willing to pay for a ride. Uber is the middleman connecting both parties, and it takes a fee. In 2016, all of those fees added up to over 5.5 billion dollars in net revenue, yet Uber is not (yet) profitable.[226]

By now, you know that blockchain is all about getting rid of the middleman. So is it possible to have services similar to Uber without Uber in the middle?

That is, at least, the idea brought forward by La`Zooz in 2014. This start-up developed an algorithm, prior to the release of the Ethereum blockchain, to match drivers and passengers in a decentralized fashion.

According to their website,[227] La`Zooz enables real-time car sharing with the ambition of increasing occupancy of cars and reducing the number of cars on the road. It enables drivers to fill their empty seats with La`Zooz users. La`Zooz is decentralized and owned by the community. Early adopters of La`Zooz can receive cryptographic Zooz tokens as soon as they drive over 20km[228] or for recruiting other users. Once a critical mass is achieved in a region, these tokens can be used to compensate the La`Zooz driver.[229]

The project did not succeed in reaching its ambition due to the immature technology and ecosystem back in 2014, a lack of venture capital, and the challenge of reaching a critical mass of adopters.

The future of cloud: Decentralized cloud

Today, big companies such as Dropbox, Google, and Amazon offer cloud services. When you store your information in the cloud, you are actually storing it on one of their servers. When you want to store a large amount of information in the cloud, you have to pay prices that are much higher than running the infrastructure yourself. In return, cloud service providers guarantee that your data is safe and that you can access your data from anywhere in the world as long as you have an Internet connection. Convenient, right?

StorJ[230] is a distributed ledger-based cloud service. What is the difference? Two things:

- Everyone can offer cloud services by renting out extra storage space and receiving payments.
- You can store data directly on the network, and you are the only one who can decrypt your data.

Let us break that down.

First, "everyone can offer cloud services by renting out extra storage space and receiving payments." The concept of a decentralized cloud is that everyone can offer the extra storage space on his connected hard drive to someone else. In other words, he can rent out idle storage capacity. In StorJ, this is called "farming." Other people looking for space can use your space to store their files, and in return, you get a small amount of StorJ coins sent to you. You can also decide to become a farmer, meaning that you can decide on the amount of space you are willing to rent out as well as the bandwidth you are willing to give up.

Second, "you can store data directly on the network, and you are the only one who can decrypt your data." Unlike centralized cloud services such as Google Drive, Dropbox, and Amazon that hold the keys to your data, StorJ is encrypted end-to-end so that the people storing your data cannot see what you have stored on their server. Only you possess the keys that will be able to decrypt the data. In addition, data is fragmented across different users and stored in multiple places to ensure that it is always accessible. More interestingly, everyone is now empowered to monetize the extra storage capacity he has. Other players looking into decentralization storage systems are IPFS, Swarm, and Maidsafe.

DECENTRALIZED AUTONOMOUS ORGANIZATIONS (DAO)

There is no consensus on what exactly defines a Decentralized Autonomous Organization, but we can consider it a more advanced form of Dapps, whose governance and financing options are outlined on the distributed ledger. A DAO is designed to run by itself based on a code that cannot be altered. The token holders can vote on possible decisions, which are foreseen by a DAO. Unlike a Dapp, a DAO possesses internal capital,[231] which can be managed to carry out certain activities.

DAOs are running exclusively on the Internet without any legal headquarter and can be considered stateless. This raises many questions regarding their regulations.

In 2016, one of the first DAOs was born under the name "*The DAO*," hereafter referred to in italics to avoid confusion with DAOs in general. *The DAO* can be described as a decentralized autonomous venture capital fund. *The DAO* raised a value of 150 million dollars of ether through a crowdfunding campaign. During the campaign, everyone could review the code and invest by converting ether to DAO tokens. By investing in *The DAO,* everyone agreed that "code is law" and that they were responsible for diligently reviewing the open-source code of *The DAO.* After the crowdfunding period, *The DAO* started running and DAO token holders could trade their tokens the same way as any other cryptocurrency.

Anyone willing to collect funds from *The DAO* can submit a proposal by means of a smart contract that specifies how funds will be used and how *The DAO* will be repaid. Investors, with their tokens, can then vote for the projects in which *The DAO* should invest. Based on the result of the vote, *The DAO* will or will not invest in the proposal. If a token holder is not happy with the majority choice and believes this is a bad decision, he is free to step out of *The DAO* by selling his DAO tokens.

Soon after *The DAO* was launched, an "attacker" was able to exploit the code to his advantage and came into possession of over 3 million ether, good for a value of 50 million USD, right before people realized the attack had occurred and the value of ether started to drop. The ether collected by the "attacker" was in an account having a holding period of 28 days. This gave the community time to react and vote on a solution requiring a hard fork of the Ethereum distributed ledger. By hard-forking, a large majority of the community agreed on a proposal that redistributed the ether collected by *The DAO* to a refund contract instead, where everyone who had invested ether in *The DAO* could claim them back.

Hard forks happen from time to time to upgrade a blockchain and allow new features. However, this hard fork became controversial when a group of people continued mining the old fork, claiming that the hard fork did not respect the immutability principle of the Ethereum distributed ledger by which code is law and a contract cannot be altered. The group mining the old fork grew, partially out of ideology, probably also a bit out of speculative purposes. As this number grew, two independent cryptocurrencies emerged: ether (ETH), the hard-forked cryptocurrency redistributing the ether collected by *The DAO,* and "classic ether" (ETC), allowing *The DAO* to run even if attacked. Both were valued separately as explained in the section "Cryptocurrencies at war" in Chapter 15.

Ultimately, in August 2016, the attacker was able to get his gains in ETC, valued multiple times lower than ETH but still worth a little less than 10 million USD.[232] By the end of May 2017, ETC was valued around $17. If the attacker still held his ETC at that time, they represented a value of around 60 million USD. Not bad for a one-day job. Moreover, this number is assuming he did not short ether before the price went down due to the attack he was planning.

You will notice that the word attacker was put between quotes; this is because there is controversy about whether he should be considered as such. In the end, he used the code to his favor in a context where "code is law" and where everyone investing in *The DAO* was supposed to do the required due diligence. From the other investors' point of view, his actions felt like an attack because they did not see the security breach in the code, and what happened was not in line with the spirit of *The DAO*. This example shows the limit of "code is law" as a concept, namely managing unforeseen events that do not reflect the intent of the code. Ultimately, this is a learning point.

This interesting instance, however, should not fool you about DAOs as a concept. In this case, *The DAO* turned out differently than expected, but well-coded DAOs operating correctly can provide unprecedented levels of trust in terms of governance.

Chapter 17

Potential to redefine the real world

MACHINE-TO-MACHINE PAYMENTS

In our digital age, humans are not the only ones connected to the Internet. Numerous devices such as smartphones, physical sensors, and chips are all connected to the Internet too. The number of connected devices that send information and make decisions to make our life easier keeps growing. The world in which these devices are networked together is known as the Internet of Things (IoT), and it creates a vast number of opportunities and services. Connected devices could show available parking slots on your smartphone or order maintenance parts as soon as sensors indicate an upcoming failure. Your future home could adapt the mood of a room based on the activities in your online agenda or your stress level, monitored by a sensor.[233] A smart-refrigerator could help you keep track of the products stored inside, informing you what items you need to replenish when you are at the grocery store.

Connecting the dots between the Internet of Things (IoT) and smart contracts creates a new world of possibilities. This section will provide a few examples.

A washing machine paying for you

Samsung and IBM[234] collaborated on a demonstration of proof-of-concept for a washing machine that automatically places an order to buy detergent as soon as the level of detergent gets low.[235] This in itself is nothing new for people who are familiar with IoT. What is new is that there is an Ethereum smart contract connecting you, the machine, and the detergent supplier. In this smart contract, you can set multiple rules (i.e., the maximum price, delivery method, etc.) but more importantly, the smart contract now pays the supplier instead of you paying the supplier. The supplier and user both receive a notification that the re-order point has been reached and a payment has been executed. The supplier can then start dispatching the order based on information provided by the smart contract, like the preferred detergent brand.

Slock.it, a lock for your Airbnb apartment

Slock.it is a start-up that prototyped a smart contract running on a lock (or, as they call it, a "slock"). Different rules and conditions can be encoded in the slock, forcing it to behave in a certain way. These rules are transparent and can be reviewed by anyone on the network.

During the Devcon1 conference, Christoph Jentzsch from Slock.it showcased[236] a connected door-lock running a smart contract managing the reservation of an Airbnb apartment. With a Slock, the owner can set the conditions for a booking, such as the amount of a deposit and/or the price per day. The guest can accept these conditions by paying the Slock and setting the dates of his trip. The idea is that the booking can be processed if the apartment is still available. The guest is then empowered to open or close the door by providing a signature from the same private key. He could also ask the contract to accept other users' signatures, such as friends or family members. When the guest leaves the apartment, the contract will send the collected money to the owner of the apartment and the remainder of the deposit to the guest.

We can imagine that additional features could be set, such as cancellation fees or contracting and paying a housekeeper for the apartment after the guests leave.

Beyond the door of an Airbnb apartment, Slock.it locks could make it possible to rent, share, or sell anything and empower the sharing economy by combining distributed ledger technology and the Internet of Things.

Conclusion

These are only a few examples where connected machines are empowered to pay other machines based on pre-programmed sets of rules. The breadth of applications is endless: warranty smart contracts, batteries and plugs that sell your energy to anyone willing to charge his car at your place and pay with cryptocurrencies,[237] or a smart contract negotiating which advertisements will be displayed on your TV and how much advertisers are willing to pay to place their ads.[238]

Just like any connection between the digital and physical world, it is important to reflect on how the link between the physical object and its digital representation on the blockchain will be made waterproof. Chips storing a pair of private-public keys that generate signatures can help to ensure traceability of goods. Still, it is one thing to have a lock that opens when presented with the right signatures; it is another to have that lock on the promised apartment.

DLT FOR BUSINESSES

Distributed ledger technology could be used to benefit not just the society. Businesses are also actively investing in the new world of opportunities and disruption DLT has to offer. Various new flows of payment can be constructed around the new models for storage, ownership and exchange of data, coin distribution, and decentralized governance.

The banking industry was the first to investigate the potential of blockchains. The numerical and deterministic nature of their business makes it very suitable to DLT, in particular to transfer value and write smart contracts. Today, we see banks working in consortiums on solutions bringing efficiency gains and transparency. Sometimes, the DLT will enable them to reduce the power of their intermediaries. But is this the preliminary step before we, the people, get rid of the banks? Maybe for some cases, such as payments, but banks have many more services to offer than payments alone.

Digital identity platforms based on distributed ledger could reduce the onboarding cost of new clients. Complying with all know your customer (KYC) onboarding checks can result in high costs. Thanks to the layer of trust brought about by DLT, players might be interested in paying the customer or other players a fraction of their current cost to receive a comprehensive and trustworthy profile that can be used to automate the checks. This cost would be lower than the current total cost of the onboarding checks each player has to comply with individually.

Besides banking, many industries will be impacted. Peer-to-peer insurance or automated claims processing could change insurance companies. The pharmaceutical and healthcare industries could use DLT to reduce counterfeited drugs and prescriptions and improve collaboration between firms or third parties.

Initial coin offerings are frequent for start-ups who wish to collect money to fund their projects. This new form of crowd-sourcing money and governing organizations in a decentralized fashion, such as DAOs, creates a completely new business paradigm.

The introduction of new coins can influence industries, making new opportunities possible. Collaborations between pharma-companies and healthcare providers could incentivize people to live healthier via a distributed ledger, resulting in lower healthcare costs for society. Cryptocurrencies have already been used to light a connected lamp thousands of miles away.[239] Self-renting cars that open their doors as soon as you pay them will be possible in the automotive industry, eventually supplemented with a DLT business model taking into account contractual agreements for maintenance, etc.

Other applications exist in music, telecom, real estate, logistics, law enforcement, scientific research, government, energy, retail, and so on. We can see start-ups popping up investigating solutions for every industry.

Smart contracts have great potential to make businesses more efficient and transparent, but they operate with cryptocurrencies, while most businesses report in fiat currency. Therefore, a tokenized fiat currency, eventually issued by a central bank, operating on a distributed ledger would enable people and businesses to transact peer-to-peer and benefit from the trust and efficiency gains smart contracts have to offer. It would also provide accountancy on the fly and auditability by design for part of a company's operation, the other part remaining unchanged. Until cryptocurrencies become fully adopted, such a tokenized version of a fiat currency would offer only a pragmatic solution to benefit, in the short term, from some of the features the blockchain technology has to offer. Such a solution does not respect the decentralized ideology for which cryptocurrencies were designed, as it would remain under the control of a centralized institution, and cannot compete with the trust decentralized currencies can offer.

Use-cases exist in almost every industry, and while it is not too difficult to prove that the technology works to serve the businesses' purposes, there are a few challenges in bringing them to life. The first challenge is that public distributed ledgers are often not scalable enough to support large streams of data. Moreover, with future transaction costs being unpredictable, it is hard to make a business case when looking beyond a few years.

Therefore, companies often look into permissioned distributed ledgers between multiple players, also called a distributed ledgers consortium. This is probably the best road to take until public distributed ledgers mature and become scalable. However, there are challenges to be faced here too, such as the formation of a consortium, the regulatory environments, privacy issues, and finding a consensus mechanism on which all players of the consortium agree. Many players in the consulting and industry landscape are positive that a solution exists to address these challenges.

DLT TO DISRUPT FINANCIAL AUDITS?

The outcome of an audit of financial statements is really just an opinion about whether these statements present a fair view of a company's financial situation. Typically, auditors provide "reasonable assurance" that the financial statements are not "materially misstated." In other words, auditors give a stamp of approval on the financial statements, which is useful to investors who are considering investing in the company.

In order to validate a financial statement, an auditor performs three main types of tasks: (1) ensuring that accounting standards have been followed, (2) ensuring that internal control mechanisms work correctly, and (3) collecting sufficient evidence (i.e., invoices, bank statements, etc.) to materially support the numbers in the financial statement. For this third step, the auditor will take a sample of the company's financial records and collect outside information about them to ensure that they are accurate. For example, the auditor might verify a transaction by looking for corresponding withdrawals from the company's funds or by contacting the person on the other end of the transaction and verifying that they received the money. While this is certainly interesting for the pockets of auditors, we might question whether there is a more efficient way to perform the audit.

Today, the accounting of large companies is done by double-entry bookkeeping. In double-entry bookkeeping, each journal entry requires a minimum of two records (one debit and one credit minimum) that equal each other. As a way to verify that no money has been forgotten, the total of the debit and credit balances should always be equal to zero. For example, when company A sells a product for $50 paid immediately in cash by the customer, they will book a $50 debit record on their revenue account and a $50 credit record on their cash account.

In a world where one or multiple cryptocurrencies are legal tender and where companies are allowed to do their bookkeeping in these currencies, transactions would be recorded on a distributed ledger. A company could use a hierarchical deterministic wallet to allocate a payment address to every account of its balance sheet. Since all transactions would occur on a distributed ledger, all transactions would be traceable and would be recorded in the company's accounting as they occur, resulting in a single version of the truth. Accountants will no longer have to type every invoice into an accounting software, and the days when expensive auditors came in to reconcile the company's balance sheets will be over. Accounting and reconciliation will be achieved by design.

With DLT, the auditing of accounts could be done in a much more efficient and reliable way than it is being done today. However, as mentioned, auditing is more than just checking for material invoices recorded in a balance sheet. The first part of the auditor's job (i.e., ensuring that accounting standards are followed) would remain, and the second part (i.e., ensuring that internal control mechanisms work correctly) would still require an audit. However, DLT is ready to take over the third and most redundant part of an auditor's job.

Of course, before getting there, many questions need to be addressed. Although companies disclose aggregated numbers in their financial statements, they do not necessarily want their competition to see all the details. A cryptocurrency with enhanced anonymity might help to solve this problem. Other questions include what type of distributed ledger would be needed and who the nodes would be. Will it be the distributed ledger of a currency, which only exists as a cryptocurrency (fully virtual), or will it be a distributed ledger managed by a central bank, which also provides fiat currency as we know it (basically, a crypto-version of fiat currency)?

Still, the ability to keep accounts in the crypto-form of a currency would make it easier for businesses to benefit from the potential distributed ledgers have to offer. Businesses would be able to leverage smart contract applications in an easier way. Transactions could be performed more efficiently and recorded in the company's accounting records immediately. If designed properly, there is even the potential for governments to collect taxes and enforce regulatory compliance automatically.

YOUR IDENTITY ON A DLT?

Looking back through history, the first document to be used like a passport appears in the Hebrew Bible, which dates back to 450 BC.[240] In 1414, King Henry V of England created a document to help his citizens prove who they were when they were abroad—the first ID document inscribed into law.[241] However, until World War I, most people did not have an ID document. ID documents were imposed by European governments for security reasons during World War I. The measure remained in place after the war, but passport standardization only happened in the 1980s. Identity documents are therefore quite a recent phenomenon, and the use of identity still differs largely from one country to another. In this section, we will look at different examples from different regions, which may or may not reflect what is happening in your state or country.

Today's form of identity

In our modern society, government ID cards are not mandatory in many countries. Often, a good and standardized identity is where everything starts. Most identification documents are issued by centralized parties, whether it is a government, a state, a bank, or a credit card company. It is not unusual to show a driver's license to rent a car, your ID to get into a club or buy alcohol, or an electricity bill to prove your residency address.

By showing identification documents when asked, we often give away more information than necessary. Why do you need to show a driver's license to buy alcohol while the only information needed is whether you have crossed the legal age to buy alcohol? Why do you need to give your government ID to get a paper saying that you can drive? Why does someone on the Internet ask for your bank documents to trust that you are a real person?

Today, the transmission of information through the Internet is established in many countries. Yet, we are often required to provide paper documents in order to prove our identity. Sometimes these documents can be scanned and sent over through the Internet; sometimes an original paper version or copy needs to be provided by hand. With some effort, most of these documents can be falsified.

Some more advanced documents come with a chip containing a private-public key pair generating legal binding signatures. When these documents are linked to a centralized database, which is often the case, they can collect personal movements. Private or public institutions holding this information can peek into someone's life and do profiling. Even more dramatic is the fact that these centralized systems can be subject to security breaches. In 2014 alone, transaction fraud with credit cards, another bank identity document, cost retailers 32 billion dollars according to a LexisNexis report,[242] which is an increase of 38% compared to 2013.

We provide our identity to too many institutions and websites. Most of the time, these different institutions do not communicate amongst themselves, and all of them keep a duplicated record of our information. We struggle to keep track of who owns what information about us. Often, as time passes, this information becomes outdated, requiring us to provide updated details to whoever requires them.

In many situations, we do not need to know who you are to entitle you to drive a car, pass through a gate, open an account, or place an order. Why do we give so much of ourselves away? Why do we give information to centralized parties that could be compromised? What if we could have full control over our identity and give away only what we need to in a secure way?

Estonia has been at the forefront of identity innovation and has not tried to centralize information about its citizens. Rather, it lets the different government agencies and businesses use their own databases, creating a decentralized network of databases tied together by a platform called X-Road. X-Road is not only making queries to the different databases but also transmits large data sets and performs searches across several databases in a secure way.[243] For example, when a child is born in a hospital, it is automatically registered in the population registry, which communicates the birth to the health insurance funds, preventing the hassle of paper work while saving time.[244] According to e-estonia.com, "All outgoing data from the X-Road is digitally signed and encrypted. All incoming data is authenticated and logged."

Besides X-Road, Estonia created an e-ID, allowing their citizens to authenticate themselves online in a user-friendly way. The e-ID opened the door to new applications for their residents, such as paying for public transport with an e-ID connected to a driver's license or your health insurance.

Finally, Estonia is pioneering by being the first country issuing an e-Residency ID allowing people to sign, encrypt, and transmit documents electronically, as well as to establish an Estonian company online and administer it from anywhere in the world. Estonia's e-Health authorities will be the first ones to use a blockchain to securely store and govern health records of its citizens[245] giving them a transparent and complete view of their health data.[246]

Building an identity on a distributed ledger

In the world of distributed ledgers, you could create as many identities as you wish. For example, you might create a distinction between your private identity, your public identity, and your online identity within a firm.

Today, we have many identities. You might have banking cards, loyalty cards, club cards—all forms of identity linked back to one individual: you. With DLT, you could have one master identity that you keep private at all times and from which you derive multiple other identities serving one or multiple purposes. These other identities should not be linkable to your master identity, which is too precious to be shared with anyone else.

For each identity created on the distributed ledger, you (or your business or avatar) start from scratch and build a chain of evidences and endorsements stored on a blockchain. For example, when you graduate from a university, the university can endorse you with the obtained degree, creating an immutable record that will forever be tied to your identity. When you apply for a job, you will not have to find your diploma to show it to your employer, and your employer will not have to contact the university to check the authenticity of the piece of paper. The employer will be able to see that one particular university endorsed you with the required degree.

An identity can also be endorsed by another identity. It is then up to everyone to decide the level of trust they attribute to the endorsements. In certain cases, the other identity could be entitled by a central institution to endorse specific elements. For example, the government may endorse a certain identity (could be the current issuer of driver's licenses) as eligible to endorse another identity (e.g., an individual) with a driver's license. In this world, governments will only be one of the many endorsers in which people, more or less, have faith.

As the owner of your identities, you can reveal your different endorsements depending on the situation. The sharing of information can be, but should not necessarily be, recorded on a distributed ledger.

At the European borders, refugees struggle to prove who they are and where they came from because they had to flee their homes without any documentation to certify their identity, degrees, or history. However, with a blockchain stored over the globe, they would be able to prove who they are as long as they carried the private key of their master identity with them.

You could choose that the private key of your master identity be derived from your biometrics, such as fingerprints, iris patterns, facial maps, or a combination thereof. With the ever-decreasing cost of analyzing someone's DNA,[247] the DNA might one day serve as a usable biometric as well. However, according to Tyler Welmans, digital identity and blockchain specialist at Deloitte Digital, using biometrics as a private key would be a bad decision as biometrics can be obtained by others. Therefore, it is better to use a private key that would be used to generate a signature proving one's identity. Biometrics, combined with an additional input could be useful and serve as a second authentication factor.[248] Finally, when you have the feeling that your identity is compromised (i.e., someone else has your private key), you could notify this on the distributed ledger, which could trigger an identity protection procedure.

Belgian citizens have different options to save for their pension. One of them consists of funds saved by their employers. When employees change jobs, they receive a precious document they keep until they retire, which states their future benefits. When the day of retirement arrives, they are responsible for claiming their benefits from each of the insurance firms their past employers subscribed to. A distributed ledger solution would provide transparency on the different pension plans an employee collected throughout their career and smart contracts could, eventually, automate the payments.

Deloitte[249] goes one step further by giving objects an identity and allowing identities to be attached to other identities. As such, someone can attach his vehicle to his identity. The car will unlock when presented with the identity of its owner. When the car is for sale, the owner can sign a transaction transferring the ownership to a buyer. We can imagine a smart contract facilitating the transfer by exchanging money and ownership. When objects are given an identity on the blockchain and events related to the object are stored on a distributed ledger, it becomes easier to track their history. Has it been rented out? Is there an insurance claim covering damages?

Considerations

Using distributed ledger technology to redesign identity is a controversial subject and touches one of the most precious aspects of our existence. It is much broader than a technological solution and many questions are to be raised.

What attributes define an identity? Are all people willing to be in charge of managing their identities? Do we need a global standard, in the age of the Internet, or is the search for a consensus driving us away from implementable solutions?[250] What happens when negative endorsements are stored in relation to one identity? Can identity be stolen, lost, or compromised? What is the plan when that happens? What is the social risk?

Having an identity on a distributed ledger can be useful for certain purposes, but online identities are not required for all. A report[251] from the World Economic Forum explains that different identity architectures serve different needs going from an internal identity (e.g., employees having access to a building) to distributed identities that serve large-scale purposes.

As we discussed in Chapter 7, security standards evolve as computers become stronger. How can we guarantee that information will be stored safely forever? Is there a period of time after which it is okay for information to become public? How can we guarantee that our private keys will be secure until the end of our lives and ideally, beyond? What about privacy and the right to be forgotten? Technical solutions exist to these questions, but are they enough?

Therefore, many questions related to identity have to be debated among identity experts, philosophers, and sociologists, and not by technologists alone.

In conclusion, it is difficult to assess to what degree DLT can help us to get a fully distributed identity for life. There is, however, reasonable reason to believe that the technology can be used to improve efficiency and reduce friction in many processes. Different players from the same industry (e.g., banking or telecom) could, for example, set up a shared distributed ledger amongst them that would enable a customer to easily share and update already-provided information for different products or different players, avoiding queues, repetitive onboarding questionnaires, and potential back-and-forth paperwork.[252]

Having a single master key is one thing, but if someone wants to have multiple unrelated identities on the blockchain, he will need different private keys (which could possibly all come from the same master key). Therefore finding a practical solution to store, manage, and recover private keys is critical for cryptocurrencies and DLT identities to be widely adopted. Some of us would certainly like to be in full control of the private keys of our identities, but others might not trust themselves enough to manage the keys to their identities. In the second case, trusted institutions could be responsible and held accountable for managing the keys. One scenario could be that multiple signatures (read identity checks) will be required to validate a message (see multi-signatures in Chapter 9). Each of these private keys could be managed by different platforms or institutions, such as social media websites or banks. David Birch, Director of Innovation at Consult Hyperion, goes as far as saying, "In the future, banks will be a place where you store your identity, not your money."[253]

DLT FOR BASIC INCOME

The continuous robotization of the fourth industrial revolution *might* reduce jobs and provoke even more inequality than today. Also, distributed ledger and artificial intelligence might wipe some businesses and parts of the service economy off the map. In a world with little jobs left for humans, a basic income might become necessary to compensate those without a job. The advocates of basic income also argue that it would give equal freedom over people's time and equal opportunity to everyone. Many prominent thought-leaders have made statements in favor of a basic income, including Elon Musk and Martin Luther King.[254] [255] [256] [257]

The term "basic income" has been used by many people in many different forms. What I am writing about here is a combination of the concepts of basic income and helicopter money, operated by a cryptocurrency.

Basic income is an unconditional amount of money given to anyone and financed by a redistribution mechanism. Helicopter money is the creation of money out of thin air to be immediately redistributed to everyone. Imagine a cryptocurrency with a monetary policy (protocol) that states that every citizen can receive, unconditionally, an amount of coins every month that is large enough to meet the basic needs of life. What would you do with it? Rather, what would you stop doing?

A basic income? Are you crazy?

This book is not aimed at convincing you of the benefits of a basic income. Like everyone who is new to the idea, you might be thinking: how can a basic income help our society move forward when everyone receives money for doing nothing? We have all been there. The answer lies in the question: "What would we stop doing?"

In today's society, or at least in certain countries, many programs exist to give equal opportunities to those who have less: pension programs, unemployment benefits, and the like. With a basic income, these programs, and the cost they represent for the taxpayer, would disappear. We also know that inequality and the lack of financial resources lead to increased criminality and insecurity, which lead to more policing and work for the justice system,[258] a cost ultimately paid by the taxpayer. It is, however, unproven and impossible to prove that a basic income would reduce criminality, as this needs to be studied empirically.

A basic income would tackle the problem of growing inequality we mentioned in Chapter 14. In this regard, the protocol could state a redistribution mechanism collecting a percentage of everyone's coins to be redistributed every month. We will call this "redistribution tax." In this system, both the rich and poor would receive the same basic income but the richest people would pay more "redistribution tax" than the amount they receive from the basic income, while the poor would receive more basic income than what they pay in "redistribution tax." Hence, the rich might stay rich because they collect additional coins from the poor, who are willing to exchange coins for produced goods or services. The hope is that the basic income would bring equal opportunity to everyone and limit the current growth in inequality where we see that, *de facto*, the very richest people do not necessarily pay more taxes than the middle class does.

There are many questions to address before implementing a basic income. Research often shows interesting and counter-intuitive arguments in favor of basic income.

The role of DLT

Basic income on a distributed ledger would be achieved by means of one address per citizen registered on the network and can build on the identity solution proposed in the previous section. Potentially that address should receive a couple of identity endorsements—for example, endorsements from the doctor who delivered the baby, the government, immigration controls, etc.—and go through a couple of checks and balances to avoid fraud.

Once the address is verified, the individual will begin receiving his "income," a given number of coins sent to the address each month. He could then use his coins to pay for goods and services. The income can vary depending on the country in which the person lives, which would be defined by his identity endorsements.

Eventually, the protocol could be set up in a way that the current income inequality between countries disappears over the decades. It could also propose a pre-encoded redistribution mechanism, within a country or globally.

The protocol running the cryptocurrency could state that the number of coins in distribution increase by 2% annually through the creation of new coins, for example, thereby creating a pre-programmed stable money emission, which is supposed to foster economic activity.

A word of caution

Questions about basic income remain. Who will do the jobs no one is willing to do but are necessary for the collective group? Should part of the coins be distributed to a fund that pays out additional coins to the people doing this type of work?

Psychologists, sociologists, and economists would have to minutely study the impact and the metrics, as well as all the social and societal dimensions impacted by a basic income. The numbers and working described above do not take into account the future research that needs to be done on the basic income idea and its financing. As mentioned earlier, this book is not taking a position on whether our society needs a basic income but, if we decide to move toward a basic income, distributed ledgers should be investigated as a technology enabling it.

A mechanism would also need to be designed to transfer possessions from the current economy to the distributed ledger economy.

Finally, the consensus mechanism will be critical and should be secure, credible, sustainable, and achieve exactly what it is meant for: consensus. Easy? Not so much. Worth investigating? Absolutely!

DLT FOR NEW FORMS OF GOVERNANCE AND DEMOCRACIES

A brief history of democracy

The birth of democracy goes back to Athens, Greece in the sixth century BC. The word "democracy" comes from the combination of the Greek words "*demos*" meaning "people" and "*kratos*" meaning "power" or "rule," literally resulting in "the people hold the power" or "ruled by the people." At that point in time, Athens had a direct democracy where people came together in the presence of a rule maker, shared their concerns, and voted on new rules or laws.

Over time, many parts of the world were governed by emperors, aristocrats, monarchs, and religious institutions. Then, in 1787, the United States broke the mold by drafting a democratic constitution, which would become effective in 1789. A little later, the French Revolution abolished the French monarchy, and the republic was born. In the next century, more countries became democracies and, step-by-step, voting rights were expanded to the unemployed, women, and ethnic minorities.

Democracies also brought conflicts. The first and second world wars were results of democratic voting systems. Franklin D. Roosevelt therefore said that "democracy cannot succeed unless those who express their choice are prepared to choose wisely. The real safeguard of democracy, therefore, is education." We will come back to Roosevelt's statement later.

Today's democracies are under pressure

In the 21st century, most democracies are indirect (also known as representative democracies) and elections are held at defined intervals, every couple of years. Many of us vote for politicians affiliated with parties we trust to represent us. Sometimes, the power within these political parties can be quite centralized by a few people at the top of the political party, who might influence the way the members of the party vote.

A consequence of a direct democracy is that a majority of elected representatives own the power. In advanced democracies, this majority of elected representatives make decisions in favor of the majority of the population, while minorities are protected with checks and balances and minority rights.

We saw in Chapter 14 that trust in politics has been continually decreasing during the last decades and that people are feeling less and less represented by their representatives. We also saw that, depending on the country, people have some measure of power over the laws implemented by their country. Let us take the examples of Switzerland and the United States.

Switzerland has a semi-direct democracy where decisions are taken at three levels: municipal, cantonal, and federal. At the municipal level, people can vote on the construction of new buildings.[259] At the cantonal level, people can vote on education[260] or the opening hours of petrol stations.[261] Topics that are not covered at the cantonal level or might require the whole country to align are decided by the federal government. Laws drafted on the federal level are discussed amongst cantonal governments, political parties, non-governmental organizations (NGOs), and associations of the civil society.[262] The outcomes of these discussions are taken into account before a law is passed. After each law is passed, the people have a veto right; if 50,000 citizens (~1.2% of the electorate) ask for a referendum within three months, a referendum is held.[263] As a consequence of this system,

Switzerland's power is quite decentralized with a large part of the power lying at the cantonal level.

Contrasting with the Swiss example, Harvard professor Larry Lessig mentions in his TEDx Talk[264] that some democracies are no longer representing the people, and he uses the example of the US where, prior to the primary election, candidates need to raise funds to run their campaign in what he calls a "money primary." During this money primary, candidates tend to behave in ways that will help them collect the required funding. He comes to the conclusion that 0.02% of the American population has the financial power to decide who will run a campaign. Although it is difficult to find multiple sources coming up with the number of 0.02%, we can fairly assume that a tiny portion of the population can have the required influence to define who will run a campaign. After this "money primary," people can vote on the remaining candidates in the primary. In other words, the people can choose their future president, but only out of a selection of candidates made by a powerful elite.

The opportunities and threats of the Internet

Today, new technologies, such as the Internet, enable bottom-up revolution by the building of online communities and instant information sharing. This has already resulted in manifestations and revolutions across the world, such as the Arab spring.

The technology today would make it theoretically possible to have large-scale direct democracies, where citizens could draft laws themselves and vote on these laws. However, expecting citizens to vote directly, in an educated manner and on every law is not realistic. Not everyone is equally involved in following all happenings nor do they have the expertise to make a judgment on every law.

This brings us to the concept of liquid democracies (also known as proxy voting), where one can delegate his vote to someone he trusts, who can, in turn, delegate it to someone else. He can also decide to vote himself on matters he cares about. In case he no longer trusts the person he delegated his vote to, he can redeem it. This process would create much more accountability amongst vote-collectors and we can imagine that the people who collect the most votes would be the ones sitting in a government.

The ability for anyone to spread information through the Internet might also have more controversial effects.

An instance of this is the emergence of "fake news." Fake news websites create fictional content about news items or personalities with the aim to grab the attention of the reader and generate clicks. During the months prior to the 2016 US election, this phenomenon accelerated and fake news articles spread on social media tended to generate more reactions and engagement than legitimate news stories.[265][266] According to a Pew Research poll,[267] 64% of US adults said they believe fake news "has caused a great deal of confusion about the basic facts or current events." Whether fake news had an actual impact on the election remains uncertain. As a result of the controversy over the impact of fake news on the outcome of the 2016 American election, tech giants such as Facebook started to combat fake news with fact-checkers to flag potential fake news articles.[268] We might expect more fake-news flagging in the future, at least to a certain degree because the tech giants also benefit from the clicks generated by these sensational articles.

Another controversial debate in many elections, including the latest US presidential election, is whether voting machines have been hacked or are hackable.[269] To this day, it is unclear if machines have ever been hacked, but it is clear that e-voting requires developments in security systems[270] and that vote counting is currently managed by central authorities with limited transparency toward the citizens.

This brings us back to Franklin D. Roosevelt's quote that "democracy cannot succeed unless those who express their choice are prepared to choose wisely. The real safeguard of democracy, therefore, is education." Today, we might want to say that, in an information-based society, the real safeguard of democracy is transparency: transparency in the information and education we receive and transparency in the setup and execution of the voting process.

DLT as an enabler

Assuming we maintain indirect democracies as we know them, DLT can bring transparency in (1) the funding of political campaigns and (2) the finances of public administrations.

By making the funding of political campaigns through a distributed ledger mandatory, people would have transparency about how political campaigns are funded and how these funds are used.

Public finance could also be made transparent with budgets denominated in cryptographic currencies allocated to governmental departments. This would enable people to track how public money is actually distributed and spent at a granular level, opening new opportunities to discover where and how budgets could be reduced. This increased transparency might help people have a better understanding of the government's expenditure, and when appropriate, highlight their disagreement. For transactions requiring more anonymity, such as paying for security measures or private investigations, we might imagine that the signature of multiple appointed people would be required. Ultimately, we can imagine that smart contracts enforce the people themselves or their chosen representatives to vote on the budget allocation.

Besides transparency, DLT is a good tool to hold politicians accountable and enable new forms of democracies, such as direct democracy or a proxy-voting system. Based on a distributed ledger identity, citizens of a country could be granted the eligibility to participate and vote in a set of elections. When political decisions are to be taken, each participant can cast his preference. In a proxy-voting system, every citizen entitled to vote would receive a revocable token. He can use this token to vote or delegate his vote to whomever he wants. He would be able to revoke his token as soon as he believes this to be necessary. Eventually, every citizen could receive multiple tokens for multiple purposes (e.g., one token for decisions related to education, one related to immigration, one for economic decisions, etc.). This would create more accountability to the people collecting vote tokens. We could also imagine that smart contracts define the period for which a representative can hold our token, creating a certain form of stability. This would also prevent people from revoking their tokens to take a particular decision based on emotions related to a recent event.

This system would operate in a decentralized way, hold politicians (vote-collectors) accountable, and provide transparency on the validity and outcome of votes. Smart contracts could define the salary of politicians, maybe depending on their level of activity or reputation score. Eventually, whenever applicable and feasible, smart contracts could be proposed to enforce the laws that were voted on. Laws could also have an expiration date or require a certain number of votes for renewal, making the regulatory system leaner.

Such a system would enable everyone to play a role in politics and enable people to build a reputation over time. More importantly, it would create a form of democracy where laws are not passed only by the elite or the influence of a group, but which gives the power back to the people.

Finally, a distributed ledger could create transparency on the information one was exposed to, as well as trace the sources of information within an article. Sources referenced by the article could endorse it if they are quoted correctly. We could also check if the author of an article has the proper background to make judgments about current events. In the future, we might imagine a world where websites and information are no longer stored on centralized servers but on a decentralized cloud where all access to information could be recorded, creating more transparency about who accesses what information.

Today, people are voting content up or down every day, but there is limited traceability of who votes for what. Still, as Santiago Siri[271] pointed out, these votes are "limited to editorial use." In the future, we might link these votes to the reputation of the person who voted up or down, and they might become part of a global survey for global decision-making. We could imagine that the scoring we see depends on the different sources we decided to trust. This would create a reputation-based Internet. This system could, on one side, provide a better customer experience, as it would bestow a certain level of trust in the quality of the information we are provided with. On the other hand, it is not foolproof and could be dangerous, as it creates a people-centric view of truth and could lead to more polarization when people reinforce themselves against currently established sources of truth.

Distributed ledgers and their transparency in the setup and execution of (1) voting processes, (2) public-finances, and (3) the sources of information we use might help us in safeguarding democracies in an information-based society, but of course, DLT poses some risks too and should be treated carefully.

Breaking borders

From childhood, we were taught to live in a world with borders. Language borders, national borders, continental borders, etc. The Internet, however, has brought us closer together. We can nowadays connect with one another and keep contact more easily than before. A teenager in Asia Pacific now listens to the same music as a teenager in America. Courses from leading universities, which were once reserved for the elite, are now being offered online for free and are accessible to everyone. The generations that grew up with the Internet have more in common than any generation from before the Internet.

The Internet has created, with the exception of a few countries, a borderless platform where information can be shared. People inform themselves, travel, and trade cross-border more than ever before.

Bitcoin and DLT can facilitate a good part of this. When smart contracts make it possible for someone to receive a loan from investors located anywhere in the world, the world becomes more integrated and national identities less relevant.[272]

However, political and economic borders still define the way we live and the political system we are part of, whether that is a democracy, a monarchy, or an authoritarian regime.

Country borders shape law, trade, free movement of people, religion, education, taxation, fundamental rights, and public transportation. Some countries even filter the information on the Internet. The same borders create systems trying to influence other systems, leading to conflicts.

Our birth defines our borders and thus the political, economic, and educational system in which we live. It defines the passport and opportunities we will be granted. Within these different borders, citizens can have more or less power over and responsibility for their destiny, but what if we could break borders and open a new dimension bringing equal opportunity to all?

Bitnation

We saw in the identity section of this chapter that Estonia is pioneering Internet residency with their e-Residency program. At the end of 2015, Estonia started a partnership with Bitnation for public notary services to Estonian e-Residents.[273]

Bitnation is a DLT-based project suggesting a more competitive market for governance by allowing everyone to join an existing virtual nation or create a new one.

Susanne Tarkowski Tempelhof, founder of Bitnation, says:

Bitnation allows people to choose the virtual nation they want to be a citizen of and the laws they want to follow. You can choose whether you want to be a capitalist or a communist, live according to the civil laws, common law, or the laws of religion, or create your own set of laws.[274] You can also reuse an existing Bitnation source code to create your own nation.

This multitude of available universes and imaginable worlds from which one can choose is supposed to improve the citizen's satisfaction with the services provided by different virtual nations. Besides its ambitious vision, Bitnation provides some more concrete services, such as generating an ID on a distributed ledger or generating a blockchain Emergency ID for refugees, aiming to facilitate the lives of refugees in Europe.[275]

An example of possible services is the use of a smart contract to record your marriage on Bitnation. That smart contract could foresee a shared account or be tied to a childcare contract or house ownership, etc.[276] More than an example, one of the first instances of marriage recorded on Bitnation happened between two citizens of Estonia's e-Residency program.[277] They chose a marriage contract under the lax family law of Ontario, Canada. This contract was stored on the Bitnation blockchain-based public notary, and when the digital signatures of both bride and groom were affixed, they kissed.[278] It is unclear what the legal value of the marriage is, but Susanne Tarkowski Tempelhof hopes that more and more citizens will consider virtual nation services over time as the phenomenon grows, just like Bitcoin is considered a currency by the people using it.[279]

In some regards, Bitnation shows many similarities to role-playing websites on the Internet. The difference is that Bitnation operates in a decentralized way and records information in an immutable way. Moreover, smart contracts can manage cryptocurrencies without the trust in a website administrator. These elements create the basis for something more credible and sustainable.

Caution

More direct forms of democracies would most likely reduce corruption and empower the citizens. However, it is important to realize what the pitfalls of a too-direct democracy could be.

A direct democracy where people could decide on everything immediately could be dangerous. A heavily shared event could trigger immediate and emotional laws while losing track of the bigger picture, and these laws could have undesired consequences. A political system's credibility might suffer from such instability. This is why DLT solutions should consider time and stability factors when being implemented.

Should everyone be able to vote on everything? Are we ready to trust ourselves? To empower everyone? Or would we rather have a system where experts in their fields decide for us, with a much larger depth of knowledge and vision?

How do we ensure that network effects do not make it too difficult for parallel alternatives to exist? How do we shift from one system to another? How do we connect a virtual system with real-world consequences to one in which smart contracts and DLT do not apply? Who will write all this code? If we allow people to vote on budget allocation, how do we avoid people from being too selfish? How do we ensure solidarity if multiple blockchains are tailored to the needs of a portion of the population, separating them from the rest of the world? How do we manage diversity and minority?

Conclusion

In this section, we addressed how distributed ledger technology could be used to improve indirect democracies by making them more transparent and making politicians more accountable for their actions. We discovered how DLT could empower new forms of democracy, such as direct or liquid democracies, we raised some contingencies to these systems, and we discussed how some of these contingencies might be addressed. Finally, we took a look at new virtual nation-states operating beyond current borders and highlighted the ideology of Bitnation, which consists of letting people choose the system in which they want to operate while increasing the competition amongst nation-state services.

Democracy is, by definition, always a work in progress. History teaches us that when hard times come, humanity can re-invent itself, often from the bottom-up. In the short term, the best way to avoid instability, while experimenting with and fine-tuning the new forms of democracies that the Internet and DLT have to offer, might very well be to integrate them into our current political system. For example, a political party could start by setting up a distributed ledger where each member of an electorate is empowered to participate in a voting process. They would then vote proportionally in favor or against the laws proposed in the assembly.

THE PROMISES OF BLOCKCHAINS

In this chapter, we discovered that the technology behind Bitcoin has a lot more to offer than cryptocurrencies alone.

Blockchains cannot be altered, making them a safe place to store precious information. They enable accounting on the fly and auditability by design. They provide the desired level of privacy over our personal data, while also creating more transparency about ownership. Ultimately, blockchains return the ownership of your data to whom it belongs: you. Better yet, you can finally start monetizing it.

DLT has the potential to revolutionize every aspect of our society. Smart contracts will streamline administrative processes. Dapps and DAOs can reshape the future landscape of the sharing economy. DLT redefines the way we think about identity and provides everyone with new accesses to services, making political borders less important. It is the perfect tool to provide a basic income and ensure more equality and social peace in a world that is entering a continuous, fast-paced technological evolution.

Blockchains allow for new forms of governance, giving the power back to all people, creating a fairer, more transparent society that engages all people equally and makes politicians accountable for their behavior. Citizens, administrations, and businesses will benefit from the security and efficiency brought by blockchains. However, it does not stop there. Blockchains can foster competition amongst public services, and maybe even provide better services to all, independent of where you were born or where you live.

As with every new technological achievement, DLT raises many questions. What will be the best consensus mechanism to allow for a shared and equal validation power? Can we manage diversity on a blockchain? How can we avoid the negative pitfalls while leveraging the positive potential it has to offer?

It is generally admitted that, in the current setup, the more the distributed ledger is used, the more reliable it will be.

Permissioned blockchains make wonderful things possible amongst chosen players. While they might save lives when used by pharmaceutical and healthcare players, the true potential of blockchain lies in the public blockchain. Our current storage capacity, however, limits the scalability of public blockchains, but upcoming advancement should enable a less distributed and more decentralized storage of public blockchains.

Public blockchains uphold big dreams, and their destiny lies in our hands. The future is bright; it is ours to make, carefully.

THE PITFALLS OF BLOCKCHAINS

Although Bitcoin presents many exciting promises, they will not become reality overnight. If you have read this book carefully, you know that blockchains face challenges such as scalability, technical and ecosystem immaturity, price volatility of tokens/cryptocurrencies, limited adoption to reach a critical mass of users, lack of understanding and education material, and lack of user-friendliness. None of these challenges are impossible to overcome, but overcoming them will take time.

Besides challenges, blockchains, like any new technology, also bring a few dangers. Removing the creation of money from the hands of central institutions sounds like an appealing idea to libertarians, but what is the impact of countless cryptocurrencies with floating exchange rates? In the introduction of this book, we explained that money rules our lives and can be considered a peaceful tool to avoid anarchy. By removing trust from central institutions and placing it in a protocol, which can evolve only through forks and/or consensus, a certain confidence is created in monetary policy. However, by the same stroke, a certain flexibility is lost. This flexibility allows for the adoption of monetary policies aligned with social context, the stimulation or slowdown of economic growth, and the financing of projects and economies.

Blockchains never forget. They are designed that way. All data, transactions, and contracts are permanent. Every action uploaded to the blockchain might stay there forever. Are we ready for this? Some cultures, such as Europe, have a tradition of being concerned about privacy. How do we make blockchains forget? How do we make them compliant with the "right to be forgotten" and general data protection regulations (GDPR)? Do we want them to be compliant in the first place, or would we rather live in an open world where everything is transparent? Solutions exist to leverage the blockchain technology as a trust layer and store a limited amount of information in the blockchain, but there will always be some permanent trace.

Blockchains and cryptocurrencies come with a wide range of levels of anonymity. Some are transparent and easily auditable by the public; others enable anonymous transactions. We discussed how these anonymous cryptocurrencies, combined with anonymous browsing services, offer unprecedented tools to safeguard online privacy, for better or for worse. While they can be used for good causes, they can also facilitate illegal and criminal activities.

Smart contracts and decentralized forms of governance create further automation and integrated business logic. Since everything can be tied together in an immutable fashion, a bug or unexpected event might lead to unstoppable disturbance, at least, until the contract runs out of fuel. In addition, since contracts might be callable forever and refueled at any time, they might serve unintended purposes in the future. In Chapter 16, we explained how to mitigate these risks with the help of suicide functions. Contracts could also foresee that before triggering other events, human approval is needed.

The invention of programmable algorithmic logic has reshaped the world over the last decades, for better or for worse. Automation has led to job losses and to the creation of new jobs. Blockchain and decentralized or distributed computer systems are another milestone that have their pros and cons. Their novelty lies in the fact that they are not dependent on any central party that could manipulate information, reverse its decisions, or even shut it down. They are novel because their logic is unstoppable. This unstoppable nature makes programming ethics more important than ever before. The ethical principles for programmers redacted by the Association for Computing Machinery is often referred to as a standard and includes elements such as: avoid harm to others, respect privacy, avoid discrimination, ensure adequate testing and review of software, and accept full responsibility of your code.[280]

The idea of creating one blockchain that serves multiple purposes is sometimes referred to as building a world computer, which is maintained collectively. This world computer, which we could interact with, would be based on programmable algorithms and, therefore, could not integrate all the complex and diverse aspects of humans. The world computer, and the multiple autonomous agents sitting on it, would be ruled by procedures describing the functioning of society and the options humans have in it. Privacy standards would be set, and room for diversity, innovation, and freedom would be limited. The emergence of a world computer could not happen overnight; it would be a slow process where a blockchain, supported by a strong ecosystem, became mainstream and gained such a strong network effect that operating without or outside of it would be very difficult. A bit like the Internet, or the smartphone.

Conclusion

Satoshi created a currency made of bits and bytes that could exist outside of the hands of a central administration. From a functional point of view, the Bitcoin Blockchain is a combination of different elements enabling the transfer of something digital, most often a token representing a cryptocurrency such as bitcoins, without copying it and without going through a trusted intermediary. It is secured by cryptography and has an incentive system, which played an important role in its adoption, especially for the early adopters. It is an immutable, transparent, and decentralized system that keeps track of who owns what when. Its consensus mechanism dictates the rules by which it operates and allows for embedded monetary policies.

Bitcoin and alternative cryptocurrencies enable reliable payments over the Internet from one person to another without the need of a trusted third party. Depending on the chosen cryptocurrency, fees are low compared to the fees for international payments made through traditional banking. By managing your own wallets, you can become your own bank. Cryptocurrencies and their protocols are open-source, and everyone can participate, propose changes, and decide what course the system should take. More importantly, cryptocurrencies enable the financial inclusion of the 2 billion people who currently lack access to financial services.

From a monetary point of view, we saw that Bitcoin is too young to be considered as money but has what it takes to become a good currency in time, although its acceptance is limited today. Remarkably enough, Bitcoin seems to serve the function of a safe haven. Bitcoin's fungibility and transparency are raising questions but also represent a tremendous potential for a fairer society. Indeed, thanks to the increased auditability of blockchains, corruption could be reduced and processes made more efficient.

In the short term, Bitcoin's acceptance will likely remain low. In the event of instability in the financial system or a breakthrough in some of Bitcoin's challenges, it might become more widespread in the medium term. Nevertheless, in the long term, it is unclear what the impact of Bitcoin's limited supply will be, how the market price will fluctuate, and what the transaction cost will be. Still, it is hard to believe that Bitcoin will disappear, and with alternative cryptocurrencies emerging, sometimes better than Bitcoin, cryptocurrencies could one day form the basis of our financial system. It will give us freedom of currency.

Likely, cryptocurrencies with different features and purposes will coexist, potentially competing against each other. A key element to a stable future with cryptocurrencies will reside in the non-transportability of power from one cryptocurrency to another. Today, this power is defined by the consensus mechanisms.

Overall, the future for cryptocurrencies is bright, and they could form the foundation of a new world. The collaboration and experimentation in the blockchain ecosystem are mind-blowing. Each initial coin offering gives birth to a new project with stakeholders using their tokens as a cryptocurrency for services or other purposes.

But more than cryptocurrencies alone, the blockchain-based cryptocurrencies bring to value what the Internet brought to information: complete decentralization and peer-to-peer transfer of ownership of digital assets.

Self-executing smart contracts are another game changer that enable the transfer of digital assets based on pre-encoded and unchangeable rules securely signed by the parties involved. Smart contracts hold the potential to further automate certain types of collaboration between companies and/or individuals, to make data, transactions, and business logic more reliable and transparent, and to remove the need for current trusted parties.

Today, the main hurdle for smart contracts is the lack of a recognized, mature cryptocurrency, or tokenized fiat currency, which can be used as legal tender. Without this, it will be difficult for non-cryptocurrency users to leverage the true potential of smart contracts.

Although public blockchains are powerful trustless systems with many strengths, they also have some weaknesses and challenges, such as their dependence on private keys, their current scalability limitations, and, to a certain degree, their lack of standards.

To conclude, we can state that blockchain technology is not only reshaping the notion of currencies, it is also reshaping the notion of contracts. Redefining these two elements is touching upon the very essence of how we, the people, and our businesses and society operate. The first examples are the emergence of decentralized applications and decentralized autonomous organizations. These applications and new forms of organizations can redefine some fundamental pillars of our current society, such as our identity, the definition of a business, and the working of our democracies. Like many new technologies, blockchains open the door to a new paradigm, if we want it.

Bitcoin has changed the notion of currency and allowed us to envision a new world. This change might be exciting to some and frightening to others, but in the end, everyone should remember that, throughout history, money has taken on many forms and that, today, money is nothing but the value we collectively give it. In an ever-changing world, we might as well cease to believe in a particular currency tomorrow and realize that, in the end, the only currency we have is time. Let us use it wisely.

I have more for you...

It is likely that I will write complementary chapters to this book. I believe my readers should get free access to all that I might publish in this context. If you are interested, you can subscribe to *The Reader's list* on www.bitcoinblockchainbook.com/more/. By subscribing, you will be notified via email as soon as additional chapters are ready, with instructions on how to access them. You can also opt in to get exclusive access to the latest thinking, links to learn more, and the most important updates. All for free. Join *The Reader's list* by using the following password: 62pU7e

This book will likely be translated into other languages. If you want to subscribe to a waiting list for your preferred language, feel free to leave your email behind on www.bitcoinblockchainbook.com. You will be notified once the selected version is ready.

I will undoubtedly post relevant news and latest insights related to the new paradigm and applications that blockchain brings. If you do not want to miss out, follow me on social media channels.

Finally, do not hesitate to share your thoughts on this book with me on social media. I will be very happy to read them and will appreciate your help in giving this piece of hard work the success it deserves.

Twitter:	@JLVerhelst
LinkedIn:	Jean-Luc Verhelst
Facebook page:	Jean-Luc Verhelst
Instagram:	BitcoinBlockchainBook

#Bitcoin #Blockchain #Book

Appendixes

Appendix 1: Block Header

Appendix 2: Merkle Tree

Appendix 3: Gartner's hype cycle 2017

APPENDIX 1: BLOCK HEADER

A block header contains the following fields. All of them can be considered as constant except the Nonce that iterates to find a valid hash.

Field	Purpose	Updated when...	Size (Bytes)
Version	Block version number	You upgrade the software and it specifies a new version	4
hashPrevBlock	256-bit hash of the previous block header	A new block comes in	32
hashMerkleRoot	256-bit hash based on all of the transactions in the block	A transaction is accepted	32
Time	Current timestamp as seconds since 1970-01-01T00:00 UTC	Every few seconds	4
Bits	Current target in compact format	The difficulty is adjusted	4
Nonce	32-bit number (starts at 0)	A hash is tried (increments)	4

Source: https://wiki.bitcoin.com/w/Block_hashing_algorithm

APPENDIX 2: MERKLE TREE

A Merkle tree is a structure used to efficiently store and find transactions within a block. The Merkle root is at the top of the tree and all the transactions are at the bottom.

Let us assume we have four transactions, T_A, T_B, T_C, and T_D, which are stored at the bottom of the tree. Each of these transaction is hashed to form H_A, H_B, H_C, and H_D where H_A is the hash of T_A, H_B the hash of T_B, etc.

The hashes of the transactions are then combined to form a parent hash. For example, H_A will be combined with H_B and hashed to form the parent hash H_{AB}. At the same time, H_C will be combined with H_D and hashed to form the parent hash H_{CD}. There are now two hashes at the parent level: H_{AB} and H_{CD}. These two hashes will be combined to form the parent hash H_{ABCD}. Since this is the last hash of the tree that has hashed all the lower hashes, it is called the transaction root hash.

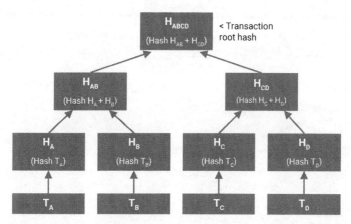

When the number of hashes at one level is uneven and leaves one hash alone, this hash is combined with itself to form the parent hash. For example, let us assume we have only three transactions, T_A, T_B, and T_C, which are stored at the bottom of the tree. Each of these transactions is hashed to form H_A, H_B, and H_C. H_A is combined with H_B to form H_{AB} as in the previous example, but H_C is left alone. Therefore, H_C will be combined with H_C to form the parent hash H_{CC}. These two parent hashes will then be combined to form the transaction root hash H_{ABCC}.

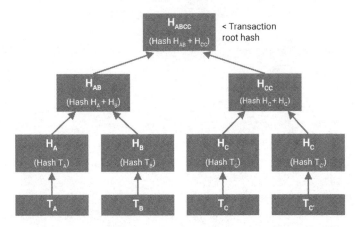

The transaction root hash will be stored in the header of the block (see Appendix 1) and will therefore be an element leading to the root hash of the block. For this reason, if one single transaction was changed, the root hash of the block would be different. If we take a closer look, we would notice that the transaction root hash has changed. From there it would be possible to investigate which branch is different from the other block, all the way until we identify the transaction that is different.

Transactions are stored in a Merkle tree to efficiently prove that a transaction is included in a block. With a Merkle tree structure, it is possible to provide a limited number of hashes to prove that a transaction is included instead of scanning through the whole list of transactions. This is particularly useful to SPV wallets that want to download minimal information but still ensure that the transactions related to the wallet are valid. By downloading only the block headers and the root paths to their transactions, an SPV wallet can prove that transactions are well stored in the Blockchain.

APPENDIX 3: GARTNER'S HYPE CYCLE 2017

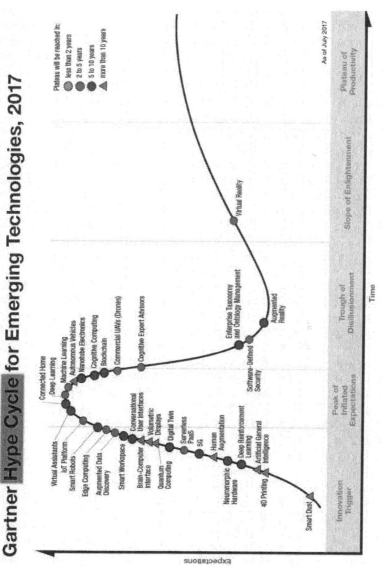

Source: Gartner

Notes

1. Original title in Dutch: "Innovatie en disruptie in het economisch recht"
2. The paper was shared via the Cryptography Mailing List and can be viewed at: http://www.mail-archive.com/cryptography@metzdowd.com/msg09959.html
3. https://bitcointalk.org/index.php?topic=195.msg1617#msg1617
4. Nakamoto's first post is visible on the P2Pfoundation forum: http://p2pfoundation.ning.com/forum/topics/bitcoin-open-source. He later became active on the Bitcointalk forum: https://bitcointalk.org
5. http://www.coindesk.com/information/who-is-satoshi-nakamoto/
6. A function is a programmed procedure that performs the same algorithm every time it is called. It can receive information to treat as input and returns a value as output.
7. This is called a collision in cryptography. All functions in cryptography can have collision; the art of a strong hashing function resides in the enormous number of guesses one must make before finding a collision, and thus this unlikelihood of finding a collision.
8. Open source means that the code is publicly available and can be reviewed by anyone. It is 100% transparent.
9. Based on testing conducted in August 2010 with IBM, https://usa.visa.com/run-your-business/small-business-tools/retail.html
10. A bit is a zero or one in computing language. Together, 256 bits offer 2^{256} (roughly 1 followed by 77 zeros) possible combinations.
11. Addresses are inspired from https://en.bitcoin.it/wiki/Technical_background_of_version_1_Bitcoin_addresses (consulted July 10, 2016) where you can also find further information on the used functions.
12. In fact, there will be a signature for every transaction input. More on transaction inputs in Chapter 6.
13. Going short in finance consists of betting that the price of something will go down
14. July 2017
15. GHash.IO, *Bitcoin mining pool GHash.IO is preventing accumulation of 51% of all hashing power* https://ghash.io/ghashio_press_release.pdf
16. Bershidsky L., *Did Ukrainians Almost Take Over Bitcoin?*, http://www.bloombergview.com/articles/2014-01-14/did-ukrainians-almost-take-over-Bitcoin- April 23, 2014

17. Curtis J., *Mining pool 'in control' of Bitcoin hit by DDos attack*, http://www.cbronline.com/news/social/mining-pool-in-control-of-Bitcoin-hit-by-ddos-attack-4293920, consulted June 20, 2014

18. Quentson A., *Bitcoin Mining Pool Ghash.io DDos-ed in Response to threat of 51% attack?*, http://www.cryptocoinsnews.com/news/Bitcoin-mining-pool-ghash-io-ddos-ed-response-51-attack/2014/06/15, consulted June 06, 2014

19. Buterin V., *Bitcoinmagazine.com*, https://Bitcoinmagazine.com/articles/Bitcoin-is-not-quantum-safe-and-how-we-can-fix-1375242150 - consulted June 2016

20. Further reading on Lamport Signatures: https://gist.github.com/karlgluck/8412807

21. Buterin V., *Bitcoinmagazine.com*, https://Bitcoinmagazine.com/articles/Bitcoin-is-not-quantum-safe-and-how-we-can-fix-1375242150 - consulted June 2016

22. Alan Szepieniec (PhD Researcher in Cryptography at the KU Leuven), July 2016

23. Alan Szepieniec (PhD Researcher in Cryptography at the KU Leuven), July 2016

24. Pieter Wuille at the Scaling Blockchain conference in Hong Kong, December 7, 2015 - https://www.youtube.com/watch?v=zchzn7aPQjI

25. Off-chain bitcoin payments are bitcoin payments that happen on alternative platforms and require only a limited number of re-transactions in the Bitcoin Blockchain.

26. Technically speaking, Johanna is rewriting a transaction waiting for John's signature to be broadcasted. The new transaction uses the same input but sends a higher amount to John. The transaction will be broadcasted once the channel is closed.

27. The complete white paper can be found at: https://blockstream.com/sidechains.pdf

28. Written by Adam Back, Matt Corallo, Luke Dashjr, Mark Friedenbach, Gregory Maxwell, Andrew Miller, Andrew Poelstra, Jorge Timón, and Pieter Wuille

29. Peer-review with Luke Dashjr, May 2017

30. Routing tables facilitate communication on networks. In this case, they would keep track of the different existing channels and how to transfer cryptocurrencies across channels.

31. https://lightning.network/lightning-network-paper.pdf

32. https://bitinfocharts.com/comparison/bitcoin%20cash-hashrate.html

33. https://blockchain.info/charts/hash-rate

34. https://www.coindesk.com/bitcoin-cash-closes-profitability-parity-original-blockchain/

35. https://www.coindesk.com/bitcoin-cash-returns-profitability-amid-mining-adjustments/

36. August 15, 2017

37. April 2017

38. http://www3.weforum.org/docs/WEF_Internet_for_All_Framework_Ac celerating_Internet_Access_Adoption_report_2016.pdf, consulted August 16, 2017

39. https://motherboard.vice.com/en_us/article/xy5evk/meet-the-man-running-the-only-bitcoin-node-in-west-africa, consulted August 16, 2018

40. https://blockstream.com/satellite/howitworks, consulted August 16, 2017

41. https://blockstream.com/satellite/faq/, consulted August 16, 2017

42. https://blockstream.com/satellite/blockstream-satellite, consulted August 16, 2017

43. https://en.bitcoin.it/wiki/Thin_Client_Security

44. The initial chaincode at the master level is an input generated from random data. As from the next level, the chaincode is generated from a function hashing the parent key, the previous chaincode, and the index of the child key.

45. *Mastering Bitcoin*, Andreas

46. Coin Desk, how to store your Bitcoin – consulted June 1, 2016 - http://www.coindesk.com/information/how-to-store-your-bitcoins/

47. Coin-mixing is a method of mixing Bitcoin transactions in order to make them less traceable. A mixing service receives different transactions from different users (the initial owners), then sends the funds of these transactions to multiple addresses before sending them back to an address controlled by the initial owner. The multitude of transactions splitting and merging bitcoins recorded on the Bitcoin Blockchain is supposed to increase the difficulty in retracing transactions.

48. Near-field communication (NFC) is a technology allowing devices to communicate in a contactless way.

49. Blockchain is the technology behind Bitcoin but there is also a wallet company based in Luxembourg, called Blockchain, which operates the website Blockchain.info. In this case, we are referring to the wallet provider.

50. "A brute force attack is a trial-and-error method used to obtain information such as a user password or personal identification number (PIN). In a brute force attack, automated software is used to generate a

large number of consecutive guesses as to the value of the desired data."
- https://www.techopedia.com/definition/18091/brute-force-attack

51. You can generate a paper wallet online at
https://bitcoinpaperwallet.com/

52. Some offline generators can be downloaded at
https://github.com/cantonbecker/bitcoinpaperwallet

53. https://en.bitcoin.it/wiki/Paper_wallet#Generation_of_secure_keys

54. https://ihb.io/paper-wallet

55. In this case, we use the term digital currencies instead of
cryptocurrencies because a few currencies are not backed by a
distributed ledger or by cryptography and, as a consequence, do not fall
under the denomination of cryptocurrencies.

56. Dougherty C. and Huang G., *Mt. Gox Seeks Bankruptcy After $480
Million Bitcoin Loss*, http://www.bloomberg.com/news/2014-02-
28/mt-gox-exchange-files-for-bankruptcy.html, consulted May 2, 2014

57. Wilson S., *Mt. Gox finds 200,000 Bitcoins in 'forgotten' wallet*,
http://www.telegraph.co.uk/finance/currency/10713243/MtGox-finds-
200000-Bitcoins-in-forgotten-wallet.html n, consulted May 26, 2014

58. http://blog.wizsec.jp/2015/04/the-missing-mtgox-bitcoins.html

59. https://cdn.omise.co/omg/whitepaper.pdf

60. http://www.coindesk.com/reality-chinese-trading-volumes/

61. http://in.reuters.com/article/china-bitcoin-idINL3N0JX2FH20131218

62. Automated teller machines

63. Phone Interview, Jean-Wallemacq, Belgian Bitcoin Foundation

64. Phone Interview, Moe Adham, BitAccess

65. Phone Interview, Moe Adham, BitAccess

66. http://www.ebtm.be/buy-sell

67. Phone interview with Arnaud Kodeck, EBTM

68. Phone interview with Arnaud Kodeck, EBTM

69. Phone Interview, Moe Adham, BitAccess

70. Wikipedia, *Silk Road*,
http://en.wikipedia.org/wiki/Silk_Road_(marketplace) – consulted
May 18, 2014

71. Kar I., *What companies accept Bitcoins?*,
http://www.nasdaq.com/article/what-companies-accept-Bitcoin-
cm323438 - consulted June 6, 2014

72. http://www.coindesk.com/tesla-model-3-bitcoin/

73. https://spectrum.mit.edu/continuum/mits-bitcoin-experiment-is-
underway/ consulted August 14, 2016

74. Gill R., Video: Holland's Bitcoin Boulevard Celebrates Two Successful Months, http://www.coindesk.com/video-hollands-Bitcoin-boulevard-celebrates-two-successful-months/ - consulted May 27, 2014

75. "Exchange risk exists (...) when a financial transaction is denominated in a currency other than that of the base currency of the company. (...) The risk is that there may be an adverse movement in the exchange rate of the denomination currency in relation to the base currency before the date when the transaction is completed." Wikipedia, consulted August 14, 2016.

76. Skype interview with Patrick van der Meijde, December 2016

77. https://www.cryptocoinsnews.com/bitcoin-boulevard-bitcoin-part-everyday-life-dutch-neighbourhood/

78. Skype interview with James Walpole, BitPay. January 6, 2017

79. Skype interview with James Walpole, BitPay. January 6, 2017

80. Skype interview with James Walpole, BitPay. January 6, 2017

81. Email exchange with James Walpole, BitPay. January 17, 2017

82. Skype interview with James Walpole, BitPay. January 6, 2017

83. Smallest storage unit on a computer, represented by 0 or 1

84. Beattie A., *The History of Money: From Barter to Banknotes*, consulted June 4, 2014, http://www.investopedia.com/articles/07/roots_of_money.asp

85. Moffatt M., *Money*, consulted June 4, 2014, http://economics.about.com/od/termsbeginningwithm/g/money.htm

86. Weatherford J., *The History of Money*, New York, Crown Publishers, 1997, p22

87. Weatherford J., *The History of Money*, New York, Crown Publishers, 1997, p31

88. Weatherford J., *The History of Money*, New York, Crown Publishers, 1997, p32

89. Weatherford J., *The History of Money*, New York, Crown Publishers, 1997, p199-203

90. http://www.consilium.europa.eu/uedocs/cms_Data/docs/pressdata/en/ecofin/136487.pdf

91. https://www.usatoday.com/story/money/business/2013/07/29/bank-of-cyprus-depositors-lose-savings/2595837/

92. https://www.rt.com/business/cyprus-crisis-bailout-deposit-631/

93. The European troika is a decision group formed by the European Commission (EC), the European Central Bank (ECB) and the International Monetary Fund (IMF).

94. *Russia Today*, https://www.rt.com/business/cyprus-crisis-bailout-deposit-631/ - consulted July 2013

95. Andresen G., *Gavin Andresen on the Present and Future of Bitcoin*, 2014, http://www.econlib.org/cgi-bin/fullsearch.pl?query=Andresen%20on%20Bitcoin, (EconTalk, Posdcast)

96. Author's experience in the Philippines

97. In Keyna, more than 45% of money transaction are done through M-Pesa (a cellphone-based money transfer service) while 30% are done by hand.
Source: The World Bank, *Mobile payments go viral: M-PESA in Kenya*, http://web.worldbank.org/WBSITE/EXTERNAL/COUNTRIES/AFRICAE XT/0,,contentMDK:22551641~pagePK:146736~piPK:146830~theSitePK: 258644,00.html - consulted June 17, 2014

98. Messenger call, Jean-Gregoire Orban de Xivry

99. A full report from Deloitte concerning supply chain challenges for retail banks and their structure can be found at:
http://www.deloitte.com/assets/Dcom-Canada/Local%20Assets/Documents/Insights/Innovative_Thinking/2013/ca_en_insights_optimizing_the_retail_bank_supply_cha in_102913.pdf, - consulted June 15, 2014

100. Unlike standard formatting, zero-fill formatting overwrites every bit on a hard drive to zero. It is estimated that a hard drive has to undergo three cycles of zero-fill formatting to make it impossible to recover any data.

101. Weatherford J., *The History of Money*, New York, Crown Publishers, 1997, p25-27

102. https://en.wikipedia.org/wiki/Superdollar#Confirmed_sources

103. Galt J. *BitcoinMagazine.com*, https://bitcoinmagazine.com/articles/is-bitcoin-headed-for-a-break-in-fungibility-1450823559 - consulted June 2016

104. Galt J. *BitcoinMagazine.com*, https://bitcoinmagazine.com/articles/is-bitcoin-headed-for-a-break-in-fungibility-1450823559 - consulted June 2016

105. Thousand millions of millions in the American system.

106. Campbell D., *Trust in politicians hits an all-time low*, http://www.theguardian.com/politics/2009/sep/27/trust-politicians-all-time-low - consulted 6/8/14
Pew Research center, *Public Trust in Government: 1958-2013*, http://www.people-press.org/2013/10/18/trust-in-government-interactive/ - consulted July 7, 2014

107. https://rbi.org.in/Scripts/NotificationUser.aspx?Id=10683&Mode=0

108. Author's personal experience in India

109. http://timesofindia.indiatimes.com/india/2-die-in-country-wide-rush-to-junk-banned-notes/articleshow/55374158.cms
110. http://indianexpress.com/article/india/india-news-india/arvind-kejriwal-lashes-out-at-bbc-reporter-questioning-him-on-demonetisation-4384031/?campaign_id=A100
111. http://www.dnaindia.com/india/report-demonetization-with-no-cash-on-hand-4-lakh-trucks-stranded-on-highways-2273414
112. http://www.firstpost.com/business/demonetisation-farmers-fear-loss-of-crops-and-income-after-currency-ban-3111694.html
113. http://www.cnbc.com/2016/11/15/india-rupee-restriction-boost-bitcoin-digital-currency.html
114. https://www.theguardian.com/world/2016/dec/15/venezuelans-on-the-removal-of-the-100-bolivar-note-thoughtless-dangerous
115. https://www.washingtonpost.com/news/global-opinions/wp/2016/12/15/declaring-war-on-common-sense-venezuela-bans-its-own-money/?utm_term=.c969f12e0b6f
116. http://www.coindesk.com/assange-bitcoin-wikileaks-helped-keep-alive/
117. https://europa.eu/newsroom/highlights/special-coverage/eu_sanctions_en - consulted September 10, 2016
118. http://www.consilium.europa.eu/uedocs/cms_data/docs/pressdata/EN/foraff/135804.pdf - consulted January 08, 2017
119. Verhelst J., The Bitcoin e-currency : historical genesis, current situation and empirical analysis compared to traditional currencies and commodities
120. https://www.cryptocoinsnews.com/ghostsec-isis-bitcoin-wallet-worth-3-million/
121. http://www.wienerzeitung.at/_em_daten/_wzo/2016/01/25/160125_1356_europol_dokument_aenderungen_in_der_verfahrensweise_mit_is_terroranschlaegen_pdf_englisch.pdf + http://europeanmemoranda.cabinetoffice.gov.uk/files/2017/07/10977-17-ADD-2.pdf
122. http://www.wsj.com/articles/alternative-currencies-flourish-in-greece-as-euros-are-harder-to-come-by-1439458241
123. http://www.investopedia.com/terms/s/seigniorage.asp
124. http://www.worldbank.org/en/news/video/2016/03/10/2-billion-number-of-adults-worldwide-without-access-to-formal-financial-services
125. https://www.ft.com/content/c5d08c5c-339c-11e6-bda0-04585c31b153
126. http://bruegel.org/wp-content/uploads/2016/06/pc_2016_10-1.pdf

127. Recent events include the transatlantic trading agreement. On the other hand, the Ukrainian conflict tends to reinforce old trading barriers.
128. For example, credit cards offer not only a faster payment method but also extra protections to their users at the cost of higher transaction fees.
129. Getting smart on smart contracts, CFO Insights, Deloitte Development LLC.– June 2016
130. https://www.youtube.com/watch?v=GplUE1NGqgA
131. Denoël T., *Pourquoi Albert Frère investit dans les terres agricoles*, http://www.levif.be/info/actualite /belgique/pourquoi-albert-frere-investit-dans-les-terres-agricoles/article-4000304793506.htm – consulted May 17, 2014
132. The blockchain is one of the more secure and world's more widespread database. Some people use the blockchain to store valuable information (i.e., Dutch notaries for storing the hashtag of documents). Source : Spaes T., *De pro's en contra's van de Bitcoin*, http://deredactie.be/cm/vrtnieuws/videozone/programmas/devrijemar kt/2.31526?video=1.1838058 – consulted April 6, 2014
133. http://www.forbes.com/sites/katiegilbert/2014/09/22/why-local-currencies-could-be-on-the-rise-in-the-u-s-and-why-it-matters/#3e56201e27b0
134. http://www.forbes.com/sites/katiegilbert/2014/09/22/why-local-currencies-could-be-on-the-rise-in-the-u-s-and-why-it-matters/#3e56201e27b0
135. http://www.lemonde.fr/economie/article/2015/05/22/en-complement-de-l-euro-les-monnaies-locales-seduisent-de-plus-en-plus_4639088_3234.html
136. http://www.euskalmoneta.org/fr/ensemble-soutenons-leuskara-grace-a-leusko/
137. https://www.youtube.com/watch?v=mpE8UMMZa9w
138. http://www.euskalmoneta.org/fr/ensemble-soutenons-leuskara-grace-a-leusko/
139. http://www.euskalmoneta.org/fr/ensemble-soutenons-leuskara-grace-a-leusko/
140. https://letstalkpayments.com/which-countries-are-close-to-a-cashless-world/
141. http://www.worldatlas.com/articles/which-are-the-world-s-most-cashless-countries.html
142. De Redactie, *Terzake*, http://deredactie.be/permalink/2.32224?video=1.1892263 – 27/2/14

143. http://www.tijd.be/nieuws/archief/Opnieuw_cyberdiefstallen_via_bank en_platform_Swift.9804437-1615.art?highlight=swift

144. http://www.tijd.be/nieuws/archief/Bankenplatform_Swift_heeft_cyber veiligheid_verwaarloosd.9799381-1615.art?ckc=1&ts=1484491732

145. IOCTA 2016, *Internet organized crime threat assessment*, Europol report, the Hague, p.44. (https://www.europol.europa.eu/activities-services/main-reports/Internet-organised-crime-threat-assessment-iocta-2016)

146. This has been the case in the Netherlands, from where Bitcoin start-ups are interested to operate but the national bank has warned companies not to work with Bitcoin start-ups. Source: Skype interview with Van de Berg R. *Tax Lawyer at Baker & McKenzie Amsterdam N.V.* (2014) following publication "Fiscaal beleid overheid rond bitcoin remt innovatie", Dutch Financial Times, June 17, 2014.

147. https://www.asfi.gob.bo/images/ASFI/DOCS/SALA_DE_PRENSA/Notas _de_prensa/2017/N_20_Nota_Prohibici%C3%B3n_de_uso_y_circulaci %C3%B3n_de_monedas_virtuales.pdf

148. https://bitcoinmagazine.com/articles/bolivian-authorities-arrest-60-cryptocurrency-promoters/

149. Perkins Coie report, Virtual Currencies: International Actions and Regulations

150. http://fortune.com/2017/02/12/bitcoin-markets-china-regulation/

151. http://calvinayre.com/2016/12/07/business/russias-finance-ministry-delaying-bitcoin-bill-late-2017/

152. http://www.cnbc.com/2017/06/01/bitcoin-russia-regulation.html

153. Perkins Coie report, Virtual Currencies: International Actions and Regulations

154. http://uk.reuters.com/article/us-venezuela-bitcoin-idUKKCN0HX11O20141008

155. https://bitcoinmagazine.com/articles/venezuela-seems-be-cracking-down-bitcoin/

156. https://bitcoinmagazine.com/articles/venezuela-seems-be-cracking-down-bitcoin/

157. http://www.newsbtc.com/2017/02/23/surbitcoin-business-next-week/

158. http://www.eba.europa.eu/documents/10180/657547/EBA-Op-2014-08+Opinion+on+Virtual+Currencies.pdf

159. http://www.eba.europa.eu/documents/10180/657547/EBA-Op-2014-08+Opinion+on+Virtual+Currencies.pdf

160. http://data.consilium.europa.eu/doc/document/ST-15605-2016-INIT/en/pdf

161. Roger Van de Berg, email exchange July 2017

162. https://bitcoinmagazine.com/articles/regulation-bitcoins-germany-first-comprehensive-statement-bitcoins-german-federal-financial-supervisory-authority-bafin-1391637959/

163. http://www.cnbc.com/id/100971898

164. Financial Crimes Enforcement Network (FinCEN), *History of Anti-Money Laundering Laws*, http://www.fincen.gov/news_room/aml_history.html [hereinafter AML History]. – consulted June 5, 2014

165. https://cointelegraph.com/news/property-money-or-currency-what-is-bitcoin-and-why-it-matters

166. IRS Notice 2014-21

167. https://www.irs.gov/irb/2014-16_IRB/ar12.html

168. Rubin R. and Dougherty C., *Bitcoin Is Property, Not Currency, in Tax System: IRS,* http://www.bloomberg.com/news/2014-03-25/Bitcoin-is-property-not-currency-in-tax-system-irs-says.html - consulted June 7, 2014

169. Van de Berg et al., *Decision on Landmark Case Regarding the VAT Treatment of Bitcoin,* Bloomberg BNA - Tax Planning International (Indirect Taxes) - Volume 13

170. http://curia.europa.eu/jcms/upload/docs/application/pdf/2015-10/cp150128en.pdf

171. Moore A. G., Crossing the Charm, New York, PerfectBound, 1991 – page 9

172. https://blockchain.info/fr/charts/hash-rate, consulted May 13, 2017. One Gigahash is equal to 1 billion hashes.

173. http://www.nytimes.com/2016/10/12/business/dealbook/central-banks-consider-bitcoins-technology-if-not-bitcoin.html?_r=0

174. https://www.cryptocoinsnews.com/european-central-bank-is-open-to-blockchain-technology/

175. https://bitcoinmagazine.com/articles/bank-of-england-chief-economist-blockchain-based-digital-currency-issued-by-central-banks-could-replace-cash-1443028299

176. Assuming no legal measures decide to ban the Internet.

177. Numbers on July 22, 2016. Source: https://cryptolization.com/

178. https://www.youtube.com/watch?v=fE_oWNEDh_k

179. August 15, 2017

180. Coinmarketcap.com, consulted August 15, 2017

181. The "pump and dump" of altcoins is similar to the pump and dump of penny stocks; both having relatively small market capitalization. You can buy a lot of coins at a cheap price, and then create a buzz about the coin to attract other investors willing to buy the coin. As more and more

investors buy in, the price increases (pump). While the price increases, the initial buyer starts selling his coins (dump). Ultimately, people realize that there was a lot of buzz about nothing, and the price decreases.

182. January 2017
183. https://peercoin.net/assets/paper/peercoin-paper.pdf
184. https://chainz.cryptoid.info/slr/
185. The full list of metadata posted in the transaction can be consulted at https://solarcoin.org/en/viewing-transactions-on-the-solarcoin-blockchain/
186. Facetime interview with Jean-Gregoire Orban de Xivry, Early adopter of Solarcoin and Founder of Solarly, a start-up bringing solar energy to African villages.
187. Email exchange Ryan Taylor, February 28, 2017
188. Email exchange Ryan Taylor, March 5, 2017
189. https://www.dash.org/team/
190. Email exchange with Bas Wisselink, Nxt Foundation, February 27 2017
191. Francisco Cabanas, Monero, Email exchange March 14, 2017
192. https://blockchainhub.net/blog/infographics/monero-in-a-nutshell/ consulted December 29, 2016
193. https://en.wikipedia.org/wiki/Monero_(cryptocurrency) consulted December 29, 2016
194. Ripple.com December 29, 2016
195. https://ripple.com/xrp-portal/
196. https://pando.com/2014/08/15/ripple-settles-with-estranged-founder-jed-mccaleb-outlining-a-metered-sale-of-his-xrp-holdings/
197. https://ripple.com/xrp-portal/, consulted March 14, 2017
198. Email exchange with Daniel Kraft, February 27, 2017.
199. https://nameid.org/?
200. http://bitcoin.stackexchange.com/questions/273/how-does-merged-mining-work
201. Remember, the coinbase transaction is the transaction in which the miner allocates newly generated bitcoins to himself.
202. Or another cryptocurrency backed by many times more computing power.
203. http://bitcoin.stackexchange.com/questions/3472/what-is-the-story-behind-the-attack-on-coiledcoin
204. https://bitcointalk.org/index.php?topic=56675.msg678006#msg678006
205. This example is inspired from Peercoin
206. https://blog.ethereum.org/2014/01/15/slasher-a-punitive-proof-of-stake-algorithm/

207. https://blog.ethereum.org/2015/08/01/introducing-casper-friendly-ghost/

208. https://solarcoin.org/en/important-update-to-solarcoin-currency-wallets/

209. Email exchange with Nick Gogerty, Founder of Solarcoin

210. http://docs.bitshares.org/bitshares/dpos.html#:

211. https://www.nem.io/NEM_techRef.pdf

212. https://cointelegraph.com/news/proof-of-importance-nem-is-going-to-add-reputations-to-the-blockchain

213. As explained https://bytecoin.org/blog/proof-of-activity-proof-of-burn-proof-of-capacity/
     White paper can be found at https://eprint.iacr.org/2014/452.pdf

214. Iddo Bentov (Cornell University)

215. https://bitcointalk.org/index.php?topic=731923.0

216. https://en.wikipedia.org/wiki/Proof_of_Space

217. Email exchange with Nick Gogerty, May 12, 2017

218. This was the case for Chancecoin, one of the first altcoins to experiment with burning.

219. This assumes that the mechanism to go from private key to address is the same on both chains.

220. http://www.coindesk.com/everledger-blockchain-tech-fight-diamond-theft/

221. https://techcrunch.com/2015/06/29/everledger/

222. https://blog.oraclize.it/understanding-oracles-99055c9c9f7b, consulted April 16, 2017

223. Martin Swende, peer-review, May 2017

224. https://github.com/DavidJohnstonCEO/DecentralizedApplications/blob/master/README.md

225. http://blockchainhub.net/dapps/

226. https://techcrunch.com/2016/12/21/uber-losses-expected-to-hit-3-billion-in-2016-despite-revenue-growth/

227. www.lazooz.org

228. http://bitcoinwiki.co/using-the-blockchain-for-decentralized-ride-sharing-with-lazooz/

229. https://www.indiegogo.com/projects/la-zooz-real-time-social-ridesharing-app#/

230. https://storj.io/

231. https://blog.ethereum.org/2014/05/06/daos-dacs-das-and-more-an-incomplete-terminology-guide/

232. http://www.altcointoday.com/ethereum-classic-funds-of-the-dao-hack-are-moving/

233. https://www.youtube.com/watch?v=LVlT4sX6uVs
234. See https://t.co/mAMFrXCTiX for more technical details
235. Find demo at https://youtu.be/U1XOPIqyP7A
236. https://www.youtube.com/watch?v=49wHQoJxYP0
237. See Blockcharge
238. Find demo at https://youtu.be/U1XOPIqyP7A
239. https://www.youtube.com/watch?v=qlBQfv85g6I
240. https://en.wikipedia.org/wiki/Passport
241. https://en.wikipedia.org/wiki/Identity_document#History
242. https://shocard.com/cpt_news/identity-management-on-the-blockchain/
243. https://e-estonia.com/component/x-road/
244. https://www.youtube.com/watch?v=9PaHinkJlvA
245. https://bravenewcoin.com/news/e-estonia-initiative-progresses-with-blockchain-partnerships/
246. http://pwc.blogs.com/health_matters/2017/03/estonia-prescribes-blockchain-for-healthcare-data-security.html
247. https://www.genome.gov/sequencingcostsdata/
248. Tyler Welmans, Blockchain and Digital Identity specialist Deloitte, Email exchange May 2017
249. https://www.youtube.com/watch?v=zpO7eH5FYdo
250. http://www3.weforum.org/docs/WEF_A_Blueprint_for_Digital_Identity.pdf
251. http://www3.weforum.org/docs/WEF_A_Blueprint_for_Digital_Identity.pdf
252. https://www.youtube.com/watch?v=IoQqchIoA-k
253. https://www.youtube.com/watch?v=hS15p5V3slg
254. http://www.businessinsider.com/elon-musk-universal-basic-income-2017-2
255. http://www.businessinsider.com/bill-gates-basic-income-2017-2
256. http://www.doorbraak.be/nl/etienne-vermeersch-men-schijnt-onvoldoende-te-beseffen-wat-er-op-ons-afkomt
257. https://medium.com/basic-income/why-milton-friedman-supported-a-guaranteed-income-5-reasons-da6e628f6070#.m0dlnxi4s
258. https://www.weforum.org/agenda/2017/01/why-we-should-all-have-a-basic-income?
259. https://www.youtube.com/watch?v=_wYywEW9aTY
260. https://www.swissinfo.ch/eng/cantons-and-municipalities/29289028
261. https://www.youtube.com/watch?v=_wYywEW9aTY
262. http://direct-democracy.geschichte-schweiz.ch/
263. http://direct-democracy.geschichte-schweiz.ch/

264. https://www.youtube.com/watch?v=PJy8vTu66tE
265. https://www.buzzfeed.com/craigsilverman/viral-fake-election-news-outperformed-real-news-on-facebook?utm_term=.sy4Wm32Kp#.jh3oARMge
266. http://www.pcworld.com/article/3142412/windows/just-how-partisan-is-facebooks-fake-news-we-tested-it.html
267. http://www.journalism.org/2016/12/15/many-americans-believe-fake-news-is-sowing-confusion/
268. http://www.independent.co.uk/voices/facebook-fake-news-fact-check-google-ad-save-journalism-a7645706.html
269. http://www.independent.co.uk/life-style/gadgets-and-tech/news/us-election-rigged-hillary-clinton-hacked-donald-trump-russia-edward-snowden-a7437181.html
270. http://www.europarl.europa.eu/RegData/etudes/ATAG/2016/581918/E PRS_ATA(2016)581918_EN.pdf
271. https://www.youtube.com/watch?v=UajbQTHnTfM
272. https://blockgeeks.com/blockchain-voting/
273. https://e-estonia.com/estonian-government-and-bitnation-begin-cooperation/
274. https://www.youtube.com/watch?v=M4Dg3mO3cAc Susanne Tarkowski Tempelhof
275. https://bitnation.co/refugee-emergency-response/
276. https://www.youtube.com/watch?v=fEfgCdy1mwE
277. https://www.bloomberg.com/view/articles/2015-12-01/i-attended-the-first-official-digital-wedding
278. https://www.bloomberg.com/view/articles/2015-12-01/i-attended-the-first-official-digital-wedding
279. https://www.bloomberg.com/view/articles/2015-12-01/i-attended-the-first-official-digital-wedding
280. http://www.acm.org/about-acm/acm-code-of-ethics-and-professional-conduct

Full table of contents

About the author

Jean-Luc Verhelst is a Strategy Consultant working for Monitor Deloitte and is a founding member of BlockchainHub Brussels, a non-profit think tank and information hub part of the global BlockchainHub network. He holds an applied Bachelor's degree in Information Technology and a Master of Science in Business Administration.

In 2014, his master thesis on Bitcoin received the award for best financial thesis of Belgium by ING Bank. In 2016, he won the world's largest blockchain hackathon in Dublin. He is recognized as a global blockchain expert within the consulting firm Deloitte and has facilitated and conducted the first EMEA and US trainings. He is currently involved in the development of blockchain projects in multiple industries.

Finally, Jean-Luc is a well-regarded speaker within the Belgian Bitcoin and blockchain community. He is known for his ability to explain technical topics in an inspiring and understandable way, coming up with innovative use-cases while being knowledgeable on the more technical aspects.

Twitter:	@JLVerhelst
LinkedIn:	Jean-Luc Verhelst
Facebook page:	Jean-Luc Verhelst
YouTube channel:	jeanlucverhelst
Instagram:	BitcoinBlockchainBook

www.jeanlucverhelst.com
www.bitcoinblockchainbook.com

Contact is possible via www.jeanlucverhelst.com